In our post-EHR, consumer-driven model, in order to achieve the triple aim of healthcare is case... ...data. Big Unlock is incredibly timely and im... ...rested in learning about the potent... ...re, lower costs, and anchor care on the pat...

Travis Good, MD, Founder and CEO, Datica

This is a very timely book on the huge possibilities that lie ahead for the digital transformation of healthcare. The role of a wide range of emerging data sources, the challenges in harnessing the data for insights, and the opportunities for creating new digital health experiences are explained clearly in a structured way. Paddy is a technology veteran who understands healthcare and I have had the pleasure of witnessing his work for many years. Readers will benefit from the valuable insights from his personal experience in growing and managing healthcare technology businesses. This is a book for everyone interested in how emerging technologies and data will impact our healthcare system in the future.

Eliel Oliveira, CIO, Louisiana Public Health Institute

A very welcome and pertinent book at a time of great change in the healthcare industry. Clear exposition of complex ideas in jargon-free language.

Siddhartha ("Sid") Chatterjee, Ph.D. | Chief Technology Officer, Persistent Systems

We, consumers, have expectations of healthcare that far exceed what the system can deliver at this time. We want high quality, affordable, personalized care as and when it is needed – and we want to know that we are doing what may prevent us from ever needing this care. Putting this "we" at the center of the way the healthcare system operates is the objective of value-based care – healthcare that is about being well, or providing accessible, high quality, meaningful care as and when it is needed. In his book, Paddy describes the changing landscape of the healthcare industry today and the central role of data and analytics to unlock the value in value-based care. Paddy taps into experience and interviews to explore what it will take to unlock insights from the myriad of sources in the market and deliver on the "triple aim" of health care – better health outcomes and care experience at a lower cost by economically viable digital health organizations.

Barbra Sheridan McGann, EVP, Business Operations, Healthcare, Life Sciences, Public Sector, HfS Research

The healthcare system is inefficient - payment models are intractable and often provide counterproductive incentives; clinical decision making is based on partial information as a result of data interoperability barriers and medical errors are common; and operational processes are intransparent, complex and drive cost. In all cases, the data is there, but not available, not interchangeable, or lack the integrity required for advanced analytics. The challenge is magnified by explosions of wearable or genomic data. Promises lie in AI, patient consumerism, digital health, and - ironically - in cost escalations driving a need for change. In the Big Unlock, Paddy illuminates these trends and challenges and provides a roadmap for what could be.

Wido Menhardt, Healthcare Technology Leader

This book is a culmination of Paddy's knowledge of the industry, insights gleaned from industry leaders and baked in with trends in technology and the healthcare industry to make this a compelling read. If you want to know how analytics are shaping the healthcare industry - along with other macro shifts shaping the industry - you need to read this book.

Abhijeet Pradhan, Healthcare Technology Executive

THE
BIG
UNLOCK

Harnessing Data and
Growing Digital Health Businesses
in a Value-based Care Era

PADDY PADMANABHAN

ARCHWAY
PUBLISHING

Archway Publishing books may be ordered through booksellers or by contacting:

Archway Publishing
1663 Liberty Drive
Bloomington, IN 47403
www.archwaypublishing.com
1 (888) 242-5904

ISBN: 978-1-4808-5458-1 (sc)
ISBN: 978-1-4808-5460-4 (hc)
ISBN: 978-1-4808-5459-8 (e)

Library of Congress Control Number: 2017916631

Print information available on the last page.

Archway Publishing rev. date: 11/9/2017

Contents

Foreword

One of the landmark achievements of healthcare IT over the past decade has been the near total penetration of electronic health record (EHR) systems in the healthcare economy. While the early impetus was primarily to take advantage of meaningful-use incentives, we are now seeing a transformation of healthcare that requires a much deeper understanding of the role of EHRs.

For one, the data residing in EHR systems must be tapped into fully. The vast amount of unstructured data in EHR systems is a data goldmine waiting to be tapped. In the past few years, we have seen the emergence of a multitude of data sources including the Internet of Things (IoT) data, such as wearables, genomic data, and social determinant data. Increasingly, the data is coming at a high velocity; for example, streaming data from smart medical devices that require real-time analysis for timely interventions in managing chronic conditions such as diabetes.

As healthcare moves towards a value-based care era, the role of data in population health management, patient engagement, and revenue-cycle management will be more important than before. Along with new data sources, we are seeing the emergence of new technology infrastructure models to store and process the avalanche of data and new methods of analyzing the data. The term big data analytics has given way to more sophisticated techniques such as artificial intelligence and cognitive computing.

The speed of change of technology and healthcare is unprecedented. Coupled with the rise of consumerism, many individuals and organizations have become exasperated trying to determine strategy, let alone solutions. It used to be that organizations had the luxury of months to develop a strategy and then execute solutions over the course of three to five years. Today that time period has shrunk to the point where we are leveraging agile processes in strategy development and execution.

While serving as a leader in one of the nation's largest faith-based systems, we found ourselves working on strategy on a continual basis. The challenge was to develop a business intelligence system that could easily adapt and pivot without knowing all the changes the organizations would experience. We deployed a flexible architecture that could respond to the chaos of healthcare and helped guide the organizations in making sound business and clinical decisions.

At Cleveland Clinic, we are helping lead the revolution in digital medicine, and the ability to assimilate and analyze data in real-time is foundational to our effort. While the shelf life of strategy has shrunk considerably, we must still anticipate the future and, to the extent possible, create it. Central to our strategy is our collaboration with IBM Watson and directing our scientists, technologists, and caregivers to focus on solutions. Consuming data from disparate and heterogeneous sources, we are able to transform healthcare with predictive and prescriptive analysis. We continuously look to build out and strengthen our foundation so we can become resilient and responsive to economic market forces and the continuous adoption of best practices.

Healthcare IT solution providers are working closely with enterprises to help transform the technology and applications infrastructure in order to meet the emerging needs of consumerism, improved health outcomes, and organizational efficiency. There is a thriving ecosystem of digital health startups, fueled by venture capital, that is trying to tap into the opportunity.

However, the path toward value-based care is neither easy nor quick. Technology-led innovation in healthcare faces many obstacles, including funding models, evidence of improved healthcare outcomes, and preparedness for change. Healthcare has not traditionally been a pioneer in technology adoption, but more of a fast follower. The lack of interoperability among systems and growing threats of cyberattacks are among the major challenges that impact the rate of change in healthcare.

The cost of healthcare in the United States is the highest in the world by far, and there is not much evidence that healthcare outcomes are better than in any other country. In fact, studies show it is the opposite. We are at the cusp of an unprecedented opportunity to transform healthcare by unlocking data and using advanced analytics technologies to develop and deploy insights for improving outcomes and reducing costs. This book is timely, in that it not only outlines the drivers of the opportunity for enterprises and technology providers alike, but provides a framework for understanding how to create value with the Big Unlock.

The work is just beginning.

Edward W. Marx
Chief Information Officer
Cleveland Clinic

Introduction

This book is based on my experience of nearly two decades in healthcare, as a technology executive and later as an analytics entrepreneur. I have tried to provide a view into how the unlocking of existing and emerging data sources is creating unprecedented opportunities. The book draws from around sixty opinion pieces I wrote in *CIO* magazine from January 2015 until early 2017. The primary audience for the book consists of technology business executives looking to identify and expand growth opportunities in digital health. Health system executives seeking to understand emerging technology solutions will also benefit from the insights into how the landscape is changing with the huge inflow of venture-capital (VC) money into digital health startups and innovation programs by leading health systems.

The premise of digital health is the creation of new, engaging platforms that will drive improved healthcare outcomes while lowering costs and enhancing patient experiences. To do this effectively, digital health programs must rely on applications that deliver insights from a variety of data sources, structured and unstructured, and from a variety of clinical and non-clinical sources. The unlocking of these insights also relies on advanced analytical methods, for which stakeholders in the digital health ecosystem have to leverage new approaches and new technologies. The challenges in the journey towards value-based care and advanced analytics include data interoperability, information security and privacy, and most importantly a revenue and business model for new digital health solutions. Done correctly, this will unlock profits for everyone, starting with the healthcare consumers who now bear increased financial responsibility for their healthcare.

The Big Unlock refers to the massive opportunity unfolding in healthcare from the digitization of patient medical records and the emerging tsunami of data from a wide range of medical and non-medical sources, especially unstructured data such as text and speech. Collectively, these data will enable the unlocking of insights for improving the quality of care, reducing costs, and creating new sources of value for healthcare providers, consumers, and technology firms. In this book, I have developed a framework for understanding the competitive landscape of digital health solutions and a set of key principles, which I call universal themes, for success in the digital health marketplace.

The book is meant to be a reference document for digital health startups and their venture capitalists, technology firms with a strategic focus on healthcare, and healthcare IT leaders who are keen to understand the solution provider and emerging technology markets. For each of these stakeholder groups, the book provides insights into increasing revenues and profits, while creating a sustainable competitive advantage from the Big Unlock. Finally, the book is a primer for anyone interested in understanding the exciting transformation of healthcare under way and the important role of data and analytics in this transformation.

The book contains insights from interviews and conversations with dozens of C-level executives whom I have had the privilege of working with over the years. This is a view from the trenches that informs corporate strategy, product strategy, technology strategy, and revenue strategy.

This book focuses on business-to-business (B2B) technology markets in healthcare that address the information technology needs of healthcare enterprises. Healthcare B2B technologies play a key role in the economics and delivery of healthcare—primarily providers (physicians, clinics, hospitals, and health systems) and commercial payers (national and regional health insurance companies).

1 Healthcare Data and the Forces Driving the Big Unlock

If data is the new oil, digital health is the new oil refinery.

After the massive effort to digitize patient medical records under the Affordable Care Act and the Health Information Technology for Economic and Clinical Health (HITECH) Act during the Obama administration, the next stage of evolution for healthcare is to unlock the value of the data. Healthcare data is getting bigger all the time. A typical five-hundred-bed hospital today generates fifty petabytes of data.[1] The pace of growth of data is exploding, and our ability to digitize and analyze it is struggling to catch up. Many enterprises to consider themselves to be data rich but insight poor.

Along with this, the rate of change in the way we are digitizing and analyzing the data in the health space is accelerating. Big data analytics is expected to be a $187 billion market by 2019, according to research firm IDC.[2] Healthcare is a fast-growing segment that is expected to be a $43 billion market by 2024.[3] According to the widely read annual report on Internet trends in May 2017 by Mary Meeker of VC firm Kleiner Perkins, healthcare is at a digital inflection point.[4] The rapid growth of healthcare data (48 percent annual growth as of 2013) and the accumulation of digital health data from a variety of sources is leading to a generation of new and improved insights for driving healthcare outcomes. New data sources such as wearables and the Internet of Things (IoT) present new opportunities and challenges; research firm Gartner predicts that twenty-one billion IoT devices will be online by 2020.

The growing volume of data and the emerging opportunities for value creation by generating new insights make big data the new oil. What is driving the exploration of the new oil is the healthcare industry's shift to value-based care (VBC).

The per capita cost of healthcare in the United States in 2015 was around $9,900, the highest in the world by a wide margin, with the sector accounting for a fifth of the gross domestic product (GDP).[5] The higher costs in the United States are not necessarily producing better outcomes.

The Institute of Healthcare Improvement (IHI), a not-for-profit organization, defines the triple aim of healthcare as improving the patient experience of care, improving the health of populations, and reducing the per capita cost of healthcare.[6] To achieve this triple aim, the healthcare sector needed to be made accountable. As the largest payer of healthcare services, the federal government decided to use the biggest lever it had—payment reform.

VBC shifts financial risk while increasing accountability in the healthcare system. It challenges health plans, health systems, and pharmaceutical companies to change their mind-sets about their revenue models. The most important aspect of this shift, besides providers getting used to not being paid for volume, is the unlocking of insights from data to improve healthcare outcomes and reduce costs. With an estimated $35 billion in taxpayer money paid out as meaningful-use incentives over the past eight years to digitize health records,[7] the need of the hour is to unlock insights from the data to drive improved healthcare outcomes. The key competencies required are data aggregation and analysis to drive physician productivity, care management, and patient engagement. Creating the digital and analytical infrastructure required to navigate this transition to VBC is the biggest opportunity in front of the healthcare sector and technology-provider community.

The transition to VBC is neither easy nor assured. It involves significant financial risks in upfront investments, radically new ways of approaching healthcare delivery, and a culture shift that emphasizes the role of data and insights for care decisions. While it is widely acknowledged that healthcare is an area of tremendous opportunity for big data analytics, innovation has been slow due to margin pressures, a risk-averse mind-set, and market-related factors.

A study by Quest Diagnostics (Quest) and analytics company Inovalon, based on a survey of healthcare payers and providers, indicates progress toward VBC but also points to the opportunity for further alignment between health plans and providers to advance VBC.[8] Despite the industry's progress toward VBC, the vast majority of payments still flow through the fee-for-service (FFS) system. Within healthcare, adoption levels for VBC models fall on a wide spectrum between large, integrated networks operating on accountable care models and smaller independent and rural health systems holding on to FFS. The Quest report indicates that, while 82 percent of physicians and health-plan executives agreed the transition to VBC will continue regardless of policy changes, only 29 percent of physicians and health-plan executives said they believe healthcare in the United States is value-based. This percentage was a marginal increase from the findings of the previous year.

At the time of writing, healthcare policy in the United States is in a state of tremendous flux and uncertainty. However, behind the scenes, the shift to VBC is quietly taking place, driven by the 2015 Medicare Access and CHIP Reauthorization Act (MACRA), a bipartisan piece of legislation that creates incentives to move away from FFS to value-based reimbursements. Neal Singh, CEO of Caradigm, a GE Healthcare company that provides population health management solutions, says, "Just over a year ago, nobody was talking about MACRA, and now, everybody is talking about MACRA because, guess what, whether you like it or not, the healthcare provider's compensation is going to be heavily influenced by MACRA over time. The levels of risk are going to change over time as well. The Centers for Medicare and Medicaid Services (CMS) is very clear about where they want to lead healthcare. The formats may change, the names may change, the types of payment systems may change, but the fact is that the laws of economics will not change. The laws of economics are fundamentally saying that the current system of basic FFS is not sustainable."[9]

As all these pieces evolve rapidly, the healthcare industry is looking at implementing systems designed to be future-proof in relation to policy changes. A big part of that is putting in systems that will be able to deal with the exploding volume and variety of data and generate insights in real-time for improved healthcare outcomes and reduced costs of care.

We are in the very early stages of the effort to unlock the value of the data. Much of the data remains locked in proprietary third-party vendor technologies (more on that later), and the investment required to unlock insights and the returns required to justify these investments have yet to line up. The biggest challenge by far remains interoperability between various proprietary EHR systems. Efforts to promote data sharing through health-information exchanges (HIE) have also not been as successful as expected, for a variety of reasons.

At the same time, we have new data sources coming online, such as the IoT and genomic testing, to name a couple. These new data sources are emerging as important factors in the Big Unlock.

In early 2017, the *New England Journal of Medicine* (*NEJM*) published the results of a survey of healthcare executives who were asked what the most useful sources of data were expected to be in five years.[10] Clinical data, and specifically EHR data, was seen as the most important data source by far, indicating the enormous focus by healthcare enterprises on optimizing their investments in EHR systems over the past several years. However, the expected rise of patient-generated and genomic data provides interesting insights into what is emerging as important data.

Today, we are seeing a convergence of demand- and supply-side forces that are unlocking the potential of advanced analytics. Some of these are

- increasing importance of analytics for enterprise growth and profitability;
- falling prices for data storage and computing capacity;
- acceleration of technology-led innovation; and
- alternate payment models and the transition to population health management.

A nagging question that keeps coming up in boardrooms is what the return on investments is on new technology investments, especially digital health, is. The answers are not clear today. A survey of nearly four hundred CEOs and senior managers across sectors by research firm Gartner indicated they rate the productivity gains from breakthrough technologies to be "very low" in the next five years.[11] It may be too early in the game to fully appreciate the potential benefits of these technologies.

Some of the factors driving the sentiment are

- demonstration of the ability of digital health solutions to improve outcomes and deliver financial returns;
- data security and interoperability challenges;
- operationalization of digital health and analytics solutions in clinical workflows;
- ability to adapt to new data sources such as wearables, IoT, genomic data, and patient-generated health data (PGHD); and
- talent acquisition and retention.

Value creation in analytics today is focused on a couple of areas: data integration and insight generation through the use of predictive models for managing clinical outcomes, especially in the context of population health management (PHM). I call this the *zone of activity*. However, most health systems lack a plecosystem—an integrated platform ecosystem approach (more on this later) to derive benefits from advanced analytics by incorporating them into the clinical workflow in hospitals.

In recent years, expensive and complex analytical tools and technology have become accessible and affordable to people and businesses. The computational horsepower needed to conduct analysis on vast amounts of data has also dropped significantly in recent years in line with Moore's law (coined by Intel cofounder Gordon Moore in 1965, the law broadly states that the computing capacity that can be packed into chips has doubled every year since their invention while computing costs have halved).[12] With storage and computing capacity becoming very affordable and practically available on tap, analytics is no longer constrained by scalability and affordability.

IBM Watson Health, Amazon Web Services (AWS), and Microsoft Azure machine learning as-a-service are examples of how complex technologies and analytical models are being made available freely for teams to build solutions on.

This trend is putting the power of advanced analytics in the hands of increasing numbers of non-technical executives and individuals, creating a democratization effect. My colleague Larry Boyer and I explored this in detail in a paper on the democratization of analytics[13] and came up with the following key observations:

- Analytics is becoming pervasive as complex analytical tools allow businesses to collect and process vast amounts of diverse data.
- Automated processes have substantially replaced manual processes, and new tools that perform activities that were not possible earlier are now widely available.
- We are entering an era of democratization of analytics driven by the acceleration of technological innovation and the open-source movement, among other factors.
- Advanced analytics and machine learning that were previously available only to chief information officer (CIO)

organizations and specialized units have become accessible to individual users at a fraction of the cost.

- Although organizations still need appropriately qualified people to review the analytical reports carefully, enabling more people to do more analysis can help leaders make better decisions and operate businesses more efficiently and effectively.

- When hiring data scientists, organizations need to have clear expectations, especially when the hiring managers themselves do not understand clearly what the term *data scientist* means.

Much has been written about the huge shortage of data scientist talent and the pursuit of *unicorns*—analytics superheroes who can single-handedly wrangle the biggest and most complex data sets to deliver insights that translate into increased profits for the enterprise. Despite a lack of clarity and direction with advanced analytics programs, large enterprises have nevertheless been falling over each other to hire as many of these individuals as they can.

There is no doubt a giant bottleneck on the supply side of data scientists; as with all such situations, creative solutions are emerging to restore balance through a "reversion to the mean" in data scientist-speak. The embedding of advanced analytical models and algorithms in emerging analytics platforms is one such trend that reduces the need for data scientists. Better data-management tools to integrate, normalize, and standardize data will also reduce the need for scarce and expensive data scientists, whose work often revolves around the unglamorous but necessary aspects of analytics, such as data preparation.

As with most innovation and new technology programs, adoption rates and effectiveness will vary across and within sectors. Typical factors influencing this dynamic are an industry sector's historical approach to cutting-edge technologies, focus (or lack thereof) on top-line oriented innovation vs. cost reductions, and ROI considerations, just to name a few.

Even within healthcare, the focus may be on research and development (R&D) in pharma, claim expense control among payers, and clinical outcome improvement in providers. Accordingly, stakeholders take widely varying approaches to investments in big data. Regardless of the use case, approaches toward the stewardship of enterprise-level data vary widely, and organizational "data silos" are a common feature across the sector.

Healthcare has been suboptimal in its ability to unlock insights from data. Some of the top issues include the following:

- **Inflated expectations.** Health systems have been sold the idea that big data is the silver bullet for PHM. However, ROI from analytics has been hard to quantify, which has led to leadership taking a cautious approach to investments.

- **Data-management challenges and interoperability among systems.** Perhaps no other topic has been beaten to death more than this, with some technology vendors taking an enormous amount of heat for data blocking, a practice that deliberately prevents access to systems and applications that require such access to enable new and improved approaches to healthcare.

- **Lack of cooperation among stakeholders.** While the role of Chief Digital Officer (CDO) has become more prominent, data silos continue to exist, leading to data bottlenecks that impact the ability to harness data for improved insights.

- **Operationalization of analytics.** Many analytics solutions are offline, meaning they operate in a standalone fashion, and analytics is not integrated into day-to-day clinical workflows.

Big data programs are more about people than about technology. While CDO and Chief Population Health Officer (CPHO) roles are on the rise, the challenges related to organizational alignment, change management, and data governance have not gone away. Within organizations, effective use of data is stymied by management silos; the disconnect between CIOs and the lines of business hampers the collaboration required for improving patient outcomes. Healthcare governance models are evolving slowly, with the role of CDO still relatively rare. The absence of centralized governance and the lack of collaboration weaken the data even further as individual groups choose to work with the limited data available within their silos.

Several forces are driving healthcare to accelerate the pace of big data analytics programs. In the short term, the path will be different for different players in the market, based on their needs and maturity levels. Health plans will seek to align incentives, mitigate financial risks, and keep premiums in check. Providers will focus more on improved care coordination and patient engagement. Life sciences companies will look to maintain innovation pipelines while adjusting to performance-based contracting models and demonstrating efficacy and robust healthcare economics. However, within each sector, enterprises will be at various levels of maturity, like vehicles driving at different speeds on a multi-lane expressway.

Several workarounds are emerging to address the challenges related to interoperability, as market participants coalesce around common standards such as fast health interoperability resources (FHIR) to enable data exchange and analysis across the healthcare ecosystem. Cloud-based models that are Health Insurance Portability and Accountability Act of 1996 (HIPAA)-compliant and secure are becoming increasingly more accepted as enterprises recognize that, in many cases, cloud environments can be even more secure than their legacy environments.

The biggest challenges in front of healthcare are IT security and the new menace of ransomware which has emerged as a potent disruptor of healthcare operations, with the potential to put patient lives at risk. Healthcare has historically underinvested in technology modernization, and the chickens seem to be coming home to roost. The migration of enterprise workloads to cloud environments managed by providers such as Amazon and Microsoft—who operate with high levels of IT security in their data centers—can potentially mitigate this risk for healthcare enterprises. However, healthcare's migration to the cloud has been slow, and there are no failsafe guarantees even in an AWS or Azure environment.

The ability to derive value depends on an individual institution's access to large amounts of data within and across health systems that enable benchmarking and pattern analysis. Healthcare is a fragmented sector with very few models for data sharing and collaboration. The big EHR vendors, with their broad market footprint, have made a limited amount of progress with data-sharing among their client organizations. Vendor-agnostic initiatives like HIEs remain regional, with restrictions on data use governed by the individual members of the exchange.

In the future, the highest-value use cases in big data analytics in healthcare will combine the power of predictive analytics with the rapid proliferation of data. Data from wearables and smart medical devices, unstructured data such as text and speech, genomic data, and social determinants will be among the vast and diverse sources of data that will be ingested into data lakes built on open-source technologies such as Hadoop, or on-cloud service provider environments such as AWS. Analytical tools go beyond merely reporting historical events and trends, predicting outcomes while learning through cognitive capabilities. New platforms such as IBM Watson Health will deliver insights and recommendations from massive repositories of knowledge in addition to the data.

The story that is unfolding in front of us is the opportunity of a generation. No sector is as broken as healthcare. No sector is more exciting to be in today.

1.1 Payment Reform and VBC

The FFS revenue model of healthcare, stable for decades, is being shaken to its foundations. The entire healthcare sector is moving away from reimbursements based on volumes to payments based on results. Welcome to the era of VBC.

The US Department of Health and Human Services (HHS) has set a goal of tying 50 percent of Medicare FFS payments to value through alternative payment models (APMs) by 2018.[14] The HHS states that APMs and payment reforms that seek to deliver better care at lower cost share a common pathway for success: providers, payers, and others in the healthcare system must make fundamental changes in their day-to-day operations that improve quality and reduce the cost of healthcare. The HHS is pushing for a shift to person-focused and population-based payments that will, in concert with other reforms, result in an expansion of high-value care in the United States.

Ed Marx, a nationally renowned CIO who currently leads the IT function at Cleveland Clinic, believes that VBC is here to stay, and the only way to survive and potentially thrive in this era is to be much more data driven than we have been in the past. He believes that being smart about leveraging data is a must-have in the immediate term and not a nice-to-have anymore.[15]

Alternate payment models in the emerging VBC era are driven by MACRA.[16] MACRA was passed in 2016, and its key features include

- the merit-based incentive payment system, which would apply to all eligible clinicians that Medicare pays under the physician fee schedule, and
- incentives for clinicians to participate in advanced APMs.

Essentially, MACRA overhauls Medicare's payments by requiring financial risk-sharing by clinicians (something that has caused much anxiety and confusion among the physician community). Health systems will need to invest in technology, analytics, and other new capabilities to succeed in the new payment model. Payment reform under MACRA may well be the one big factor in definitively transitioning the healthcare sector from FFS to a value-based era.

An important factor in the growth of alternate payment models is the active involvement of patients in partnership with healthcare providers in achieving their health goals. New, technology-based approaches to increase patient engagement will rely on data about clinical and patient experience measures. Financial rewards for patients for their active participation in health and wellness will be the norm, and a corresponding incentive for healthcare providers will budge them to help achieve these goals collaboratively.

On the flip side, healthcare providers accustomed to the FFS model are now having to get used to alternate models of payment that depend on the quality of healthcare outcomes. The CMS readmission risk-management program that imposed penalties on health systems exceeding the threshold for avoidable readmissions may have been an important milestone in driving providers to focus more on healthcare outcomes. It also laid the foundation for PHM as an approach to care management and care delivery.

As of late 2016, an estimated 25 percent of commercial healthcare dollars flowed through APMs associated with PHM initiatives,[17] which is an indicator of the progress of these new models toward incentivizing healthcare providers to change their economic preferences toward risk-based payment models. While it is still a relatively small percentage of overall revenue dollars for healthcare, it is a rapidly growing share of future revenues and one that all healthcare enterprises are actively preparing.

A survey by PHM company Caradigm (part of GE Healthcare) in late 2016 indicated that most health systems are in the early stages of participation in the CMS Bundled Payment for Care Improvement (BPCI) program, but expect to increase their participation in the next one to two years. Importantly, a majority (60 percent) of respondents indicated that they view BPCI as a key part of their shift to VBC, and aim to use BPCI as a means to improve healthcare outcomes and reduce the costs of care.[18]

Understanding the various APMs is important as they drive behavior that impacts the business models of healthcare enterprises and technology solution providers alike. Before exploring APMs, it is useful to understand the dominant payment model today, which is FFS.

Fee-for-service. This is exactly what it sounds like—healthcare providers get paid for providing a service such as a blood test, doctor's visit, or magnetic resonance imaging. The crucial thing to understand is that the person receiving the service is not paying for the service, which is typically a health insurance company. This misalignment is widely understood by many as the reason for perverse incentives that drive up healthcare costs. FFS continues to be the dominant mode of payment for healthcare services today, although that is changing quickly.

Here are three widely proposed and increasingly popular APMs:

Accountable care organizations (ACOs). As the name implies, these entities are designed to take accountability for healthcare outcomes and in return become eligible for incentives based on improved outcomes. These are groups of providers across different settings—primary care, specialty physicians, hospitals, clinics, and others—who come together to jointly share responsibility and sign up to hit quality benchmarks for a large patient population. Through improved coordination and elimination of unnecessary medical expenses, such as duplicate tests, these entities are expected to deliver better care at lower costs. ACO participants stand to gain upsides from shared savings but can also face penalties if they miss their targets. The ACO model has had mixed success for a variety of reasons; however, all indications are that the model will continue to remain an option for healthcare providers willing to take risks for increased returns. The biggest beneficiaries are patients who benefit from more focused and coordinated care.

Bundled payments. A healthcare bundle is an estimate of the total cost of all the services related to a certain problem, like a knee or hip replacement. The bundle includes the costs over a period from acute to post-acute care and includes everything from diagnosis to treatment to recovery for the episode. For example, a hypothetical thirty-day bundle for a hip replacement surgery could be estimated at $10,000. However, prices could vary widely across states (an analysis in 2013 found that a hip replacement could cost between $10,000 and $125,000 across the country).[19] These variations notwithstanding, health insurers continue to look at bundles as an alternate payment option to mitigate financial risks. Providers, for their part, can improve margins on the procedure by keeping their costs under control and are in fact incentivized to do so, which is precisely the point of the payment model in the first place. The role of data and analytics in managing bundled payment contracts has increased as health systems look to identify points of care that are not delivering expected outcomes or have excessive costs. An example of this is the role and costs of skilled nursing facilities (SNF) in post-acute care and the tradeoff between additional lengths of stay at an SNF vs. home-based care for improving outcomes.

Patient-centered medical homes (PCMH). The American College of Physicians defines a PCMH as "a care delivery model whereby patient treatment is coordinated through their primary care physician to ensure they receive the necessary care when and where they need it, in a manner they can understand."[20] A PCMH comprises highly coordinated teams of caregivers including primary care professionals, physicians, nurse–practitioners, and other specialists. The team works closely to improve care coordination with each other, as well as with patients and their caregivers. In the PCMH model, an additional payment is layered on to compensate for the extra effort of care coordination. This extra money can be used to deploy productivity-enhancing technology, hire specialist agencies for special care needs, home visits, remote monitoring, and a host of other things that aim to reduce the likelihood of rehospitalization or other complications. The operating principle is that the incremental savings from better-coordinated care justify the extra monthly payments and benefits all stakeholders, mitigating financial risks for payers.

How have these models done so far? As a VBC model, the ACO has arguably gained the most traction, at least judging by the body of evidence from the past few years. Around three-fourths of the 220 early Medicare ACOs renewed their contracts in early 2016, indicating growing confidence in the ability-managed risk-based contracts. Commercial ACOs have continued to climb steadily and stood at over 1,300 in early 2017,[21] up from around 850 in early 2016.[22] Even so, ACO contracts cover only around 10 percent of the US population, with varying levels of penetration across states, indicating significant room for growth.

ACOs represent a fundamental shift from the traditional one-on-one patient care model practiced by physicians, who had no reason to consider population-level health-outcome management in an FFS payment era. PHM indicates a shift to a many-to-many care model, with ACO contracts being the commercial manifestation of these shifts. The real challenge for healthcare providers now is to develop strong PHM capabilities supported by technology enablers, analytics platforms, and robust data.

Health systems, health plans, and healthcare technology companies have to plan for this new VBC era and develop technology and analytics capabilities that enable them to manage risk, control costs, and thrive in a performance-based payment model. There is a significant opportunity for the right kinds of solutions that can unlock insights from population health data in all its current and emerging forms.

This focus on PHM is an important aspect of the Big Unlock, which we will explore in detail. The shift toward PHM has significant implications for healthcare enterprises and their technology providers alike.

While the payment landscape shifts from traditional FFS payments to an outcomes-based financial incentive framework, the burden of increased risk is a shared responsibility. Financial incentives may spur improved care coordination, not just among care providers but also between providers, payers, and other parts of the ecosystem.

The success of an outcomes-based financial model will depend on a data infrastructure that enables maximization of VBC reimbursements and sets the course for sustainable growth. Healthcare enterprises that proactively embrace the new value-based payment models and manage shared risk will be the ones that survive in the long run.

An interesting dynamic in healthcare is that some parts of the market are more aggressively embracing the shift to VBC, while others are still holding on to the traditional FFS model.

Neal Singh, CEO of Caradigm, says, "I do not think the market is changing consistently. Some markets are embracing the move toward VBC faster than other markets. I think it always comes down to the economic factors in play. We see that wherever there is a higher Medicare and Medicaid patient population, health systems are moving faster to VBC. We are seeing large employer plans with more negotiating power doing value-based contracts that are driving more and more risk toward providers. This, in turn, is incentivizing or forcing change among providers. Of course, in areas where economic incentives are lacking, there is still FFS that providers persist. I think it is a mix, but we are moving toward VBC in a very big way."[23]

With the CMS's goal of achieving at least 50 percent of Medicare payments to VBC contracts, there is no doubt a significant shift among providers toward taking on risk-based contracts. A widely accepted notion in healthcare today is that the shift toward VBC is a train that has left the station. The question is: how fast is the train moving?

Says Lidia Fonseca, CIO of lab test leader Quest Diagnostics, "In healthcare, it takes time before things transform. So, while it is still a fee-for-service world, we will see more and more of a shift toward VBC."[24]

A significant factor in the shift toward VBC is the alignment (or lack thereof) between participants in the healthcare ecosystem. A Quest Diagnostics study published in May 2017 indicates that while 70 percent of health-plan executives said there has been progress toward better alignment, only 47 percent of physicians agreed.[25] Even if market participants were to achieve alignment around the need for VBC models, the execution of accountable care and APMs depends heavily on the adoption of technology tools and innovation. The Quest survey finds that EHR systems are not closing the gaps. Tellingly, a vast majority (70 percent) of clinicians do not see a link between EHRs and improved healthcare outcomes.

According to L. Patrick James, MD, Chief Clinical Officer for Health Plans & Policy, Medical Affairs at Quest Diagnostics, "One of the most striking findings of the study is that physicians question the value of EHRs, but they would be willing to spend more time with them if they could ultimately gain patient-specific insights in real-time."[26] Quest has developed a range of innovative data products, many of them in partnerships with companies such as IBM Watson Health, Inovalon, and others that are embedded directly in the daily workflow of a physician and provide the real-time insights that Dr. James talks about.

The ability to obtain real-time insights at the point of care could be the most important factor driving the shift toward VBC. The vast majority of health systems remain deeply committed to their EHR systems, given the enormous investments of money and effort into these implementations over the past several years. EHR data will remain the predominant source of patient information in the next five years, and extending the capabilities of the EHR systems capabilities could unleash value.

Ultimately, the level of investment by health plans and healthcare providers in health IT innovation may be the key to accelerating VBC adoption. In an uncertain policy environment, many health systems are unwilling to commit to innovation programs, a sentiment further reinforced by the costs and efforts involved in experimenting with new technologies and solutions. The current EHR systems do not meet the complete needs of a healthcare sector in transition toward a data and insight-driven future. Also, well-known interoperability issues with these systems pose a challenge for integrating emerging non-EHR data sources such as wearable and sensor data, genomic data, and social determinant data.

The key to accelerating innovation may be the burgeoning digital health startup ecosystem that has raised billions in VC money over the past few years. In today's marketplace of innovative new digital health solutions, which I will discuss later in this book, new solutions often struggle to establish a business case and find paying customers who are willing to buy based on expected returns from a value-based reimbursement model. Establishing the kind of rigorous evidence required to gain acceptance in larger health systems for broader deployment is a related challenge, which I will discuss later in the section on the competitive environment. Moreover, the VC funding industry, struggling to find a clear path toward a profitable exit for their portfolio companies, is taking a pause on new investments and is increasingly concentrating fund allocation toward later-stage rounds of financing, leaving early-stage digital health companies gasping for oxygen.

Intense competition in the startup ecosystem will ensure that a set of winners will eventually emerge, battle-hardened and well-positioned to transform healthcare. Some of the catalysts for that transformation will be the increase in healthcare consumerism and price transparency, the relentless downward pressure on FFS reimbursements, and creative use of technology-led innovation to unlock insights from the coming explosion of data.

1.2 Population Health Management

The healthcare analytics market is expected to grow at a compound annual growth rate of 15 percent through 2020, with the biggest area of growth in PHM.[27]

As of 2014, a mere 1 percent of the US population accounted for 23 percent of the total health expenditure, and around half the population accounted for 97 percent of the total health spending. People over the age of fifty-five accounted for over half the health spending while representing 28 percent of the total population.[28] The good news is that a large section of the population is healthy. The bad news is that this trend is not sustainable for the long term.

The Affordable Care Act (ACA or Obamacare) made the healthcare sector think differently about how care is delivered and paid for. The focus was clearly on cost containment, specifically on bending the cost curve to bring it under the rate of general inflation. The government used the single biggest lever available to it as the largest payer for healthcare services—payment mechanisms. In the previous section, I discussed how FFS payments are being replaced by alternative payment systems, where providers are required to take on financial risk for managing healthcare quality at a population level, with significant upsides for improved outcomes.

When the CMS introduced readmission penalties a few years ago, health systems were jolted out of their complacency with the status quo of FFS. When hospitals that had been penalized for breaching readmissions thresholds were listed publicly, health systems began to take notice of the risks of financial losses as well as reputational damage. They launched a furious race in the technology vendor community to deliver analytical solutions that could predict readmissions and help health systems avoid penalties. PHM grew from these beginnings and is now a well-established set of practices that focuses on managing entire patient populations with the goal of improving overall health outcomes while keeping costs under control. The emergence of PHM as a practice has also underscored the importance of emerging data sources as well as the technologies and tools to unlock value from the data.

The demand for healthcare services is growing because of aging populations (think of the more than seventy million baby boomers entering retirement),[29] the increasing prevalence of chronic diseases such as diabetes, and the growing expectations of healthcare consumers for the latest medical technologies and higher quality of treatment. Concurrently, cost pressures are arising from the need to do more and higher-quality work with fewer resources (not just financial—there is a shortage of qualified clinicians at a national level). Margin pressures are also increasing due to lower reimbursements and increased risks. All these factors are moving healthcare inexorably toward a healthcare delivery model that focuses on hospitalization prevention and increased engagement via mobile devices and remote sensors. Care management practices are now geared to intervene with the most high-risk patients based on risk-profiling and stratification using advanced analytics.

The growing demand for healthcare services and the shortage of financial and human resources is forcing healthcare IT to adapt and accelerate the build out of capabilities to unlock value from the digitization of medical records achieved through the implementation of EHR systems. At the same time, data sources are expanding and data is exploding, leading healthcare enterprises to explore alternate models such as cloud-based solutions for gathering and analyzing data.

As the digitization of patient medical records over the past several years creates an electronic health record backbone for the nation, the new gold rush will be about unlocking the value from EHR systems, in part by combining these systems with emerging data sources. We are now awash with data; not just EHR data but also data from remote sensors and devices (IoT), social determinant data (age, income, demographics), and other forms of structured and unstructured data. One of the big goals of PHM is to turn the data into meaningful insights, putting patients at the heart of personalized care.

A few years ago, the big technology initiatives were about "big data". Now, it is PHM (never mind how big or small the data is). From an information technology and data analytics point of view, PHM refers to the aggregation of patient data from multiple sources (structured and unstructured), and the analysis of that data to deliver insights that trigger actions to improve clinical and financial outcomes. PHM goes even further and seeks to improve health outcomes by risk-stratifying populations and identifying individual patients to be targeted for interventions.

The technologies available today that can enable the Big Unlock have come a long way from simple business intelligence (BI) tools of the last decade to cognitive computing, artificial intelligence (AI), and other advanced analytics tools. These tools can provide a comprehensive view of each patient within a population and help providers uncover insights into care gaps and disease progression to help improve clinical outcomes while lowering costs. These analytical insights are integrated into care management and other healthcare delivery processes to ensure the desired outcomes.

The landscape of PHM solutions is large and growing. As data sources increase, the opportunity for niche technology vendors and startups continues to expand. Healthcare enterprises, for their part, are becoming active participants in the innovation ecosystem by funding and supporting promising startups with unique solutions. I will discuss several examples in later chapters. The foundational principle of PHM is to create a single, unified EHR with analytics and decision-support tools for patients.

PHM has largely focused on clinical and claims data on patients. Both have limitations. At a basic level, claims data captures information on discrete encounters, whereas clinical data misses important financial information that can shed light on patient populations. An important development is the realization that, what affects health outcomes is very often associated with factors outside the traditional boundaries of healthcare delivery. The conversation is increasingly around social determinants including health behaviors (e.g. tobacco use), demographic and economic factors (e.g. employment, education, and income), and physical environment (e.g. air quality, crime rates, and access to transportation). Patients, for their part, are becoming active participants in their healthcare and are reporting data from wearables and other personal devices. All of these data sources are vital to enhancing the understanding of a patient's medical history and condition. PHM practices that expand their patient engagement programs to account for all of these data sources are beginning to show improved outcomes.

Despite the exciting possibilities for unlocking insights from data, the fact remains that healthcare data is messy, incomplete, and unreliable, especially as it relates to emerging and unstructured data sources. Healthcare data sets tend to be small relative to other sectors, such as retail and consumer finance, and a good chunk of the data often has to be thrown away due to data integrity and data sufficiency issues. However, every effort has to be made to analyze the data as best as possible because while investing in improved data capture and aggregation. Analysis of data, even with all the limitations described above, may provide incremental insights which can inform intervention and treatment options that may not otherwise be evident. Moreover, advanced analytical methods such as natural-language processing and cognitive computing rely on learning, for which data in any shape and form is important.

As the healthcare sector transitions to VBC, APMs such as ACO and PCMH will rely heavily on PHM practices to deliver quality outcomes. PHM is already the norm and will expand in range and sophistication in the coming years.

PHM solutions in the marketplace have to deal with integration and sharing of data, something which is less a technical challenge and more an issue related to conflicting and powerful proprietary and departmental interests. The interoperability of data between major EHR systems and other PHM solutions has been a big constraint in the adoption and acceleration of PHM solutions.

The promise of PHM can also be realized only when the analytical insights and improved care management practices effectively engage patients and make them active participants in their care. Digital health programs that focus primarily on the patient engagement aspects of PHM have received a tremendous boost in the past couple of years. Digital health startups have raised billions in funding from venture capitalists looking to benefit from the wave of interest in everything digital, from patient engagement to telemedicine programs, the IoT, and more. The digital transformation of healthcare is expected to make healthcare more efficient, eliminate friction in the provider-patient interface, and accelerate innovation in care delivery. However, this transformation relies on the technology ecosystem's ability to unlock insights from a vast and growing number of data sources.

For technology firms, especially those used to selling to CIOs, the PHM space is a new landscape with new decision makers and new titles to navigate. CPHOs and CDOs are among the new stakeholders they have to know and understand.

1.3 The Rise of Healthcare Consumerism

Consumers are dissatisfied with their experience with healthcare.[30] In most consumer-oriented industries, consumers have high expectations and provide feedback almost instantaneously. For instance, in the music industry when someone likes a band's live performance, they come back for more shows; otherwise, they do not. In sharp contrast, healthcare consumers have not only come to expect poor service, they almost always come back to the same hospital for care. To the healthcare system, it made no difference.

In the traditional employer-based model of healthcare coverage, which continues to cover the vast majority of the US population, the disconnect between the provider, payer, and consumer meant that the consumer did not know or care about what it cost to obtain a healthcare service. Since there was limited financial exposure and premiums were pretty much the same across the board—at least for healthy individuals—there was no incentive for consumers to be conservative about consuming services. By the same token, there was no incentive for healthcare providers or payers to care much about the quality of service or outcomes. In the triad of patient, provider, and insurer, there was a strong partnership between patient and provider but a general mistrust defining the remaining two relationships.

The dynamic between healthcare consumers and the healthcare sector has changed in the past couple of years, with increased deductibles and copays on the back of skyrocketing premiums and runaway drug prices. In light of increased premiums, deductibles, and out-of-pocket costs, patients have no choice but to become informed consumers of healthcare services. The newly arisen healthcare consumer has created a need for transparency around healthcare costs, something healthcare providers have long sought to avoid.

Health insurance premiums have far outpaced income growth due to several reasons, including the high medical costs of the newly insured under the ACA, which have necessitated premium increases by health insurance carriers. In addition to these premium increases, there have also been increases in out-of-pocket expenses, including copays and deductibles.

Faced with this, the American consumer has had no choice but to start looking for other options. The rise of consumerism is a direct consequence of the transition from FFS to VBC, which has resulted in a dramatic shift of risks, with consumers at the receiving end. Consumers have to spend several thousand dollars out of pocket before they can expect their insurance carriers to pick up the tab.

There is no doubt that we have entered the era of healthcare consumerism. But what is consumerism in healthcare?

Simply stated, consumerism is about putting the consumer at the center of the business model. The patient's interaction with the healthcare system is changing from being merely episodic to more of an ongoing communication. The focus is also changing from being merely transactional to more emotion-based and meaningful interactions, with high expectations around quality of experience. With healthcare costs and insurance premiums out of control, the only way for employers to reduce costs and keep premium increases in check is to incentivize employees to take care of themselves and avoid hospitalizations and unnecessary physician office visits.

The demographic makeup of healthcare consumers will now matter more than ever. The senior citizen on Medicare has different expectations than the millennial consumer.[31] Healthcare companies have to recognize these differences and market themselves appropriately.

However, healthcare is poorly prepared to become a consumer-oriented industry given its long legacy of ignoring the consumers' needs and preferences, and the unique industry structure with perverse incentives that rewarded excessive consumption of healthcare services.

The healthcare sector has traditionally been poor at delivering consumer experiences, and there are opportunities everywhere. Recognizing this yawning gap, VC investments are pouring into disruptive startups that are focusing on improving the consumer experience with the help of technology platforms, advanced analytics, and segmentation models.[32] The entry of nimble and agile software companies in redefining the healthcare experience is unleashing competitive forces that are shaking up healthcare, a sector hitherto unfamiliar with naked market forces. Ultimately, the winners will be those that can lower the costs of insurance while improving the quality of the experience by providing consumers with a range of offerings in a unified manner, enabling them to make more-informed choices about healthcare.

As the consumerization of healthcare gains momentum, the use of advanced analytics in digital marketing for patient acquisition and engagement will drive new investments in digital programs.[33] With an aim to attract and retain increasingly well-informed patients, health systems are using sophisticated data analytics to target people at the moment of healthcare need.

In the new world of healthcare consumerism, technology and

data analytics will be center-stage in determining the efficacy of patient engagement. Understanding healthcare consumers will require healthcare companies to have access to comprehensive information about their medical and non-medical data, including nontraditional data such as from social media and wearables. At the other end of the spectrum, consumers will expect enhanced engagement levels from their healthcare providers.

The shifting burden of financial responsibility toward consumers is driving them to shop around for healthcare services. New technology platforms and partnerships are emerging to help consumers and insurers alike with products designed to help drive competition and drive down healthcare costs.

The growing trend towards consumerization of healthcare services will require traditional healthcare enterprises to invest in digital technology to reach consumers through their smart devices while enabling caregivers to have real-time access to information on their mobile devices through clinical data integration. However, unlike digital health startups, traditional healthcare companies have a treasure trove of data that gives them a significant advantage over startups in truly understanding the healthcare consumer. The challenge is that many of these data sources do not work well together. This is partly due to the absence of industry-wide interoperability standards. This is also because data is emerging from nontraditional sources that have not been part of the healthcare ecosystem. An example of this would be genetic testing data and PGHD from wearables that is slowly being integrated into clinical settings for improved diagnosis and treatment outcomes.

The emerging trends of consumerism represent a tremendous opportunity for some. Companies like Leapfrog, Healthgrades, and Castlight have created platforms that provide price transparency and comparison tools. A large part of the push towards developing products for healthcare consumers came from the digital health startup ecosystem which raised $4.5 billion in VC funds in 2016 and a similar amount in 2015.[34] Dozens of VC-funded digital health startups have developed products targeting consumers directly with personal health trackers, wearables, and sensors that focus on wellness. There has been a proliferation of digital health applications over the past few years but recent data suggests that many of these firms have struggled to build sustainable and scalable businesses with business to consumer (B2C) models and have pivoted to B2B models targeting healthcare enterprises instead.

The digital transformation of healthcare, driven by the shift toward VBC, is also a mandate for improving patient engagement and adopting a new approach to healthcare marketing focused on engaging with healthcare consumers through smartphone interfaces and social media. However, there has never been a bigger need for technology to be empathetic to patients. Digital officers in healthcare are focusing on improving patient experiences and managing their online reputations to attract and retain savvy consumers.

As patients increasingly turn to independent platforms such as Leapfrog and Healthgrades to make informed choices about medical care, health systems are transforming their marketing practices to engage with this newly informed class of patients. For their part, major health insurers such as Cigna are providing consumers with price comparison and other decision tools to help them make informed choices about their treatment options.

The era of healthcare consumerism is in the early stages, with average healthcare consumers still unaware of the changes in the environment and the increasing range of choices available. While healthcare companies are widely adopting data analytics, issues such as interoperability remain formidable challenges to overcome, as are restrictions related to HIPAA that make it difficult to share data. The use of newer forms of data, such as from wearables and social media, is still in very early stages, with no clear precedents or guidelines to follow. The lack of trust remains a significant barrier as well, given the decades-long adversarial relationships among all participants.

A related challenge is that most consumers find healthcare to be too complex and find navigating through it a huge challenge. Enabling patients with better technology and giving them more control is an important aspect of the emerging relationship between health systems and their patients. Increasing consumerism also means that patients have to feel like they are partners in their healthcare. The days of a paternalistic approach to healthcare are behind us, and technology is stepping in to help patients partner with physicians.

The ongoing transfer of financial responsibility and the shift toward VBC are driving some unusual partnerships between traditional and nontraditional players in healthcare with a common purpose—increasing choice and improving outcomes. Healthcare has always looked to patients to take more control of their medical decisions. However, patients have chosen to go with a doctor-knows-best approach to their care. Now, increased financial responsibility is driving consumers to seek information and take control of their healthcare. They are increasingly consulting "Dr. Google" and other sources of information for health and cost information and then showing up at their physicians' offices with their findings and even recommendations for treatment options. Most importantly, they are now willing to share personal data including genomic data and data from their wearable devices with their physicians and expect physicians to use the data in diagnostic and treatment decisions. A case in point is that of actor Angelina Jolie who made a personal choice to undergo a double mastectomy in 2013 on the basis of a genomic test that identified her as having an 87 percent risk of breast cancer.

Physicians are becoming willing participants in these discussions, driven by a shared purpose. They are further motivated, by incentives launched last year by the CMS, to participate in shared decision making between doctors and patients. Various studies indicate that engaging in collaborative decision making is turning patients into active participants in their healthcare.

How does technology feature in this new model of doctor–patient collaboration? As the recent shift from B2C towards B2B models by many digital health startups attests, it is one thing to develop a consumer-focused application or technology and entirely another to get those consumers or their physicians to use it. Blame it on the system of reimbursements for healthcare. Many early startups were dogged and doomed by a payment system that discouraged physicians from recommending a mobile health application unless it qualified for insurance reimbursement.

Many digital health companies have realized that the route to profitability and sustainability lies in demonstrating ROI for the platform or service independently. Consumers' willingness to pay for the technologies is likely to increase physicians' willingness to recommend these innovative new digital health solutions, untethered from the system of reimbursements that drives healthcare choices.

1.4 The Internet of Healthcare (and Other) Things

Twenty-five percent of Americans owned a wearable device at the end of 2016 (a growth of 12 percent over the previous year) according to the Rock Health Consumer Health Trends Report.[35] The world of healthcare wearables is witnessing a boom fueled by heightened awareness of health and fitness. The current focus on wearables, which can take a wide range of shapes and forms, is an extension or subset of the IoT phenomenon, which includes remote sensors, monitoring devices, and medical devices capable of communicating with similar wireless-enabled devices. IoT data which is gaining a great deal of attention to the explosion of these "smart" devices may well drive the way we manage our health and wellness in the future.

Research firm Gartner estimated that some 6.4 billion connected things would be in use by the end of 2016, with some 5.5 million new things getting connected every day.[36] We are aware of the boom in health and fitness wearables, especially among healthcare consumers who are buying fitness trackers —sometimes with their employers' encouragement. While other sectors such as manufacturing have been using wearables in a wide range of applications such as safety, productivity, and workplace collaboration,[37] the IoT movement is relatively nascent in healthcare. Consulting firm Accenture published a report in early 2017 that estimates that the market for the Internet of Health Things—any object with network connectivity that can talk to another similar object in the healthcare industry—will be worth $163 billion by 2020.[38]

An important concept in this context is *connected health*. While the term means different things to different people, it is used commonly to describe the enabling of healthcare delivery through improved communication between stakeholders, mainly patients and providers, through connected devices. Importantly, the term is more than just mHealth or telehealth—two terms that are commonly used in relation to connected health.

A couple of high-level trends driving connected health include the following:

- A shift from episodic, in-person encounters between patients and providers to an anytime, anywhere mode of care delivery. In particular, millennials are defining this experience with their lifestyle and preferences, especially for asynchronous interactions through smartphone-enabled apps.[39]
- The proliferation of entirely new classes of devices (IoT) that can connect to one another in the context of a connected health program.

Connected health and IoT are distinct but interdependent movements that are gaining traction in the VBC era. Technology advances are enabling health systems to harness the full potential of IoT, and it is early days yet. Fascinating IoT applications are being developed, many through unlikely partnerships. Medical device company Medtronic has developed a diabetes-monitoring application (SugarIQ) that transmits data from wearables to the IBM Watson cognitive computing and predictive analytics platform for real-time feedback and alerts.[40] Swiss pharma company Novartis has joined with Qualcomm to develop an Internet-connected inhaler that can send information to a cloud-based big data analytics platform for healthcare providers to use in treating patients.[41]

Heightened awareness of health and fitness is driving healthcare consumers to invest in fitness trackers and monitors that can prevent expensive physician and hospital visits that now carry increased out-of-pocket costs. Excited by the possibilities, several healthcare enterprises have been running IoT pilots. However, the transition from pilots to enterprise-wide adoption is slower than anticipated for a variety of reasons.

- Humans are notoriously unreliable when it comes to turning on and off their trackers.
- The accuracy of data recorded from IoT devices is questionable given the current state of the technology; an example of which is the low reliability of data from wearable devices on the wrist which can vary based on how they are worn by the user, sweat levels and so on. Due to the various types of sensor technologies used, as well as individual differences between users, such as hair and sweat on the wrist at the time of readings, there are significant inconsistencies in the data gathered by wearables even from the same individual.[42]
- The real benefit of wearables in improving health and wellness can never be realized unless the data collected can be integrated with other medical and socioeconomic data, which will provide a complete picture that experienced medical practitioners can use when diagnosing and treating patients.
- Interoperability issues between different systems that store patient medical information, combined with data-privacy laws, continue to be big challenges.
- Patent wars involving wearable devices are likely to put a damper on VC investments, as evidenced by Jawbone's lawsuits against Fitbit for patent infringement.[43] Ultimately,

it is VC funding that will drive innovation and growth in this sector, and any adverse rulings will slow down capital flow to this fast-growing sector.

Despite the promise of connected health for improved outcomes, the growth rate for connected health programs has to overcome these challenges.

Healthcare things do not necessarily talk well to each other. Interoperability issues keep critical patient data locked up in proprietary systems such as Epic, and the makers of "things" like to operate within proprietary platforms such as Apple. The interoperability issue is being gradually addressed through the formation of consortia that are trying to set industry standards, and several innovative startups are building cloud-based applications on data gathered through a collection of application programming interfaces (APIs). The emergence of FHIR standards seems promising as more and more applications are FHIR-enabled, creating momentum for eventual independence from proprietary standards.

Errors in data capture. I have a wearable device that I use to track my activity levels, and I can say with confidence that I would not ask my physician to use the wearable data for my annual health check-up or to diagnose a medical condition. While the data capture is directionally correct, the inaccuracy is well outside what I would consider acceptable for the data to be considered "medical grade." Call them *meditoys* if you will, because they are consumer devices that have yet to mature into real medical devices.

Lack of clinical-grade digital health applications. Most digital health applications are consumer-grade, meaning they are not usable in a clinical context. However, we are now seeing a convergence of several technology trends, all of which are aimed at harnessing personal health and medical information that can be used to improve health and wellness, as well as for academic research. There are not many clinical-grade mobile applications that can connect devices for clinical use. A study by the QuintilesIMS Institute of Health Informatics (IIHI) found that, while there are over 165,000 mobile health apps available for iOS and Android, only 2 percent of these apps can connect a patient to a provider system.[44] This bottleneck in the adoption of mHealth applications has implications for patient engagement levels, as well as for quality and safety. However, the IIHI report states that one in ten apps can connect to a device or sensor, which significantly improves the ease and accuracy of data collection in a clinical setting.

The regulatory and reimbursement environment for connected health programs plays a big part in the acceleration of adoption rates. Many emerging technology solutions in healthcare are not eligible for reimbursements under the FFS framework. Disconnects between fee-based reimbursement at the physician level and the push for increased VBC models at the enterprise level create conflicting incentives between stakeholder groups. The consumerization of healthcare is also likely to draw many new entrants, lured by the opportunity but often unaware of the regulatory and compliance requirements related to healthcare data. Playing fast and loose with consumer privacy is likely to earn, at the very least, a slap on the wrist from government agencies looking out for consumer interests.

The benefits of connected health programs will accrue when the data can be analyzed to develop holistic views of patients and patient populations that can drive outcomes. The unlocking of insights from data is in an embryonic stage today—partly due to the rapid emergence of new and varied data sources in structured and unstructured formats, and partly due to interoperability challenges with the dominant sources of patient data such as EHR systems. The aggregation and analysis of diverse data sets has been the focus of PHM programs.

Eventually, healthcare will overcome all these challenges, simply because of the potential benefits of using IoT data for connected health. Technology is evolving at an explosive pace, and the regulatory and legal infrastructure has to catch up. We are seeing the very early stages of the exciting new era of wearables. One might even say that the technology is only skin-deep at this point. However, the coming of age of IoT in healthcare is under way, and technology firms and healthcare innovators are racing to harness the data and unlock its insights. This is just the beginning.

2 New Data and the Analytical Approaches to Unlocking Insights

The explosion of data sources and the growing volume of knowledge have created an unprecedented opportunity for generating insights, as well as a challenge in building the computing and analytics infrastructure for effectively harnessing the data and knowledge. To gain an appreciation of the magnitude of the issue, consider this:

- The volume of healthcare data was at 153 exabytes in 2013 (an exabyte is 1 billion gigabytes), according to the research firm IDC, which calls this a "data tsunami." At projected growth rates, this figure will swell to 2,314 exabytes by 2020.[45]
- According to a Kleiner Perkins report on Internet trends, medical knowledge, which took fifty years to double in 1950, is expected to double in three and a half years today.[46]

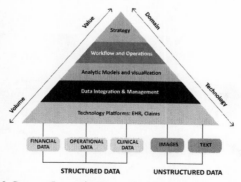

Figure 1: Damo Consulting Analytics Value Pyramid, 2017

The healthcare analytics market is estimated to be worth over $24.5 billion by 2021 according to industry research firms.[47] The market is driven by the promise of improved population health, reduced healthcare costs, and rising healthcare consumerism, with rising costs of healthcare being the biggest motivating factor. The top analytical priorities for providers are clinical analytics and data capture. Risk management, quality improvement, and digital health innovations are driving analytics in a big way.

Although the overall news is encouraging regarding the increase in adoption rates for analytics, there are some disturbing negative trends as well. Adoption levels for analytics vary widely, with larger hospitals showing greater adoption and corresponding benefits. A caveat for any analysis of adoption rates on analytics is that there may not be common definitions. The term *analytics* could refer to anything from data infrastructure to reporting to predictive modeling (see fig 1), and clinical practitioners, as well as analytics professionals, need to be circumspect about arriving at generic conclusions.

The healthcare data used in analytics and digital health programs sits primarily in proprietary EHR systems, though an increasing number of data sources are outside of them. Within EHR systems, most of the data sit in unstructured formats (such as text and clinical notes) that are yet to be fully tapped. Savvy chief medical information officers (CMIOs) and CIOs are looking past their EHR systems and putting together analytics strategies using a combination of third-party solutions and in-house expertise. The vendor landscape is maturing with solutions and offerings, and many stories are emerging of partnerships between healthcare systems and solution providers that are delivering value.

An important aspect of creating value from data is to ingest, aggregate, and analyze vast amounts of data from a wide range of sources. Lidia Fonseca of Quest Diagnostics likes to imagine the data being fed into a data lake as an iceberg.[48] At any given time, a user is only viewing the tip of the iceberg they want to see, but underneath is information waiting to be unlocked for value. With the right tools to catalog and structure the data, health systems can create the ability to provide the right insights at the point where they are needed. Fonseca sees behavioral, lifestyle, and wearables data to be a piece of the overall iceberg. She adds, "In terms of data sources we certainly have claims data, medication data, and laboratory data. Those three data sources give you some very key insights. I think you will see more and more data sources on the behavioral side, such as wearables and lifestyle data, and data on the choices that people make in terms of health and lifestyle. We are going to see more of that as we think about the shift from treating the sick to keeping people healthy. I very much believe that having the ability to integrate data from various sources is the key to be successful and that is certainly the approach that we have taken to bring all of our data into a data lake. We catalog this data and organize it and structure it, and serve it to our internal and external clients through some pretty robust visualization and reporting capabilities." The QuestQuanum™ data analytics platform she has launched is designed to deliver real-time insights at the point of care by ingesting and analyzing data from multiple data sources in a data lake running on Hadoop big data architecture.

The transformation of healthcare from a transactional to an outcomes-based model is driving the interest in multiple data sources. Payers are worried about the risks and financial exposure of value-based contracts and APMs, as well as the medical cost risks of individual members they know little or nothing about in exchange markets. Providers are worried about risk-based contracts, clinical quality measures such as readmissions, and the reputational damage that ensues from penalties and low ratings.

Enter the science of advanced analytics. Faced with the realization that analyzing historical data to understand what happened is no longer adequate, the most progressive among healthcare enterprises are developing and wielding advanced models as strategic tools for improved outcomes, reduced utilizations, and increased margins. Traditionally, healthcare has been measuring and analyzing the operational and the tactical, focusing on metrics such as revenue per bed, per member per month costs, and the like. By combining structured data analysis with techniques such as cognitive computing and natural-language processing (NLP) capabilities, health systems and health plans are addressing care quality in terms of PHM practices. New requirements like population health analytics will drive the survival of health systems and ACOs, where the whole focus is predicting what is likely to happen, especially for chronic cases that sit in the top 15 percent of the population risk pool.

Armed with predictive modeling and scoring tools, CPHOs can now have conversations with CMOs and physicians about outcomes, quality, and variability in care based on best practices; stratify populations; and manage risk pools.

C-level executives in mid-sized hospital systems, faced with stagnant-to-declining inpatient volumes, are focusing hard on costs to stay afloat. In an uncertain environment, tactical and operational analytics focusing on historical data are no longer a reliable guide for strategic decision making. Real-time predictive analytics based on the integration of data across silos is almost necessary for survival. Organizations need to be fanatically wed to data analysis to negotiate this landscape.

Drew Schiller, CEO of digital health company Validic, a leading platform for connecting patient-generated data from digital health apps, wearables, and in-home medical devices in the healthcare system, has a hands-on perspective on the ground-level reality of working with multiple data sources, especially non-EHR data sources and patient-generated data. The Validic platform works with over four hundred data sources: everything from health apps and wearables to in-home medical devices that are US Food and Drug Administration (FDA) listed, such as blood pressure monitors, glucose meters, pulse oximeters, and weight scales. The platform standardizes and normalizes the data from these different sources and provides one simple connection for easy access and use inside healthcare. Says Schiller, "If I look more broadly at the healthcare system, I see a lot of thinking is happening around how to integrate more data into the workflow of a clinician. That has been a big challenge that we have seen, so while there is a lot of data available now, in reality, it is difficult to get any information into the clinician's workflow. Every health system has a different way of thinking about health data, even within the organization. For instance, the head of endocrinology is looking for data from glucose meters, and the head of ENT is looking for the integration of data from inhalers for the asthmatic population, but they are not thinking about getting and integrating the data which is a big challenge. We are beginning to see a lot more thoughtfulness emerging on this from healthcare executives."[49] A related challenge for healthcare is developing a consistent way of running data integration programs while minimizing the number of vendor connections and interactions, optimizing EHR systems, and finding ways to unlock the data that already exists in these systems. Schiller of Validic believes we are seeing a trend of thinking holistically about data that is very encouraging.

In early 2017, the FDA allowed 23andMe, a Silicon Valley company, to market their Personal Genome Service Genetic Health Risk (GHR) tests for ten diseases or conditions. The press release stated that these are "the first direct-to-consumer (DTC) tests authorized by the FDA that provide information on an individual's genetic predisposition to certain medical diseases or conditions, which may help to make decisions about lifestyle choices or to inform discussions with a health care professional."[50] The tests, based on saliva samples, aim to provide information to individual consumers on their genetic risks for conditions such as Parkinson's disease. The company points out that GHR tests cannot determine a person's overall risk of developing a disease or condition and points to other factors such as environment and lifestyle that contribute to the development of a disease or a condition.

The FDA approval was a reversal of an earlier decision that prohibited 23andMe from offering personal genetic tests. Besides being an interesting case of a Silicon Valley company winning over the much-disliked regulatory authorities, it represented a breakthrough for an important source of data that could now be used for PHM and personalized care.

Healthcare services firms, technology vendors, and a handful of nontraditional players are coming together to develop unique, value-added offerings by combining data pools to serve the savvy healthcare consumer of the future. The acceleration of digital health adoption across generations has resulted in dramatic cost reductions for data storage and processing. The cost of sequencing a human genome, an estimated $300 million in 2000, is now down to a mere $1,000.[51] There are over five thousand diagnostic tests[52] available for genetic disorders today.

One concern that has come up regarding the use of genetic testing data is the potential for misuse. Media reports have pointed out that companies like AncestryDNA make customers sign over virtually unlimited rights to use their data.[53]

The US National Library of Medicine provides useful guidance around informed consent in genetic tests and genetic discrimination that lays out consumer rights. Though the Genetic Information Nondiscrimination Act of 2008 provides some protections, especially against insurers and employers from using DNA data to influence decisions about insurance coverage or employment decisions, future legislation could effectively overturn these protections.[54]

For healthcare organizations, it all boils down to making investments in analytics infrastructure and computing the returns on this investment. The most progressive healthcare organizations have made aggressive investments in setting up a dedicated analytics infrastructure and building teams of decision scientists and technologists who can take data and turn it into insights. Many, especially national payers, are acquiring analytics companies to give themselves a leg up on the competition. For mid-sized healthcare organizations, the options are limited. Most tend to partner with a vendor that understands healthcare and brings advanced analytics capabilities to develop the capability in-house over time. While there are no clear benchmarks on the ROI of analytics investments, by focusing on specific problems with identifiable cost implications, such as readmissions, returns can be computed using a combination of cost avoidance and reduced utilization levels.

In the next section, I discuss a few examples of how health systems are unlocking value from data and computing the ROI using innovative new techniques.

2.1 Risk Management with NLP: UPMC Health Plan

Big data analytics in healthcare has largely been about looking at claims, EHR, and other forms of structured data. NLP is an emerging area that can help unlock value from the vast amount of unstructured data that is pervasive in healthcare. In the emerging era of value-based payments, risk adjustments may well determine the difference between profit and loss for the health insurance industry.

UPMC Health Plan, the health insurance arm of the University of Pittsburgh Medical Center (UPMC), has deployed NLP-based technology and big data analytics to efficiently process millions of pieces of documentation to identify risk adjustment possibilities and capture incremental revenue.

Under the risk adjustment program for Medicare Advantage, the CMS adjusts reimbursement amounts based on risk scores that take into account a variety of conditions. The purpose is to adequately cover the costs of providing healthcare, especially to those with complex conditions. Under this program, health plans can increase revenues by submitting documents from doctor–patient interactions that justify the risk adjustment. However, they often fail to capitalize on this opportunity for a variety of reasons. The result is a potential loss of revenue for the health plan.

Despite the billions of dollars spent on digitizing medical records under the Meaningful Use provisions of the HITECH Act, the vast majority of clinical data (estimated widely to be around 80 percent) is in the form of unstructured data, such as clinical notes, audio transcripts, and images. Since unstructured data can support risk adjustment claims, big data and NLP technologies can be used to parse the information in these types of documents for evidence of incremental risk that can qualify for additional payments.

Health plans typically have large teams of certified coders (people trained on the International Classification of Diseases or (ICD-10) who review claims under the risk adjustment program. Given the nine thousand or so ICD-10 codes that map to some seventy-nine CMS hierarchical condition categories, there are simply too many combinations for humans to handle.[55] Besides being labor intensive, the process can be expensive and error prone. Besides, it is well near impossible to use a brute-force approach to process all of the unstructured data sitting in the millions and millions of documents to unearth evidence for risk adjustment.

With the emergence of NLP tools, it is now possible to process very large numbers of documents much more efficiently and identify opportunities much more accurately.

By partnering with Health Fidelity, a Silicon Valley startup that has built a big data analytics platform based on NLP technology, UPMC obtains insightful and accurate coding suggestions for risk adjustment from vast amounts of unstructured data such as clinical notes. UPMC has also made a strategic investment in the company, which has licensed the NLP technology from Columbia University, where it was originally developed. According to John Wisniewski, chief actuary at UPMC Health Plan, the technology has allowed the organization to "make more money — and keep it, which allows us to keep our premiums low."[56] The NLP platform presents coders with suggestions for possible risk adjustments based on standard terminology and robust taxonomies that identify and understand patterns using techniques such as machine learning and association mining.

The ROI on the use of NLP technology comes from improved productivity as well as increased reimbursements. The financial returns to UPMC Health Plan have been in the range of $40 million a year for the two years it has used the technology.

NLP technology and big data analytics are a means of augmenting—not replacing—human knowledge. Experienced coders take the recommendations from the platform and check them for accuracy before modifying claims to include additional information. The technology and tools thus complement the work of expert coders. By identifying and helping prioritize claims for review, and doing it in a fraction of the time it used to take, UPMC's coders have been able to increase throughput by a factor of four, leading to accelerated cash flows and increased revenues.[57]

NLP and sentiment analysis are likely to grow in importance because of the need to create context. NLP technologies are likely to become significantly more important in the future because they enable us to mine the data quickly and turn it into insights.

An important aspect of the improved accuracy is the avoidance of penalties that might arise from CMS risk-adjusted data validation audits that are intended to identify and recover improper payments. UPMC's NLP platform can remember where to find supporting documents for any claim, years after the claim was submitted and reimbursed. The platform reduces effort and costs associated with the cumbersome process of going through the increasingly frequent audits.

A final, important aspect of the use of NLP is the opportunity to improve Healthcare Effectiveness Data and Information Set scores by identifying gaps in care that can help improve health outcomes.

NLP technology is rapidly gaining ground as a technology that can recognize and analyze human commands as opposed to machine language or programming (think Siri or Alexa). Through machine learning and AI, NLP technologies can become increasingly accurate over time.

Many health plans are turning to big data analytics on unstructured data using techniques such as NLP to process vast data sets efficiently and identify hidden revenue opportunities. Those that are not getting on the bandwagon are likely to be busy writing refund checks to the CMS for improper payments.

2.2 Managing At-risk Populations for Behavioral Health: South Florida Behavioral Health Network (SFBHN)

Behavioral health issues—which include substance abuse—correlate with increased mortality, unemployment, and homelessness, among other things.

As with accountable care models in PHM, the key to reining in behavioral health costs is to understand population health risks and intervening with preventive care models that reduce costs while improving the quality of care. A couple of partnership models provide examples of how technology innovators and care providers are collaborating to address the problem.

"The behavioral health sector is not well prepared to take risks," says John Dow, CEO of SFBHN, a nonprofit that deals with the prevention and treatment of behavioral health disorders at the community level. "To begin with, unlike in a medical field such as oncology, there are no registries with longitudinal data on behavioral health patients. Additional complications include confidentiality and sensitivity of data that might hurt individuals if mishandled (such as data on criminal history and incarceration). Aggregating data can be a significant challenge that requires collaboration among stakeholders."[58]

However, behavioral health is underfunded given the scale of the problem and under-equipped regarding treatment infrastructure. The costs, relative to the size of the affected population, are disproportionately high. Consulting firm McKinsey estimates that this group represents 20 percent of the population but accounts for 35 percent of the total healthcare expenditure in the country today.[59]

To bring technology innovation to address the problem, SFBHN partnered with ODH Solutions, an offshoot of Japanese pharma company Otsuka, which developed Mentrics, a PHM platform for behavioral health. The key feature of the platform is a risk-scoring algorithm that identifies high-risk patients for targeted intervention by using predictive analytics on medical records, behavioral health data, as well as data on the individual's justice issues. Justice issues, an important aspect of the program, are an outcome of the White House's Data Driven Justice initiative, which focuses on reducing incarceration and recidivism within the population.[60] SFBHN, which has accumulated five to six years of behavioral health data, works with local hospitals to combine this data with medical records to identify and target at-risk individuals. SFBHN is careful about the confidentiality of the data and takes extreme care to comply with the government's Code of Federal Regulations (CFR) 42 regulations on the same.[61]

Behavioral health is a complicated and expensive issue in US healthcare today. It is also a field that is underfunded and ripe for technology-led innovation. It is one of those spaces with a double bottom line. In other words, the intended benefits are financial and social. As support for funding for behavioral health programs gathers momentum through legislation and technology and analytics solutions mature with data, predictive models that accurately identify early onset of dementia and other conditions can have a significant impact on reducing treatment costs.

In 2016, there were over two hundred behavioral health startups,[62] many of them funded by venture capital. Many of these startups are attracting the attention of health insurance companies looking to rein in the costs of behavioral health in their member populations by buying innovation from the market. Some of the early solution providers solutions have already been acquired by larger insurance companies, while others have received venture capital from the investing arms of health plans.

However, as in the case of digital health, many of these solutions are not based on clinical evidence and are not FDA-approved, which limits their use in clinical settings.

The lack of federal funding for behavioral health may raise questions about the business viability for many of these startups. The shortage of trained mental health professionals, especially in rural areas, can be a barrier to scale as well. The announcement by HHS in late 2016 to set aside $44.5 million to grow the pool of behavioral health professionals was very timely.[63]

As John Dow, CEO of SFBHN says, "Everyone will then be able to reap the benefits, regardless of how you define it."[64]

2.3 Unlocking Data with Unusual Partnerships: Quest Diagnostics

Quest Diagnostics, a lab test leader, is an example of a company that has successfully monetized its data and has built a set of strategic partnerships to expand its core business into the advanced healthcare analytics space. In 2016, the company launched QuestQuanum™, a set of analytics tools that unlock insights from Quest's database of over twenty billion test results combined with traditional data such as claim data, EHR data, and emerging data sources such as genetic test data and scientific literature.

A partnership between Quest and analytics company Inovalon resulted in Data Diagnostics™, an analytics platform that blends Quest's twenty billion lab test records with Inovalon's access to claim records on 130 million patients. The combined data set covers roughly one in three Americans. Providers and affiliated physicians gain access to analytical reports through a single user interface from within their EHR systems. According to Quest CIO Lidia Fonseca and Inovalon CEO Keith Dunleavy, MD, the partnership is important because it combines two massive and complementary data sets to create unique value for the provider community as well as payers and health systems transitioning from FFS to value-based payment models.[65]

Having a mountain of data is one thing, and delivering real-time insights from the data at the point of care is another. The Data Diagnostics™ platform does this effectively by providing real-time visibility to patient history and risk eligibility, especially for affiliated physicians to whom large health systems are downstreaming the risks. The platform also delivers incremental value by helping to identify opportunities to reduce and eliminate waste arising from unnecessary or duplicative tests and procedures. In that sense, it contributes to the improvement of overall efficiencies in the healthcare system. The partnership is also a template for data monetization models for other health systems, especially those with broad national reach.

Providers have limited options today for obtaining actionable insights through the implementation of big data technologies. However, most analytics programs struggle with the operationalization of analytics platforms that do not have real-time capabilities. Such platforms work offline and do not integrate into the day-to-day clinical workflow. The transition to VBC requires analytics to be front and center in point of care decisions which requires tightly integrated, real-time computing infrastructure.

Over the years, Quest has developed interfaces that connect to over six hundred EHR systems installed in provider organizations. In the absence of true interoperability between provider clinical systems, this is as close as it gets. Combined with Inovalon's complementary data sets in the cloud, analytical reports—over a hundred of these so far—generate real-time insights with a single click. A pay-per-click model minimizes costs by allowing physicians to choose only the reports they need, with the practice or health system paying the cost. The ROI is a result of better care and outcomes that help physicians qualify for additional financial incentives under value-based payment models. Minimal setup cost and ease of use have enhanced the commercial viability of the platform.

Of the reimbursement models required to increase adoption for advanced analytical solutions, Lidia Fonseca of Quest says, "For emerging solutions, it comes back to showing value which can take time. In our core business, many years ago somebody had to convince payers of the value of diagnostic testing. Similarly, when you think about some of the new advances such as the more high-end genomic and genetics testing, there is a process that we go through to show the value and make a case for why insurance should cover the tests. When you think about new analytical tools and platforms, we need to be able to work with the payers and show them, for instance by identifying patients that have a condition, that we can intervene sooner so that they do not advance to a more serious stage. That is value, because if you can intervene early, then you create a treatment path that prevents their condition from becoming a chronic or a more advanced stage condition. There is value in that."[66]

Quest has also entered into unusual partnerships. A deal with retailer Safeway provides convenient access to testing services at approximately fifty Safeway locations; another with Ancestry. com provides genotyping test services on behalf of Ancestry's AncestryDNA service, which identifies and quantifies an individual's ethnic origins based on results of DNA testing.

Genetic testing data, in particular, seems to be emerging as an important data source. In addition to Ancestry, Quest has partnered with IBM Watson Health to provide a Watson-powered genomic sequencing service for cancer patients. The Watson cognitive computing platform's advanced analytics capabilities for oncology, combined with Quest's diagnostic testing capabilities, aim to benefit cancer treatment at the Memorial Sloan Kettering Cancer Center.

Fonseca, who is also responsible for the IT infrastructure supporting the partnership, believes that the partnership can greatly benefit rural hospitals and providers who may have limited resources and access to cancer care.[67] Developing a network of partnerships has been a crucial step in the evolution of Quest from being a company known only for lab tests to becoming more of an information services company.

Quest Diagnostics is also an example of an emerging trend of healthcare organizations getting into new businesses that put them in the marketplace of technology solution providers, an aspect I will cover again in chapter five on the competitive landscape.

2.4 Future-proofing the Technology Backbone of Patient-generated Health Data: Sutter Health

The notion of PGHD is not new.

Every time a patient shows up at a physician's office and starts describing symptoms, the doctor is effectively gathering PGHD. Hitherto, this verbal exchange would form part of the basis for a doctor's diagnosis and would likely be recorded in the doctor's notes from the visit.

Along with the increase in healthcare consumerism, there is a growing awareness among health systems of the need to involve patients in their medical care. An important aspect of enabling that is to harness the continuous stream of data from wearables, sensors, and IoT devices. PGHD can provide valuable insights to clinicians in PHM and personalized medicine.

Technology has enabled patients to communicate with doctors more frequently, as opposed to the episodic mode of interaction characterized by the traditional physician's office visit. The growing use of smartphones, remote monitoring devices, and mobile health applications provides patients with new ways to share data with physicians. Data sharing on a continuous basis physicians to develop more comprehensive views of patients—especially of how they are doing between office visits, which can significantly improve outcomes in chronic disease management.

It is important to note that PGHD is not just clinical data such as health and treatment history; it is also social determinant data such as income, lifestyle, access to transportation, and a host of other factors that enable physicians to get a holistic picture of a patient. It is also important to know that some physicians have resisted PGHD in their diagnosis and treatment decisions. The reasons are many: data overload, incomplete or unreliable data, privacy and security concerns, among others.

Recognizing the value of PGHD and the role of technology in advancing patient engagement in healthcare, the Office of the

National Coordinator for Health IT (ONC) started developing a policy framework in 2015 to assess the opportunities for improving health outcomes through the collection and use of PGHD.

As a part of a two-year demonstration of the potential benefits of PGHD, the ONC contracted with a select number of technology partners for demonstration projects with different health systems. One of the projects was with Sutter Health, a large health system in Northern California.

A key consideration for the pilot project was that the technology had to be in the clinical workflow—critical for success given the work overload that most physicians face today. Partnering with consulting firm Accenture and digital health company Validic, Sutter Health deployed the Validic digital health platform to collect and deliver personal health data from mobile applications securely into EHR systems. The program enables patients to receive periodic dashboards incorporating this data. Physicians, in turn, get an enhanced dashboard with advanced interpretations of the same data, which enables a much richer discussion with patients around their care management programs. The patient dashboard also became a big motivator for patients to get engaged in their own healthcare. The Validic platform addresses data privacy, one of the barriers to using PGHD, by ensuring a secure and private data exchange between doctor and patient. An additional benefit of the program is that the increased understanding of patients enables a dynamic pull between care managers and patients to identify cases that could turn critical and stratify risk for PHM.

Says Validic CEO Drew Schiller, "Validic is positioned in this environment as the enabler for PGHD, and we were fortunate to kind of look into our crystal ball and see a future where PGHD is going to become more and more valuable in the healthcare system. We were able to build a pretty substantial ecosystem of connections between device manufacturers and the healthcare system and solidify our presence as a partner for all the folks in healthcare who are looking to make this data acceptable and actionable. We make it simple and cost-effective to bring in fragmented patient-generated health data in a way that ensures future-proofing of PGHD integration for health systems."[68]

From a healthcare policy perspective, there are several initiatives under way that could provide a boost for PGHD. The PGHD effort is part of the ONC's ten-year vision and roadmap for nationwide interoperability. The federal government's Stage 3 guidelines for Meaningful Use of EHR technology, which are set to go into effect in 2018, require hospital EHR systems to have the ability to collect PGHD from nonclinical sources. Under the newly proposed MACRA, Meaningful Use is one of the criteria for merit-based incentive payments, and this might further boost PGHD.

The challenges with PGHD relate to the lack of consistency and quality of data received from patients on the one hand, and the absence of adequate processes, protocols, and systems to ingest and analyze the data at health systems on the other. Additional challenges pertain to data interoperability. Realizing the value from PGHD depends on the ability to involve patients in care delivery, supported by a higher volume and velocity of medical data that can enable personalized care plans.

2.5 Online Reputation Management with Social Media Data: Providence Health

The rise of social media has created a new problem (and an opportunity) for healthcare providers: how to manage their online reputations.

Until now, the healthcare industry has focused exclusively on Hospital Consumer Assessment of Healthcare Providers and Systems (HCAHPS) scores to manage their organizational reputations.[69] The CMS uses HCAHPS scores to determine patient satisfaction levels, which in turn drive financial incentives for health systems. However, HCAHPS is far from adequate in capturing the overall patient experience. A part of the problem with HCAHPS—besides getting patients to respond to surveys—is that patient feedback is no longer limited to a single encounter or platform. Patients are increasingly using social media to express themselves and provide feedback on their experiences. However, most health systems do not have an effective means to capture patient feedback from social media or to integrate that data into a multichannel strategy for patient experience management.

Health systems are recognizing the changing nature of patient engagement and the increasing importance of social media channels for communication and feedback, and are going beyond traditional engagement models to become partners with their consumers in managing health and wellness.

Providence Health and Services (Providence Health), a large health system founded in 1859 that serves over eleven million patients in seven states across the western United States, looks at online reputation management as an important aspect of patient experience and a key to the long-term sustainability of the business. In a departure from the traditional "if you build it, they will come" approach to patient acquisition and retention, Orest Holubec, chief communications officer at Providence Health, has started looking at customer lifetime value and focusing on building long-term relationships with patients instead of just focusing on high-margin surgeries.[70]

Customer satisfaction and retention follow a tried-and-tested three-part formula: data, insights, and action. What if this data is woefully inadequate and fails to take into consideration the different forms and sources from which it is available today?

Providence Health knew that it needed something more than HCAHPS scores to understand the true nature of patient experience in its hospitals. Working with Binary Fountain, a company that has developed a partnership with Press Ganey (an agency used widely by healthcare enterprises to gather patient feedback using structured questionnaires), Providence Health deployed Binary Health Analytics, a holistic patient feedback management platform to manage online reputation and improve patient experience. The platform helps healthcare organizations uncover and act on patient experience insights from online ratings and reviews, social media, Clinician and Group Consumer Assessment of Healthcare Providers and Systems (CG CAHPS) surveys, HCAHPS, and other surveys. By augmenting proprietary patient survey data (Press Ganey) with crowdsourced reviews (e.g. Yelp), Providence Health enhances its understanding of patient experience to drive operational change.

Since the publication of these ratings, providers in the Providence network who are part of the program have seen a 25–29 percent surge in page views. Patients have indicated that the reviews are valuable considerations in provider selection. It is as if patients have finally found a voice, and health systems like Providence Health have tapped into a crying need in the healthcare marketplace.[71]

2.6 Targeting Consumers with Demographic Data: Lehigh Valley Health Network

At Lehigh Valley Health Network (LVHN), a regional health system in Pennsylvania that serves over 1.9 million patients, digital transformation is driven by a need to attract more patients and by PHM objectives.[72] LVHN has been driving a multichannel marketing program with aggregated data from a wide range of data sources, including proprietary data from EHR systems such as Epic, as well as commercially available demographic data such as from Experian. LVHN is also beginning to look at public data released by entities such as the CMS.

At LVHN, targeting consumers through enhanced data analytics is designed to drive patients into the network at the moment of healthcare need. By targeting commercially insured patients, LVHN can drive revenue through increased marketing leads and conversions.

LVHN has also developed new experiences for their patients, designed to gain an improved understanding of consumer engagement and preferences that drive marketing content, targeted messaging, and communication channels to be deployed. One example of this is the use of video consultations, a relatively new concept for healthcare consumers that has tremendous potential to reduce costs and improve productivity in healthcare.

With the rapid pace of digital transformation, organizational structures need to adapt as well. One aspect of this is the growing need for close alignment between IT and other functions. At LVHN, CIO Mike Minear and Vice President of Marketing John Marzano collaborate closely, recognizing that, while marketing owns the digital function, the CIO organization has deep knowledge of data and technology integration that is integral to digital transformation.

The proliferation of technologies and tools creates a need for a robust integration strategy to ensure success. As healthcare becomes more of an on-demand environment, interoperability between different systems becomes a critical factor in responding quickly to consumer demands. Keeping this in mind, LVHN is becoming a part of the CareQuality network of the not-for-profit Sequoia Project, a consortium supported by the ONC to advance the implementation of a secure, interoperable nationwide health information exchange. The network provides a comprehensive view of a patient's medical history regardless of where the patient has received treatment within the network of participating entities.

As healthcare embarks on the digital transformation journey and adopts sophisticated consumer marketing techniques, the ROI of these programs may not be immediately evident.

Despite being in early stages, LVHN has been able to identify several measures of campaign success since moving to customer relationship management (CRM) and multichannel marketing. By one measure, the cost per acquisition (the cost of acquiring one lead) for the orthopedics service line is three times lower than it was when they relied solely on traditional mass media, which is historically difficult to measure. In bariatrics, there has been a 30 percent year-over-year increase in surgeries since the multichannel marketing program launched. By looking at multiple measures, LVHN estimates that the ratio of revenue generated for each dollar spent on marketing ranges from 8:1 for orthopedics to 11:1 for bariatrics.[73]

These results indicate the transition of marketing from an expense item to a revenue generator in a traditional hospital environment and from a reactive to a proactive mode of engagement with patients and consumers, driven by data and analytics.

2.7 Social Determinants of Health: Central New York Care Collaborative

Your zip code may be the single biggest predictor of your health and mortality.

Healthcare analytics professionals increasingly view zip codes as surrogates for income, education, employment status, ethnicity, and other related data elements that are collectively referred to as social determinants of health (SDOH). These types of data are beginning to play a critical role in PHM practices.

Healthcare outcomes depend on the active involvement of patients in their care. Despite the best care protocols by healthcare providers, patients are often unable to follow the protocols and instructions due to various socioeconomic factors. An example of this is the access to transportation that determines whether a patient will show up in time for a scheduled doctor visit. The growing realization that a variety of social determinants such as access to transportation determine health outcomes is driving personalization of care.

Healthcare is focused today mostly on unlocking insights from clinical data that resides in EHR systems, as well as claims data. Emerging data sources are challenging healthcare organizations to broaden the scope of their data gathering and analysis. CPHOs in health systems are now looking at ways to leverage data from a wide range of sources to obtain comprehensive views of patient populations. These data sources now include remote sensors and devices (via IoT), PGHD, genomics data, and, more recently, behavioral health and SDOH data.

SDOH data has been a topic of interest for healthcare policymakers for a while. In a 2015 paper, the Kaiser Family Foundation explored the role of social determinants of health and health equity, especially factors such as where people are born, grow up, live, work, and age.[74] These factors directly impacted mortality and healthcare expenditures.

With healthcare transitioning rapidly to VBC, harnessing these data sources has become critically important in assessing the health risks of low-income population segments. The low-income population segments are seen to be more at risk of the adverse impacts of their socioeconomic status.

Traditional risk prediction models based mostly on structured data from EHR systems are no longer adequate for the PHM needs of the VBC era. While there is some amount of SDOH data in EHR systems, it is incomplete, insufficient, or otherwise difficult to incorporate into traditional risk-stratification models. Addressing this gap presents an enormous opportunity for health plans and health systems to progress to the next stage of evolution in their care management and intervention models.

In New York, the Central New York Care Collaborative is using social determinant data[75] as part of its PHM efforts under the state's Delivery System Reform Incentive Payment program[76] to reduce the costs of care for the state's Medicaid population. Medicaid populations are among the most vulnerable segments of the society in terms of health impact from social determinants.[77] By addressing needs such as transportation access, providers are driving improved adherence to care protocols and reducing care gaps that will result in reduced costs and improved outcomes at the population level.

Health plan Cigna is using SDOH to improve risk management models and also determine the effectiveness of specific patient engagement programs by tapping into data already available within EHR systems. While it is early days yet, incorporating SDOH into analytical models can have a tangible impact on risk-based contract outcomes.

While incremental insights from social determinant data are being seen as valuable inputs to patient engagement and management, the data is frequently unavailable. An example of this is data on access to transportation in low-income communities—a factor that has a significant bearing on health outcomes. This is the unsexy side of analytics. While the models thirst for data, it is hard work—and often not possible—to quench that thirst.

The holy grail of personalized care and precision medicine starts with a holistic view of the patient that drives care management and medical outcomes. Achieving a holistic view requires healthcare organizations to build sophisticated data integration and advanced analytics capabilities. SDOH data is often available as unstructured data that requires NLP capabilities. Patient risk assessment requires going beyond static models and working with cognitive-learning systems that continuously analyze data, deliver insights and recommend appropriate and timely interventions. Healthcare organizations that make even one small step in this direction will achieve giant leaps in performance and outcomes in a VBC era.

3 The Key Emerging Technologies that Will Unlock Data

The acceleration of the Big Unlock requires widespread adoption of a handful of key technologies that enable data management capabilities on a vast scale, advanced analytical tools that can extract insight from data from a wide range of sources, and a secure means of handling the data in compliance with privacy regulations.

In this section, I will focus on three key technologies that will have a significant bearing on the Big Unlock. Cloud computing is already widespread and growing at an astounding pace. Going forward, the computing infrastructure for large-scale analytics programs will inevitably be based in the cloud. Along with the emergence of the cloud, analytical software and methods that can process vast amounts of data and unlock insights will increasingly rely on learning systems such as cognitive computing and AI. These technologies, while robust and advanced, are inadequate when it comes to ensuring security and privacy of data, which is one of the barriers to the Big Unlock. The solution may be blockchain, a technology that is rapidly gaining ground in financial services in the form of bitcoin, an alternative currency. Blockchain technology is in very early stages in healthcare. However, its potential to enable secure data sharing positions it as one of the key technologies for the future.

While the possibilities for driving technology-led change in healthcare are exciting, long years of underinvestment in technology have left healthcare providers not only vulnerable in terms of system stability and security threats but also financially unprepared to adopt new technologies. The recent focus on PHM and shift to VBC may accelerate adoption of these emerging technologies.

3.1 Cloud Computing: Setting Data Free from Enterprise IT

The rise of cloud computing coincides with the relentless march of Moore's law, enabling us to store and process data at progressively lower costs than we could have imagined ten years ago. The dramatic reduction in data storage costs may be the single biggest factor driving the explosive growth of the cloud computing industry.

Today, any device that connects wirelessly is enabled by cloud infrastructure. Every new device is wirelessly enabled to talk to other similarly connected devices. Digital health technologies such as mobile applications, remote monitoring devices, wearables, and a wide range of medical devices connect to one another via the cloud. Cloud infrastructure is increasingly used to store volumes of data that enterprise data centers can no longer handle, and to manage unexpected surges in demand for storage and computing resources. New applications are invariably developed as cloud-based software, accessible to users through desktop or mobile interfaces in a subscription model. The cloud enables real-time sharing of data, whether it is text messages between care coordination teams in a hospital or medical images for a radiologist halfway across the world.

The cloud has probably had its biggest impact in big data analytics in healthcare by providing a technology foundation that can ingest huge amounts of data in a variety of formats—structured and unstructured—in data lakes. Open-source technologies such as Hadoop have made it easier to manage these massive data repositories and access them for analysis and development of innovative new digital health applications.

The cloud services market is growing exponentially, and research firm Gartner estimates the market for cloud services to be worth over $200 billion.[78] The healthcare sector has been increasingly embracing cloud infrastructure for enterprise IT workloads as well as third-party technology solutions.

New big data technology and analytics solutions in the marketplace are cloud-based by default. However, for enterprise workloads, the solutions are a bit more nuanced, with variations in the form of infrastructure as-a-service, platform as-a-service, and software as-a-service (SaaS). Cloud deployment models can also vary—private, public, and hybrid—and because these models imply different requirements and responsibilities, they also impact strategic technology investment decisions.

There are a handful of factors that explain the rapid rise of cloud adoption in healthcare.

The rise of digital health startups. The astounding levels of VC investments in healthcare, specifically digital health startups, have driven growth for cloud service providers such as AWS. Because of the need for speed and efficiency, these startups need ready-to-deploy technology infrastructure to build and launch their applications. On the flip side, if they fail, it is easy to unplug from pay-as-you-go agreements and unwind the operation quickly. A lot of these new solutions and applications are stand-alone consumer apps, but an increasing number are being integrated into healthcare delivery systems. Having a cloud-based architecture enables them to integrate easily using an API-based architecture without having to go through onerous processes involving enterprise IT environments.

Healthcare IT modernization. Enterprise IT in healthcare is outdated, underfunded, and vulnerable to data breaches (I discuss the security risks and implications in a different chapter). Cloud computing is a solution that lies at the heart of enterprise IT modernization. With the shift toward an information-centric care delivery model, the need to integrate multiple data sources and applications almost mandates a cloud-based architecture, albeit one that is enabled in part by open standards that support collaborative workflows and information sharing. Most importantly, a cloud-based model allows all participants in the healthcare ecosystem to leverage secure and state-of-the-art computing infrastructure at potentially lower total costs. Leading cloud providers such as AWS and Azure are investing far more in their infrastructure to keep it robust and secure than any individual enterprise can hope to achieve. However, due to a variety of factors, significant amounts of enterprise workloads need to operate on dedicated infrastructure, which has led to more private and hybrid cloud models in healthcare.

The innovation agenda. Innovation and IT modernization go side by side. Due to the ease of information sharing with external participants, cloud infrastructure is much better-suited for innovation programs, advanced analytics, and digital health experiences. Innovation by its very nature is risky, and cloud environments help mitigate financial risks by limiting the downsides from occasional failures. On the contrary, innovation programs at health systems with limited resources can get a boost by being able to stretch budget dollars with low-cost pilot programs—often involving startups and innovative digital health companies. The rise of the IoT movement, especially remote sensors, fitness monitors, and the like, make it necessary to default to the cloud to deploy connected health and digital health programs. Also, as data sources continue to explode, and all kinds of unstructured and non-medical data, text, speech, social determinant data, wearable and fitness tracker data, and other forms of PGHD come online, healthcare providers will be compelled to use the cloud as the data platform for PHM solutions. Cloud environments function as secure and scalable options for managing large-scale data management programs.

The economic benefits of cloud computing aside, cloud services offer the scalability and flexibility that are critical for the Big Unlock. Cloud service providers (CSPs) such as AWS can also provide better security and privacy for protected health information (PHI) data when compared to most health systems. The data centers managed by CSPs are highly secure environments, protected against data breaches through robust administrative, physical, and technical safeguards. They offer sophisticated data encryption and access controls that are critical for sensitive medical information that is subject to HIPAA regulations. Most CSPs now sign HIPAA business associate agreements (BAA) that provide much-needed assurance for HIPAA-covered entities that entrust patient medical information to external service providers (even if much of it is anonymized as an additional precaution).

An additional benefit of cloud-based systems is that they now offer the potential for broad interoperability and integration by using standard protocols. However, full interoperability is still a work in progress due to the large amounts of patient information locked up in proprietary EHR vendor systems. CSPs such as AWS are constantly expanding healthcare cloud services by bringing on new capabilities that eliminate additional investments and accelerate time to market.

However, there are some risks to cloud-based platforms. If breached, multi-tenant clouds can bring down an entire ecosystem of users by becoming a single point of failure and potentially exposing them to ransomware extortions that can threaten patient lives through system unavailability.

It is no surprise that the HHS has taken note of the importance of cloud computing in healthcare and has released a set of guidelines for CSPs, clarifying their role as business associates (BAs) in the context of HIPAA and healthcare data.[79]

The guidelines acknowledge the growing role of public cloud providers such as AWS and Microsoft Azure that have been storing electronic PHI (ePHI) for some years as part of their agreements with technology providers and enterprises. These CSPs are now classified as BAs and are required to sign HIPAA BAAs, regardless of the nature of the arrangement or the level of access to ePHI stored in the cloud infrastructure.

Secondly, the focus of the guidelines seems to be on information security. Given the increasing number of data breaches over the past couple of years, HIPAA BAs are more on notice than ever before.[80]

The HHS guidelines consider CSPs that store ePHI to fall under the purview of HIPAA and require both the CSP and their BA to ensure there is a BAA in place. Calling out the threat of malicious actors, the guidelines hold CSPs responsible for breaches, even if they do not have direct access to the data or are protected by "no view" clauses in their contracts. An exception granted to CSPs is that they are outside the purview of the HIPAA rules to the extent that the ePHI is de-identified according to the Office for Civil Rights rules.

The HHS guidelines also now allow CSPs to store ePHI on servers outside the United States. However, the general practice in the market between covered entities and their BAs is to house all data in cloud servers that reside in the United States, not least due to complex compliance requirements around data privacy laws in other countries, especially those in the European Union (EU).

There are a few gaps in the guidelines that covered entities and BAs will need to work through.

-   Reporting of HIPAA breaches is left to contracting parties and can potentially result in an inconsistent and incomplete picture of the nature and extent of data breaches across the sector.
-   Reconciling the US privacy laws with international laws, especially in the EU, where every country might have a different set of guidelines. HHS acknowledges these differences and urges covered entities and BAs to do their risk assessment if choosing to store ePHI outside the United States. Accessing data from locations such as India and the Philippines in outsourcing arrangements adds more complexity.
-   Certain providers (e.g. network carriers and middleware companies) may be exempt from HIPAA as conduit access providers, despite their role in transmitting ePHI. Data in

motion is as vulnerable to cyberattacks as data at rest, and accountability should be specified for such entities.

The HHS guidelines targeting CSPs can potentially eliminate many of the contentious contract discussions regarding ePHI in the cloud. Most importantly, they recognize the growing importance of cloud computing in healthcare and will help bring these entities into the broader discussion on healthcare data security and privacy.

All of these benefits of cloud technologies will unleash innovation by providing a solid, scalable, secure technology platform for aggregating and analyzing structured and unstructured data—a fundamental pillar for the Big Unlock. Vast amounts of untapped data sources will become available on cloud infrastructure as part of the Big Unlock. These include clinical notes and other unstructured forms of data (which account for 80 percent of healthcare data), genomic data that is increasingly available through personal genomic testing services, and other emerging forms of data including speech and video.

3.2 Cognitive Computing and AI: Seeking the Threshold for Accelerated Adoption

In February 2011, IBM's Watson computer made history by defeating Ken Jennings and Brad Rutter in the final round of the TV show *Jeopardy!*. That moment might also be considered the moment the term *AI* entered public consciousness (although the term was coined back in 1955).[81]

What people do not remember as well about Watson's spectacular performance on *Jeopardy!* are the answers it did not get right. In the category "US Cities," the contestants were presented with the clue, "Its largest airport was named after a World War II hero; its second largest, for a World War II battle." The answer is Chicago (O'Hare and Midway). Watson guessed, "What is Toronto?" Watson was perhaps confused by the presence of a city in Illinois named

Toronto or by the Toronto Blue Jays baseball team that plays in the American League.

A machine with a database comprising all the knowledge in the world can sometimes struggle to identify commonplace images that come easily to humans. A child knows a cat is a cat, but it took Google's Deep Mind sixteen thousand computers and a billion neural network connections to identify a cat from a set of images—with less than 75 percent accuracy.[82]

Five years to the day after Watson beat the humans on *Jeopardy!*, Google's AlphaGo program beat Lee Sedol, a young Korean who was the reigning grandmaster in the ancient board game Go. Deep learning had arrived.

Unlocking insights from digital patient records began with the big data analytics movement as a way to harness large volumes of structured data in the form of EHRs. It has since evolved to encompass all kinds of data, structured and unstructured. Accordingly, the technologies required to unlock insights have also evolved. The most promising, and perhaps the most widely discussed, are AI and cognitive computing.

Research firm IDC forecasted that spending on AI technologies would rise from $8 billion in 2016 to $47 billion in 2020.[83] The report identified healthcare as one of the sectors likely to spend the most on cognitive or AI systems. The definition of *AI* runs the gamut from virtual personal assistants (bots) all the way to intelligent automation and cognitive computing using machine learning and deep learning algorithms. Applications can be found in all aspects of a healthcare enterprise, from IT operations to precision medicine.

Perhaps the most exciting emerging technology in unlocking insights from data for healthcare applications is cognitive computing. Platforms such as IBM Watson Health have made significant progress in the use of AI and cognitive computing in oncology and genomics. Digital health firm HealthTap, which offers a platform that provides online medical consulting, launched what may have been the first AI-based app, named Dr. A.I.[84] The platform provides personalized recommendations based on cognitive insights from a database of medical profiles and knowledge gained from millions of online consultations. AI is now being applied to large volumes of data from increasingly diverse sources. The results are guiding clinicians on everything from drug discovery to diagnosis and treatment.

Healthcare enterprises are striving to become learning organizations. However, the ability of enterprises to learn effectively is limited by the ability of human beings to keep up with the increasing volumes of data and knowledge. Emerging technologies such as AI and cognitive computing are enabling organizations to augment human capacity to process information by analyzing enormous amounts data and knowledge in a fraction of the time, detecting patterns, and delivering insights and recommendations.

AI. Cognitive. RPA. Autonomics. Machine learning. Deep learning.

All these terms fly around in IT organizations as CIOs, battling marketplace uncertainties and cost pressures, look for ways to enhance enterprise performance. As with most technology trends, the hype tends to overhang reality by a significant margin in the early stages of adoption, much in line with Gartner's hype cycle theory.[85]

The signs are that the use of AI technologies has picked up momentum in healthcare. A study by consulting firm Accenture provides us some interesting data points. The market for AI in healthcare is expected to grow more than ten times in the next five years, to around $6.6 billion at a compounded rate of over 40 percent.[86] AI represents a $150 billion savings opportunity for healthcare, across a wide range of applications: robot-assisted surgery, clinical diagnosis and treatment options, and operational efficiencies, to name a few. In my firm's work with healthcare technology firms and enterprises, there is a palpable excitement about the growing demand for AI in healthcare.

The terms *AI, machine learning, deep learning,* and *cognitive* are often used interchangeably, but they are not the same. It may be worthwhile defining some of the terms that are used interchangeably and synonymously with AI.

One way to visualize the relationships is to see each of terms as a subset of one of the others. Deep learning would be a subset of machine learning, which is a subset of AI, which in turn is a subset of cognitive computing.

At the outermost layer, cognitive systems are meant to be learning systems that closely match human ability through thinking and reasoning capabilities. Just like humans, they adapt to new data, including unstructured data, and develop revised recommendations or conclusions. Advanced cognitive systems that run on massive computing infrastructure, such as the IBM Watson Health platform, can process structured and unstructured data and keep pace with the increasing volume and complexity of information. Cognitive platforms learn continuously by solving problems on an ongoing basis getting better at doing so, in much the same way humans do. The learning ability of cognitive systems is expected to transform healthcare by enabling faster and more-focused responses to healthcare needs while reducing costs.

Today, cognitive systems such as IBM Watson Health augment the ability of oncologists looking for cancer diagnosis and treatment options based on the available medical literature and patient medical data sets. It is important to note that, in today's context, cognitive systems are merely augmenting—not replacing—human judgment and decisions, and the oncologist makes the final call on how to treat the patient based on experience, instinct, and other factors that cannot be replaced by a machine. The oncologist sees, feels, and hears things when interacting with a patient that no computer can emulate in the foreseeable future. The doctor's final judgment combines this hard knowledge with empathy, intuition, and instinct.

IBM CEO Ginni Rometty refers to this relationship as "man and machine," as opposed to man vs. machine. The partnership between human and cognitive systems helps to scale and elevate human expertise. An estimated shortage of up to 88,000 doctors in the country by 2025 also highlights AI's potential to mitigate the dependency on humans and, in fact, make them more productive and efficient.[87]

"Cognitive is not a destination," says Dr. Anil Jain, Chief Innovation Officer at IBM Watson Health. "It is an enabler with a specialized underlying capability."[88] He believes that, in three to five years, almost every decision in health will be aided by technology, especially high-risk protocols such as oncology where the augmentation of a doctor's diagnosis by AI-enabled platforms such as IBM Watson Health will be inevitable.

Cognitive systems need massive amounts of data and the ability to integrate that data in different forms from diverse data sources. Cognitive systems form the underpinnings of next-generation PHM systems, which provide granular insights at the patient and population levels for clinicians and care managers to improve healthcare outcomes and reduce costs in the new era of VBC.

AI systems solve complex problems through deterministic processes (working with structured data and predetermined processes to arrive at outcomes); for example, Netflix's recommendation engines and speech recognition and NLP used by Amazon Echo. Unlike AI, cognitive systems are probabilistic and do not just generate answers to numerical problems, but develop hypotheses, reasoned arguments, and recommendations about complex and meaningful bodies of data.

Machine learning (ML) works by developing algorithms[89] that can learn from and make predictions about data.[90] We typically train machines with large amounts of data, which gives them the ability to learn how to perform certain tasks. ML is employed in computing tasks where designing and programming explicit algorithms for good performance is difficult or infeasible. ML has commonly been used to conduct predictive modeling from patient EHRs; for example, in readmission risk predictions.

Deep learning (DL) is a branch of ML that makes use of multiple processing layers and hierarchical representations to drive the learning process. DL is based on neural networks, a computing paradigm that tries to mimic the way the brain functions. Information is processed in multiple layers, with information and patterns being passed up from one layer to another to arrive at a holistic understanding of the system. Changes to any one layer will ripple through the entire system, and the accumulated knowledge is stored away as "learnings."

There is a rapidly growing body of use cases and successful applications of AI in operational and clinical areas. Here are a few examples of how AI technologies are currently being applied in the healthcare and life sciences sectors.

Health plans. Healthcare enterprises, especially health plans, have been actively applying robotic process automation (RPA) tools and AI technologies to improve productivity and efficiency in their operations. By codifying workflow rules and enabling self-learning through ontological patterns and databases, these technologies are being used in areas such as provider data management, claim approvals and exception management, fraud detection, and customer service operations.

Health systems. AI and automation tools have found wide applications in a range of functions including revenue cycle operations, diagnosis and treatment, and PHM initiatives. IBM Watson Health's engine, for example, has made significant strides in applying cognitive and AI technologies in the field of oncology and diabetic retinopathy, allowing the search and analysis of data to provide clinicians with inputs for targeted intervention options.

Life sciences. Pharma companies have started successfully applying AI tools in clinical trial phases of new drugs by automatically generating content required for regulatory submissions and reviews. On the other side of the equation, these tools are being applied in pharmacovigilance for case intake and reporting on the adverse effects of drugs. There is increasing interest in the use of AI for improving efficiencies in supply chain operations.

Across all of these segments, there are several commonly used applications, an example of which is the use of AI technologies for IT infrastructure operations to detect and remediate network errors and application failures. Another example is the use of AI in patient engagement programs, especially for managing chronic conditions such as diabetes through automated alerts and interventions based on analysis of real-time data gathered through intelligent devices and wearables.

As the use of AI technologies gains momentum, more use cases will surely emerge. As healthcare transitions from a FFS to a VBC era, the need for advanced technologies for everything from precision medicine to increased operational efficiencies and improved patient engagement will drive the adoption rates for these technologies. Many of these initial projects are in pilot phases, and, in the broader context, there is a relatively small number of healthcare enterprises that are investing in these technologies and programs. That is par for the course for new technologies in any field. Mainstream adoption may be a bit further away, and, in the current environment of policy uncertainty, many of the smaller enterprises are likely to be in wait-and-watch mode, choosing to stay with business as usual until there is some clarity.

To paraphrase a quote attributed to the sci-fi writer William Gibson, the future has arrived, only it is unevenly distributed. This may be the most accurate summary of AI in healthcare at this time.

One of the most visible applications of AI today is RPA. RPA is being applied to business operations to eliminate human intervention in basic tasks that require the application of rules to determine an outcome. A computer system user might interact with an RPA-based system to perform simple tasks, such as confirming the benefits of a health insurance policy by looking up a field in a database. This process can be scripted and does not require human intervention.

RPA is gaining ground in healthcare operations as a way to increase automation and speed up processes. Another example would be the revenue cycle and claim processing transactions that are bound by rigid rules and thus can be automated, in many cases by using bots. The use of bots is proliferating in every field, especially in customer-facing transactions. Many processes that require human intervention today can effectively be replaced by bots, which has caused much anxiety about impending large-scale layoffs, as humans are replaced by intelligent systems. However, bots address relatively lower-order skills and, in many ways, are just extensions of early efforts in the '80s and '90s to computerize manual tasks, which at the time created anxiety among office workers. Today, basic accounting functions and banking transactions are automatically posted by enterprise resource planning (ERP) software. The travel industry uses algorithms to find and present multiple airline and hotel choices based on price, schedule preferences, and other factors. No one gives this a second thought anymore, although at the time these were seen to have devastating effects on jobs within the banking and travel industries.

Even though bots and RPA have caught the imagination of industry pundits, implementing and maintaining an army of bots can be as challenging as maintaining an army of human operators. Bots need extensive configuration and constant maintenance, not least because of inconsistent processes and underlying systems that require changes. It is too early to tell how much the cost of maintaining a bot army impacts the savings that result from automation; however, as with most technology innovations, it is a matter of scale. The more the adoption, the better the business case benefits. As with most disruptive technologies, adoption rates are influenced by social and organizational factors beyond mere business case justifications.

AI and augmented intelligence tools are beginning to help physicians, patients, and staff in very tangible ways. Through improved human–machine interfaces, especially speech recognition, companies like IBM Watson Health and emerging players such as Amazon are creating rapid, low-threshold, low-effort ways of communicating that could revolutionize the doctor–patient interaction. The Amazon Echo can make phone calls or send messages. We may soon see the ability for users to say, "Alexa, call Dr. Smith," and, with some form of biometric identifiers, place a call or send a message to make an appointment. In many ways, this is AI-enabled IoT and could be the way healthcare is delivered in the future.

Despite the promise of emerging automation technologies, healthcare is in the early stages of harnessing technologies such as RPA. Barbra Sheridan McGann, EVP, Business Operations, Healthcare, Life Sciences, Public Sector, HfS Research, a firm that works extensively in the technology services sector says, "Many questions I get today are from people who tell me that they are hearing about all this new technology and RPA and AI, but do not know how to use these technologies and what the true business benefits are. They do not know where to start, whom to involve, and how to bring different stakeholders together."[91] She adds that a lot of the use cases for cognitive and AI technologies in healthcare are in the clinical area, helping detect patterns and develop treatment plans. However, these technologies are still taking hold in business operations. She believes there is great potential to bring structured and unstructured data sources together in areas such as claim operations to apply cognitive technologies to identify patterns and trigger actions to address administrative and operational aspects, ultimately impacting the financial performance of enterprises.

Many emerging technologies such as cognitive and AI are enabling platforms that are solutions looking for problems. The big challenge for many providers of technology solutions is to try to figure out not just what problems can be solved by emerging technologies, but which problems are worth solving and whether there is enough money available to use the technology to solve them. Says McGann, "You cannot start with technology. You have to start with a problem and figure out how technology can solve the problem."[92] This may explain why a survey by research firm Gartner indicated that CEOs and senior enterprise managers rated the returns from emerging technologies to be "very low."[93] The good news is that many of the same CEOs predicted that technologies such as AI will significantly impact business in the next five years.

3.3 Blockchain: Changing the Physics of Data Sharing

In May 2016, Craig Wright, an Australian programmer, claimed to be Satoshi Nakomoto, a shadowy figure in the Internet world who is widely considered to be the inventor of bitcoin, a form of digital currency referred to as cryptocurrency that is set to disrupt the world of banking and finance. More momentous than bitcoin is the development of its underlying technology, blockchain. Blockchain could fundamentally change the way we store and share healthcare data—and do it more securely—and has a potentially significant role in the Big Unlock in healthcare.

The Big Unlock has faced headwinds due to the unprecedented levels of data breaches (including ransomware) experienced by health plans and health systems in 2016. Data breaches and ransomware incidents have continued through 2017 and have almost become the new normal.[94] Recent incidents of ransomware and data breaches have pointed to the role of foreign actors, raising questions about data security in vulnerable sectors such as healthcare.

Born out of a need for an efficient, cost-effective, reliable, and secure system for recording and conducting transactions, Blockchain, an emerging technology that uses a distributed database for secure transactions, has the potential to address many of the challenges related to security and privacy of personal health information. In simple terms, Blockchain is a list of transactions, grouped into blocks and shared with members within a network (*blocks* of data linked together in a *chain*, hence the name blockchain). The data is stored in a shared, *distributed* ledger where identical copies of the data may be shared on multiple computers or nodes in a network. Through what is known as *peer-to-peer replication*, blockchain architecture gives participants the ability to share a ledger that is updated every time a transaction occurs. The peer-to-peer replication process ensures that any changes by any member in the network has the approval of every other member in the network (through a process known as *consensus*). Every event or transaction is time-stamped and unalterable after the fact, making blockchain data reliable and trustworthy.

Blockchain provides complete control to the owner of the data. Members are provided electronic keys to unlock the data, however, once a key has been provided, it cannot be revoked, and the data is locked immutably (i.e no participant can tamper with it) forever. By ensuring the provenance of data (i.e. allowing participants to know the source of the data and the various changes it has undergone over time), blockchain provides data integrity, establishes trust among participants, and enables participants to share data securely. Blockchain is also potentially more efficient than traditional ledger maintenance where multiple copies of a ledger have to be maintained and updated whenever there is a transaction. By eliminating the need for multiple ledgers (and consequently, also eliminating the need for intermediaries), as well by reducing the time required for settling transactions, blockchain can potentially reduce costs significantly.

Blockchain networks are broadly categorized as permissioned and permissionless: Permissioned networks restrict participation by invitation (the default mode for business networks, especially in regulated industries such as healthcare); permissionless networks are open, where anyone can participate (such as bitcoin markets). Equivalently, permissionless networks can be thought of as operating in a zero-trust environment, while permissioned networks operate in an environment where there is a modicum of trust among peers.

Blockchain is still a relatively new concept for many healthcare providers, but there is an emerging interest in applying blockchain to personal healthcare data in the context of research, clinical trials, and PHM. In a survey of healthcare executives by IBM's Institute for Business Value, 16 percent of respondents said they expect to have a commercial blockchain solution in 2017.[95] Blockchain could fundamentally reinvent how health data is created, protected, stored, and shared.

Even the federal government is making early moves in assessing the potential of blockchain technologies. The FDA has entered into a partnership with IBM Watson Health to explore the use of blockchain technology in oncology.[96] The partnership will help integrate data from multiple sources and provide a 360-degree view of patients. The technology will enable all participants, including patients, to share data from EHR systems as well as PGHD from wearables and smart devices. The initiative is expected to demonstrate the transformative potential of blockchain technology to enable the discovery of new drugs through evidence-based research and improve health outcomes for patient populations.

A separate initiative, known as Hyperledger, is an open-source collaboration supported by more than one hundred members and sponsored by the Linux Foundation, which is working hard to make blockchain suitable for enterprise environments in healthcare and other sectors. The initiative could democratize healthcare data and eventually put patients at the center of the healthcare ecosystem.

Perhaps the biggest impact that blockchain could have on healthcare is its potential to break down data silos. By giving consumers unprecedented control over the sharing, collaboration, and privacy of their health information, blockchain can democratize access to and use of the data for improved healthcare outcomes. It can promote shared decision making between patients and their healthcare providers and lay the foundation for longitudinal health records, which could be invaluable in medical research and public health initiatives. IBM, a Hyperledger consortium member and strong advocate for blockchain in healthcare, calls the methodology "the chain of trust," emphasizing its potential role in promoting collaboration by breaking down data silos between organizations with while keeping the data close to the vest.

Other benefits in healthcare include the ability to establish the provenance of drugs and medical equipment, which are often brought to market after going through many cross-border supply chain steps. In the event of a problem with a drug, it becomes easy to identify the source of the problem in the supply chain and isolate it before further damage takes place.

Many other uses for blockchain are emerging. Examples include matching patients for clinical trials or identifying potential donors for organ transplants and blood transfusions (where the provenance of the organ or the blood is critical for patient safety). By giving patients the rights to their data, blockchain can also ensure compliance with privacy laws.

In health systems, blockchain can potentially be a technology solution for data security, especially for patient medical records that are currently stored in monolithic EHR systems. By democratizing the storage of data among patients and their healthcare providers in distributed ledgers, the risks of data breaches can be significantly reduced. In health plans, blockchain-enabled "smart contracts" can facilitate pre-authorization and claims adjudication by disintermediating and automating payment processes (akin to a rules-based workflow) and reducing the administrative costs and time for providers and payers. In IoT, blockchain-enabled solutions can improve security and spur the unlocking of insights from interconnected devices.

Most patient data, specifically electronic medical records, sits in proprietary systems belonging to technology vendors or in data silos within enterprise systems with limited access to patients and their healthcare providers. In the future, Blockchain can potentially enable the creation of comprehensive data sets that are maintained instead in distributed ledgers to which patients and their healthcare providers have access and control. As ML and AI tools become increasingly prevalent in advanced analytics and PHM, this seamless access to data will accelerate the progress in precision medicine and personalized care. By eliminating friction, blockchain can significantly reduce transaction costs in healthcare data management.

Blockchain is not a panacea for all the problems associated with secure access to healthcare data. Data sources are becoming increasingly varied, and ML and AI platforms are struggling to keep pace. Aggregating and analyzing all that data is not easy. A related problem with blockchain is its scalability. In the blockchain world, every computer in the network processes every transaction, which is a slow way of doing things in a big data world. Some businesses may pause when they learn blockchain data is immutable and blockchain-enabled contracts run forever, with no human "at the wheel".

Blockchain received some negative press in its early days, primarily due to its association with bitcoin, which was used in illegal activities to avoid detection through traditional banking channels. Many of these illegal businesses (notably Silk Road) have since been shut down, and blockchain is making its way toward respectability and an influential role in banking and finance. In healthcare, it holds the potential to ensure data privacy and security while maintaining accuracy and integrity and giving healthcare consumers the ability to control their information.

Just like data interoperability, blockchain has to endure growing pains and adoption will progress slowly and steadily, starting with specific use cases and data sets within small networks and expanding as confidence levels and acceptability grow over time. While blockchain is an exciting and transformative new technology, the big unknown is how long it will take for it to go mainstream.

4 ...And the Forces that Will Restrain It

Even among progressive healthcare enterprises, the pathway to a digital health future, where data is treated as a corporate asset to be unlocked and mined for profits, is full of obstacles. As more healthcare reimbursement moves toward APMs, the industry as a whole and enterprises on their own will need to find their solutions to some of these issues.

One of the big barriers to healthcare innovation is the regulatory environment. By definition, regulation stifles innovation. Onerous FDA regulations have been blamed for the lack of innovation and investment in the life sciences industry, be it new drug discovery or the launch of new medical devices. Often, these regulatory burdens end up being a form of tax on innovation, which is ultimately borne by consumers.

In the world of healthcare providers, HIPAA rules determine privacy protections for patient information that can often get in the way of the free flow of data. In addition, the industry has struggled with issues of data interoperability and data blocking by dominant vendors. Some observers have accused EHR vendors of trying to monetize interoperability. There has been an industry-wide call for EHR vendors to lower the barriers to interoperability and smooth the path to innovation. At the same time, innovators cannot take for granted that they can jump on the interoperability tollway for free. This is a highly controversial and frustrating topic for many, and I discuss this in detail later in the chapter.

As digital health moves beyond EHR data to other emerging sources such as IoT data, PGHD, and genomics data, one of the big gaps is the lack of an operating model for aggregating and utilizing the data. The vast majority of personal health data is simply thrown away because there is no operating model to harness it. Physicians have no interest in receiving raw data and are looking to the technology innovation ecosystem to create intermediaries that will scrub and analyze the data to develop composite scores of patient health that can be embedded directly into their daily workflow. Significant parts of the healthcare sector, such as behavioral health, have been routinely neglected in the past, resulting in a paucity of meaningful data and a lack of an operating model to integrate this data with other sources.

As with innovation anywhere, the early adopters are the ones with the deep pockets—this includes global pharma companies looking to go beyond the pill into new areas, or large integrated delivery networks (IDN) and academic medical centers who are investing heavily to position themselves for a VBC era. We have to follow the money to spot the early adopters and hope the rest of the industry will catch up quickly.

4.1 Market Maturity: The Teacher is Ready. What About the Student?

Even though there are over 5,500 hospitals in the country, the number of hospitals that are in a position to leverage innovative solutions and successfully manage the shift to VBC is under five hundred.[97] Ed Marx of Cleveland Clinic quips that the teacher is ready, but the student is not, implying that there are more solutions available than are health systems ready to absorb them.[98] Also, while vendors have been busy developing solutions, the healthcare sector has been consumed by EHR rollouts and financial challenges, thus creating a lag between the development of new solutions and their deployment and acceptance in healthcare. EHR systems do not have all the data needed for advanced analytics and PHM, and it remains difficult to get data out of EHR systems in the right format. Despite emerging data sources and innovative analytics solutions, the challenges of working with EHR data have made it difficult for most health systems to implement advanced analytics programs. Marx believes that many healthcare enterprises have chosen to focus in the near term instead on EHR optimization programs to increase the returns on their investments in expensive system rollouts over the past several years.

Driven by the incentives from the ACA's meaningful use programs, hospital managements rushed to implement EHR systems to qualify for incentive dollars. In hindsight, many of these implementations took place without much clinician involvement or input, resulting in suboptimal user interfaces and inefficient workflows, which increased workloads on physicians to the point of burnout and suicide.[99] In one extreme case, a poorly designed workflow resulted in a medication error of thirty-eight times the prescribed dosage and nearly killed a patient at the University of California, San Francisco.[100] Now the physician community is fighting back.

A study in 2017 by consulting firm Bain indicated that more than 60 percent of the physicians surveyed believed "it will become more difficult to deliver high-quality care in the next two years as they struggled to cope with a complex regulatory environment, increasing administrative burdens and a more difficult reimbursement landscape."[101] Physicians are tired of the years of experimentation during the EHR rollouts, followed by a plethora of new and advanced technology solutions, all claiming to improve healthcare outcomes and reduce costs. A study by NEJM Catalyst found that clinicians were skeptical about the positive impact of disruptive new technologies and healthcare delivery models, with only twenty-three percent believing they would result in decreased overall costs of care.[102] Even something like telemedicine, considered favorably by C-suite executives, was seen as an additional burden and potentially even competition by clinicians. The Bain study concluded that finding a disruptive new model for healthcare delivery will take time. In the short term, the healthcare sector appears to have developed an allergy to the word *disruption*, especially when patient safety is at stake.

Physicians now want evidence that new models for care management and reimbursement will improve clinical outcomes, and want to be actively involved in the development of technology solutions that support new care delivery models. Without their buy-in, it will be hard to alter the status quo and move the system toward a broader adoption of APMs and VBC. The lack of alignment between clinicians and other stakeholders in the healthcare economy may thus have slowed down the shift to VBC. The skepticism among the physician community about the effectiveness of APMs and the fatigue and resistance to complex, technology-led changes are serious headwinds against the adoption of analytics and new digital health technology solutions.

Suresh Krishnan, Chief Technology Officer at Amita Health, a joint venture between Ascension Health, the largest nonprofit health system in the United States, and Florida-based Adventist Health, sees this a bit differently. He believes that the current mind-set of making every new technology investment immediately pay for itself through increased patient flows will change as a generational shift takes hold in healthcare and younger physicians, many of them digital natives, demand technology enablement for all aspects of their work, especially on mobile devices.[103] With most new technologies and solutions now in the cloud, legacy applications will eventually be replaced by cloud-based solutions accessible through smartphones. As a side note, Krishnan sees himself more as a chief technology orchestrator in an era of a shrinking on-premises technology asset footprint and predicts that the role of chief technology officer (CTO) may disappear altogether in a few years.

Some of the more progressive health systems have developed their own data warehousing and business analytics capabilities, and while they may not be the most advanced analytics solutions, they are arguably better than the analytics features that come out of the box with EHR systems, according to Marx.[104] Advanced analytics and digital health companies looking to break into this market also have to deal with the question of price and a business case for investment in a new technology solution. For a handful of health systems, an alternative is to take a partnership approach; an example is UPMC, which also has an investment arm that often takes a financial stake in promising new startups and technologies.

For healthcare innovators and their technology solution providers, the maturity level of the enterprise regarding technology adoption matters as much as budgets and ROI considerations. As the needle moves in the direction of VBC and APMs, the flow of investment dollars toward innovative solutions will increase among early adopters in the healthcare provider community and will likely penetrate hospitals further down in the technology and innovation curve. After all, the adoption of EHR systems took several years to reach the near-total penetration levels that we see today in the provider space. In the interim, unless tech firms are ready to play the long game and have deep pockets, they may be better off aligning with the near-term priorities for their target markets. The big question for emerging technologies and solution providers is: how long will it be for the needle to move sufficiently?

One of the big challenges for any solution that tries to unlock data for value-added insights is internal silos within healthcare enterprises. While the enterprise tends to look at data as a corporate asset, it is not something that individual stakeholders readily want to share (everyone would like to receive other people's data, of course). A lot of the work for a technology solution provider can be about breaking down the barriers between silos of care to obtain a consolidated view of patient data across the care continuum. Technology providers also have to be aware that in the absence of aligned incentives, stakeholders will resist sharing or giving up their data until they understand what is in it for them and how it is going to help them economically.

Neil Gomes, CDO of Jefferson Health, a regional health system based in Philadelphia affiliated with Thomas Jefferson University, is very optimistic. "I think there is a lot that is going to happen in healthcare and is happening already in leveraging technology. Other industries are far ahead of us for sure. There is much impatience now among both patients and even people within innovative health systems that want innovative solutions right away, but many of these new solutions take time to implement and to customize for a particular industry. In many industries when a new technology comes out, the adoption is very rapid and very quick, but because of regulations and lives at stake, it can take some time to gain adoption in healthcare. I think in healthcare there is immense promise for newer technologies. Solution providers should not lose patience and need to work more closely with health systems."[105]

With regards to emerging technology solutions for the VBC era of the future, healthcare seems to be running on a two-speed highway. There is a fast lane that academic medical centers such as Jefferson Health, Cleveland Clinic, and Johns Hopkins are on. However, the vast majority of hospitals operate in the slow lane. Which begs the question: what does it take for the system as a whole to move forward? Are we going to see the leaders pull away from the pack and the followers struggle for an extended period?

"To some extent, you do see that in any industry, there are always larger companies that are acquiring and merging and creating even larger institutions that are constantly innovating. However, in the digital and the technology space, ever since the Internet, we have seen that the equation has changed. Small startup companies revolutionize the world—I mean, where was Google ten or fifteen years ago? They were a very small company. They used the Internet and associated platforms and became this huge behemoth and transformed our lives. I do not think there is any reason that even a small community hospital in a small population area of the nation cannot innovate with technology. The technologies that they need are now available as micro services that are in many cases exposed for free to develop an application prototype or a concept. I think that it is more of a mind-set that you need a large amount of resources to innovate and be successful," says Gomes.[106]

It is precisely this mind-set that sometimes takes hold in smaller institutions that believe technology-led innovation is going to be prohibitively expensive, which leads to a self-fulfilling prophecy. As a result, these institutions continue to fall behind. The reality today is that it is possible to innovate with technology without investing millions of dollars, unlike in the early days of ERP and other enterprise software. A great example of this is how the cost of genome sequencing has fallen from millions of dollars a few years ago to a mere thousand dollars or even less. As consumer devices such as Amazon's Echo and the Apple Watch become more ubiquitous, these devices effectively crowdsource and democratize data collection, and the data can be analyzed for incremental insights that can potentially improve the quality of care.

Digital health startups have a great opportunity to drive innovation in healthcare by unlocking insights from these newly available data sources. However, they need to be cautious with their approach. Gomes, who has endured many pitches by startups, has this to say: "Well, firstly we would like these companies to come to us at a point where they have just started with the idea, but we certainly do not want to be watching vaporware. If they come in and say they would like to co-develop with us, that is a great beginning to a conversation, versus someone saying hey, we have this thing, we want to sell it to you, we want you to validate it for us. The first thing they do is they open up a PowerPoint deck and try to make you believe they have an actual working prototype when the thing you are looking at is not quite ready. It is not going to help to start a conversation that way."[107]

The good news is that this can work well for startups that work collaboratively with clients in early stages of product development by determining the clients' needs and building a platform around the needs. Many startups also make the mistake of looking at the broken healthcare sector from the outside in and believing it somehow puts them in a position to solve the complex problems of healthcare when others have not been able to. Healthcare solutions involve patient safety, workflow considerations, ease of use, and a complex payment structure that many digital health companies struggle to figure out.

Healthcare lags behind other sectors in the creative use of data for unlocking insights and is barely scratching the surface of the opportunity landscape. There is enormous potential waiting to be realized from the Big Unlock.

4.2 Defending the Citadel: IT Security, Data Privacy, and the Ransomware Threat

Which industry went from nearly zero to a billion dollars in revenues in 2016? If you guessed ransomware, you would be right. Ransomware payments were estimated at $1 billion in 2016 according to the Federal Bureau of Investigation (FBI).[108] A global malware attack that affected over one hundred thousand organizations in 150 countries in May 2017 may have delivered that kind of revenue in a single day to the cyberattackers. In 2017, this figure was expected to go up to $5 billion.[109]

An inside joke in healthcare goes that there are two kinds of CIOs: those who have been hacked and those who do not know they have been hacked. Healthcare has been in firefighting mode regarding IT security. It needs a complete building code upgrade. If you are a B2B software company that works in healthcare IT, the loud sucking sound of healthcare data breaches may be from one of your systems. There were 325 large healthcare breaches in 2016, impacting 16.6 million patient medical records, an increase of over 300 percent from the previous year.[110] Credit risk-scoring firm Experian published a report in early 2017 indicating that healthcare would be the most targeted industry for cyberattacks.[111]

In early 2015, Premera Blue Cross announced that it had been the "target of a massive cyberattack" that had impacted some eleven million records.[112] A few weeks prior to that, Anthem, another large health insurer, had revealed that it had also been the "target of a massive cyberattack." Translation: their systems were hacked, and healthcare data was stolen. In most cases, the data breaches had been taking place for a significant period before the enterprises detected them. In Premera's case, the initial data breach took place in May 2014, and, in Anthem's case, it went as far back as 2004.

In 2016, a major distributed denial of service attack—a technical term for a specific type of cyberattack—crippled parts of the Internet by targeting Dyn, a provider of domain name services (DNS). In simple terms, a DNS provider routes Internet traffic like an air traffic controller. Because the DNS provider was targeted with a flood of junk requests from a zombie army of botnets (a standard modus operandi for these types of attacks), major services such as Twitter, Netflix, and Spotify were unavailable or loaded more slowly than normal.[113]

In May 2017, reports emerged of a large-scale ransomware attack that impacted nearly fifty of the UK's National Health Service (NHS) hospitals; it was later confirmed to be part of a larger international cyberattack. Reports emerged of hospitals turning away ambulances as they feared being unable to treat patients. Hospitals lost the use of landlines and Internet connections, and several hospitals in the UK confirmed receiving demands for ransomware payments in bitcoin, with deadlines for compliance.

The attack was by a self-propagating variant of malicious ransomware dubbed WCry/WannaCry. Early indications were that the cyberattackers found vulnerabilities in devices or systems. The WannaCry malware exploited a vulnerability in Microsoft software, which some hospitals in the UK had failed to patch. The Mirai malware (a botnet that targeted vulnerable IoT devices) infected an estimated five hundred thousand Internet-enabled devices.[114] At the time, according to Rich Barger, Director of Cybersecurity Research at information security software company Splunk, "The WCry/WannaCry ransomware strain hit 11 countries in just three hours. This is one of the largest global ransomware attacks the cyber community has ever seen."[115]

An important feature of these attacks on healthcare was the apparent involvement of overseas actors, including nation-states. Nigeria and the Baltic States are well-known sources of phishing attacks. State-sponsored actors from East Asia are now said to be targeting healthcare records. North Korea was suspected to be behind the NHS attacks in May. An episode in the popular TV program *60 Minutes* reported on industrial espionage involving the Chinese government on a staggering scale. If the report is to be believed, Chinese government agents are stealing valuable intellectual property, spying on competitors, and hacking into government servers.

Attacks on healthcare are increasing for a few reasons: other sectors such as retail and financial services have become more sophisticated, with IT security processes and tools, and the value of credit card data is decreasing. As a result, the hackers have turned their attention to softer targets with more valuable data, such as the healthcare industry. Within healthcare, payers have been hit more than providers. As opposed to gathering fragmented data from individual hospitals, hackers choose to target payers because of the opportunity to gain access to state-level population medical records, or even more. A bigger target produces a better return for the risks and effort involved.

Now, the good news—IT security budgets are increasing across the board. With most of the meaningful use work and ICD-10 preparedness out of the way, data security is one of the big CEO-level issues that are getting more funding. When there is virtually unlimited funding available, there is a tendency to throw money at technology and tools. The question is whether additional investment in technologies can solve the fundamental issues of information security in healthcare by itself.

While healthcare costs in the United States as a percentage of GDP are the highest in the world, healthcare IT spend as a percentage of revenue is among the lowest across various industry sectors. Healthcare CIOs are constantly challenged to do more with less and face budget cuts year after year. They typically respond with one or more of the following actions, purely to reduce costs: outsource IT functions to an offshore provider, lay off IT staff, or postpone refreshing IT assets. The last one, in particular, has the most potential to wreak havoc on healthcare IT.

End-of-life and out-of-support software and hardware are a reality of the healthcare IT environment today. CIOs are compelled to sweat the assets as long as they can simply because there is no money available in the budget for system upgrades.

The problem is further compounded by the following:

- Explosion of data. Electronic medical record (EMR) data, consumer health data from wearables and other devices, and IoT data will soon overwhelm healthcare enterprises.
- Data integrity compromises. If hackers can access the data, they can tamper with it. The implications for patient safety arising from the use of faulty medical records are disturbing.

Fortunately, because of the high-profile nature of these data breaches, the issue of infrastructure and information security has now climbed to the very top of the CEOs' agenda in these organizations. In many ways, IT security is now a national security issue. Chief Information Security Officers (CISO) now rule. Consequently, budgets for IT security have gone up significantly. However, IT security is not just a technology problem, nor is there a foolproof solution to be found by throwing money at new technology and tools. Security breaches can often be traced to process violations, human negligence, and even willfully destructive acts by disaffected employees.

For all the promises made about IoT's ability to significantly improve healthcare outcomes through remote patient monitoring and connected-health programs leveraging smart devices, the fact that cyberattacks can cripple an entire system by exploiting vulnerabilities in one tiny corner of the ecosystem has made many CIOs and CISOs understandably cautious about opening up their firewalls.[116]

Organizations such as Group Health Cooperative (GHC), a Seattle-based health system that was acquired in 2016 by Kaiser Permanente, are focusing more on process improvement, automated incident response, and early containment.[117] GHC is extremely restrictive about exchanging medical information with other technology providers and IoT devices, thereby insulating itself from technology partners that have weak security practices. Other tactics include strengthening internal environments through simulation techniques such as penetration tests, advanced analytics for correlations, and geolocational hot-spotting (flagging systems access from unusual locations), which has recently become relevant in light of evidence indicating the involvement of nation-states in sophisticated cyberattacks.

Chris Grant, Chief Information Security Officer at GHC, believes that it is not just about technology tools. He believes that "You cannot buy your way out of trouble on this."[118]

Grant has taken an approach to combat IT security threats that provide insights into best practices emerging in healthcare IT security practices.

- **Process vs. tools.** At GHC, Grant constantly prioritizes between process and tools (in layman's terms: between firefighting and building code upgrades). His team focuses on understanding incidents, early containment, and automation at the incident response level. Using a number of detection and monitoring tools, the GHC team identifies risks and focuses on remediation areas. Vulnerability scans combined with penetration tests designed to identify specific sets of vulnerabilities, and tools such as Splunk, a technology that records and analyzes system logs, enable reuse of the data for improved security results.

- **Analytics.** Another best practice is the use of analytics for correlations and geolocational hot-spotting. Google often sends alerts when users try to log into Gmail from an overseas location. At GHC, they have taken it a step further to develop correlations between logins from multiple locations. They have created a scoring system that manages validations and exclusions based on the location disparities for the user at the time, answering potential questions like, "How can Scott be accessing his account from Florida and England at the same time?"

- **Data privacy.** This is an issue that is closely related to IT security, especially in healthcare. Health systems are required to monitor access to EMR data as a part of meaningful use requirements. Grant and his team have built a production application and framework on a platform that uses a set of medical-record access scenarios to identify potential privacy violations and triage them using a weighted score model so GHC's privacy team can take further action.

An added twist to IT security in healthcare is that it is no longer just about healthcare or medical data. Data breaches reported by Banner Health[119] and Bon Secours Health System[120] in 2016 were attributed to breaches at one of their HIPAA BAs. Healthcare is a particularly attractive sector for cyberattackers, because

a. healthcare information systems are not up to date compared to other industries, and
b. healthcare data fetches a handsome price on the black market for stolen personal information.

A survey of healthcare lawyers indicated that nearly 90 percent believe their industry is more vulnerable to cyberattacks than others.[121] In addition, healthcare enterprises operate in a rapidly expanding ecosystem of BAs that includes medical device manufacturers, known to have weak security features.[122] Vulnerabilities in a BA's information technology systems can very easily be exploited to find back-door entry points into the IT environments of covered entities such as hospitals and health systems.

Medical device companies have a unique set of challenges as well that directly impact IT security at the enterprise level. As an example, consider that FDA guidelines require medical device manufacturers to consider device security during the product development life cycle to mitigate cybersecurity risks. What happens to devices that are already in the market, especially ones that are running on operating systems (OS) that are a couple of generations older than the current versions?

Beckman Coulter (Beckman), a medical device manufacturer that has been around since 1935, has devices that stay in the market for a long time, sometimes twenty years or more, representing multiple generations of a product. Legacy OS has its challenges, says Scott T. Nichols, Director of Global Product Privacy and Security at Beckman. He refers to post-market device security management as an "onion" strategy, referring to the multiple layers at which security must be managed: the data layer, the applications layer, operating system layer, device (PC) layer, and network layer, wrapped properly with policies and procedures.[123]

According to Nichols, while it is relatively easy to manage device security for new designs and products, it is a lot harder for legacy devices out in the market. This is due to various factors including varying levels of IT security practices among users, lack of resources, and, most pertinently, varying degrees of device security practices among medical device vendors.

The FDA released guidelines in late 2016 laying out an approach to the post-market phase for medical devices, promoting "good cyber hygiene" through routine device maintenance, a risk-based approach to characterizing vulnerabilities, and timely implementation of necessary actions to mitigate emerging cybersecurity risks and reduce the impact to patients.[124] The FDA's *Postmarket Management of Cybersecurity of Medical Devices* points out that cybersecurity risk management is a shared responsibility among stakeholders including the medical device manufacturer, the user, and an array of technology providers (e.g., OS vendors, application developers, and systems integrators), many of whom are not regulated by the FDA.[125] Given the heavily regulated nature of the device industry, even the smallest changes had to go through an onerous compliance review and approval process. More recently, the FDA has provided device manufacturers with the latitude to apply security patches that do not impact patient safety, and this provides much-needed relief to the device industry to deal quickly with cybersecurity vulnerabilities.

One of the challenges for device security is the lack of industry standards or a commonly accepted security certification process for medical devices. While the health IT sector is governed by HIPAA and has Health Information Trust Alliance certification for organizations, this is not adequate for medical devices, according to Nichols. A set of standards is needed specifically for the device industry, and Nichols is involved in some initiatives and organizations trying to achieve just that. "It is also important that these standards are industry driven," adds Nichols, "so they capture the true user needs and are not just handed down as a mandate by a federal agency."[126]

In the meantime, Nichols recommends a set of best practices for device manufacturers and users, including robust and dynamic categorization of their devices and underlying software in terms of criticality and impact. He adds that systems software vendors need to better appreciate the needs of a vertical industry segment (e.g., medical devices or healthcare). He points out that what may be critical for a software vendor may not be critical for the device manufacturer or the user, and vice versa.

Medical devices and the broader category of IoT devices are emerging as important sources of data in healthcare. They enable improved PHM and remote patient management, and develop personalized care protocols, all of which are essential pillars in the shift toward VBC and lowered costs of care. Device security is a critical enabler in the future of healthcare.

The weakest link in the chain determines its strength, and healthcare companies need to continually assess their internal environments as well as their relationships with technology providers and other BAs.

While technology optimists and vendors continue to make the case (rightly) for improving healthcare quality and lowering the overall costs of care through timely interventions and prevention of hospitalizations using connected devices, health systems are cautious (equally rightly) about exposing their infrastructure and networks to malicious attacks from IoT devices.

We are on the cusp of unlocking the potential of data in the practice of evidence-based medicine and PHM. There are greater benefits than one can unfold from the use of multiple data sources, but we need to balance it with privacy concerns as well, which are governed by HIPAA.

Neal Singh of Caradigm says, "The data has become more valuable in healthcare, but data breaches have made it even harder in terms of what providers have to do in securing data. There is a whole area around governance, risk and compliance of data that is growing as well. So the first piece is how do you get the data on the patient, and how do you create that longitudinal patient record? The second piece is how do you secure that data, how do you govern the data, how do you make sure that you are in compliance with the data and how do you protect that data?"

Information security and privacy concerns play into this equation as healthcare providers start using medical information from interconnected devices, especially in cloud-based environments. Enterprise IT providers, concerned about vulnerability to hackers, are leery of exchanging data with IoT devices. While there are indisputable benefits to healthcare consumers from their physicians gaining access to medical information from a range of connected devices, there is a real threat to privacy as well. As employers start using wearables data to gather information at an enterprise level for managing healthcare benefits, collecting personal data from devices imposes a set of legal requirements on enterprises starting with proper disclosures about the collection and use of the information.

The HIPAA Privacy Rule is a set of federal standards to protect the privacy of patients' medical records and other health information. Covered entities such as health plans, health systems, physician practices, and a host of other healthcare providers come under the purview of HIPAA, as do their BAs such as technology firms. If a covered entity engages a vendor (BA), the covered entity needs to have a written BAA in place. The vendor is also directly liable for compliance with certain provisions of the HIPAA rules.

The ONC sees HIPAA as an enabler of interoperability and population health initiatives that are crucial for advancing VBC. The ONC takes pains to point out that HIPAA not only protects PHI from unauthorized access but also promotes interoperability by permitting providers to share PHI for patient care and PHM.

The related HIPAA Security Rule establishes national standards for the security of PHI and specifies a series of administrative, technical, and physical security safeguards for covered entities as well as BAs. This latter point is important because liabilities arising from unauthorized access to or breach of personal health information flows down the chain from covered entities all the way to the bottom of the BA network. We discussed, specifically, the implications for CSPs in chapter 3.

Says Neal Singh of Caradigm, "Due to the increased levels of data breaches, we have seen a shift toward improved governance, risk and compliance. We see that it is continuing to grow because if you have to govern your data, you have to know both ends of the equation.

You have to know what a user was provisioned for in terms of access and then what they are using it for. So you have to have both sides of the equation."[127]

Under HIPAA rules, covered entities such as hospitals, health insurance companies, clinics, nursing homes, and pharmacies must comply with requirements to protect the privacy and security of health information.[128] For covered entities, recent data breaches indicate that an ongoing review of their BAA is becoming critically important since the ultimate liability for these breaches falls on the covered entities. BAAs lay out all the responsibilities of the vendor as they relate to the handling of personal information, and the obligations in the event of breaches. An additional challenge has been employee error and negligence that have been major causes of data security breaches.[129]

The bottom line is that technology firms/BAAs are liable for any data breach attributed to a failure at their end. Many BAAs have no limits on liabilities and can create significant financial risks for a BA.

IT environments in healthcare tend to be outdated, and the top priority for most CISOs is the protection of the legacy environment. The joke about technology asset refresh/replacement policy goes like this: when the asset dies, it is replaced. Organizations need to transform from being good at firefighting to upgrading the building codes—identifying and remediating system vulnerabilities and configuration issues. According to GHC's Grant, penetration tests and other traditional IT security practices tend to be reactive to security incidents, with limited ability to identify key aspects of an attack by hackers. The focus of healthcare IT security functions should be the lateral movement, or system-to-system movement, of a would-be cyber criminal set on finding and exfiltrating data.

The governance model in health systems is also changing, with IT security increasingly being considered a risk function and not a technology function. However, the risk function is expected to show a strong appreciation for technology and the ability to work in tandem with CIO organizations. The talent shortage for IT security professionals will make such collaborations—with internal as well as external partners—key to success.[130]

At the same time, as enterprise IT interacts more with external systems, including cloud-based vendor platforms, connected medical devices, and the IoT, the mandate for IT security will expand to address new vulnerabilities.[131] The medical technology industry, in particular, seems unaware of the enormity of the risks that their devices can cause for the rest of the healthcare system, although that is changing rapidly. In some ways, healthcare IT security may soon need to be called IoT security.[132]

Healthcare IT firms that have been in the space for a while understand HIPAA and their obligations under a BAA. They have compliance training programs in place for associates and documented processes for dealing with HIPAA violations and data breaches.

However, the healthcare B2B vendor landscape has changed significantly in the past few years.

New technology firms are trying to get in on the opportunities opening up due to healthcare consumerism and digital transformation in the sector. The need for cost control is also driving healthcare enterprises to adopt cloud-based services and overseas operations to support critical IT systems.

Here is a sample of how these arrangements might impact IT security and expose healthcare enterprises to data breaches.

Digital health. With the emergence of healthcare consumerism, hundreds of digital health startups have sprung up to develop platforms and solutions targeting consumers, fueled by billions of dollars in venture capital. These startups are focused primarily on growth. Compliance is not a high-priority item on the agenda.[133]

Cloud migration. With the rapid movement of IT to the cloud, covered healthcare entities are finding themselves contracting with emerging technology firms that operate with cloud-based models such as AWS or Microsoft Azure. In many cases, covered entities may not be dealing directly with cloud providers, but through a BA that delivers a cloud-based service.

Outsourcing and offshoring. Covered entities such as health plans and health systems have large overseas operations teams supporting their IT environment. These teams could be vendor organizations or even captive centers (offshore operations centers owned and operated by a US entity) that are extensions of the parent entity. While no data ever leaves the United States, per regulatory requirements, offshore teams have access to production systems and databases that expose them to consumers' personal information.

Health systems are under pressure to innovate and tap into partnerships to deliver bottom-line value to the enterprise. However, they need to protect their IT systems from vulnerabilities arising from these partnerships. Many health systems are doing just that.

Healthcare technology firms, for their part, need to be aware of their obligations under HIPAA and understand that compliance is not just about IT security but also about physical and administrative safeguards. If technology firms fail to protect their systems, there can be a serious financial impact, not to mention reputational consequences, for themselves as well as for the covered entities they work for.

Healthcare is among the most vulnerable sectors for data breaches and ransomware. Disturbingly, many of the recent data breach incidents have occurred in HIPAA BAs. Healthcare's vulnerability is no longer restricted to medical information; cyberattackers are looking for any personal information that can be sold in the stolen data market.

In the world of IoT devices, the points of vulnerability have multiplied. The exciting possibilities of IoT in healthcare, expected to be a $163 billion market in 2020 according to consulting firm Accenture, are tempered by the implications of device-level vulnerabilities.[134] Medical devices, in particular, have been identified as highly vulnerable, and hacked medical devices may now be the single biggest threat to healthcare IT security. In May 2017, the WannaCry malware attack indeed impacted certain medical devices. It is possible that security breaches of this nature may make healthcare enterprises more conservative about adopting emerging technology solutions to unlock insights from data.

While short-term fixes may enable hospitals to recover their data and resume normal operations, the vulnerabilities can persist for years, with malware residing in IT systems like sleeper cells.

In the longer term, cybersecurity is more about following basic rules and processes to prevent incidents. Rich Barger of Splunk stresses the paramount need for critical enterprises to have a ransomware playbook in place for when they are attacked. The FBI and the ONC have issued detailed guidelines on how organizations can protect themselves against ransomware attacks, and how to report them when they do happen. Having a playbook is one thing, ensuring it is rigorously followed is another. Clinicians and administrators, already stretched, cannot be faulted for not being up to speed on the latest techniques of cyberattackers. Preparing an entire organization to deal with cybersecurity threats requires a fundamental culture change, and enterprises have to prepare for a long haul.

Regardless of the precautions, ransomware has emerged as the primary method of cyberattacks in 2017, and the WannaCry attack, bigger in scale and scope than anything else we had seen, may be just the beginning. On a lighter note, Barger of Splunk jokes, "One thing is for sure — somebody is going to get very rich with ransomware, or spend a very long amount of time in jail."

4.3 Interoperability: Integrate, Do Not Just Interface

A clinician once told me, "We have killed more people because we did not share data than because we did."

The Obama years were marked by a singular achievement: the

digitization of patient medical records (a huge change from the paper-based records that were an embarrassment to the most advanced healthcare system in the world, namely the United States). At the end of 2016, over 99 percent of hospitals had partially or completely implemented an EHR system,[135] and nearly 80 percent of office-based physician practices were using certified EHR systems.[136] However, despite the high penetration of EHR in hospitals, the systems did not talk to one another, largely because the administration overlooked the need to ensure that the systems were interoperable. The lack of interoperability resulted in creating a big bottleneck in the unlocking of insights from patient data for improved healthcare outcomes and reduced costs of care.

Healthcare data is exploding. However, the inability of data to flow freely between healthcare providers and the inability of patients to freely access their medical information have been matters of great concern and frustration to the ONC. The ONC described the current state of interoperability as a work in progress in their report to Congress in late 2016 on the progress since the HITECH Act was passed as part of the American Recovery and Reinvestment Act of 2009.[137] The HITECH Act launched a far-reaching effort to spur the adoption and use of information technology throughout the health system. Since then, tens of billions of dollars in taxpayer-funded incentives have been paid out to put a national EHR backbone in place.[138]

The implication of the high penetration levels of EHR systems among hospitals and physician practices is that we now have a national backbone of digitized medical records on a vast swath of the population waiting to be unlocked for value. This backbone has enabled many digital initiatives to emerge, such as electronic prescribing, online scheduling of doctor office visits, and online access to medical records. The EHR backbone has also enabled the launch of digital initiatives that support PHM through patient engagement and advanced analytics initiatives. An entire class of digital health startups has sprung up in the past few years, which in 2016 garnered over $4.5 billion in venture capital.[139]

However, much of the digitized patient information is locked up in proprietary systems that are not interoperable. In addition to identifying this as unfinished business, the ONC blames data-blocking practices as one of the major concerns for the industry. The benefits of data interoperability are undeniable, and several efforts are under way to accelerate progress toward full interoperability. Initiatives such as the Sequoia Project's Carequality initiatives and the industry standards organization HL7's FHIR[140] standards stand out as the ones most likely to succeed in establishing industry interoperability standards. In an opinion piece in the NEJM, a group of former heads of the Office of the National Coordinator for Health IT (ONC) conclude that seamless interoperability will not only improve the quality of healthcare outcomes but also promote efficiencies in resource use and costs.[141]

Says Ed Marx of Cleveland Clinic, "Data acquisition, loading and cleansing and even the governance of it is always a huge challenge, but I do not think it is insurmountable. I think while interoperability is being solved somewhat, people are still successful in making it happen, but it certainly takes extra effort."[142]

Creating digital experiences and delivering these experiences consistently to healthcare consumers and care managers via multiple channels requires data standardization and integration. With the increasing adoption of cloud-based technologies, enterprises have to find ways to combine their legacy platform investments with emerging technology solutions built on cloud-based platforms.

Modern technologies such as cloud, mobile, IoT, and big data provide the means for healthcare organizations to respond to industry disruption. However, realizing value from these technologies requires connecting them to other sources of data within the healthcare enterprise. For example, it is not enough for organizations to simply move to the cloud since cloud and SaaS technologies are only as powerful as the data that powers them. An organization that acquires a solution like Salesforce Health Cloud must be able to connect it to the EHR systems where patient data resides to realize value.

Similarly, healthcare organizations cannot simply build or adopt mHealth technologies without addressing underlying connectivity challenges.

Incorporating IoT technologies in healthcare also poses integration challenges. Information resides in more places than ever before, and under status quo connectivity approaches, each new endpoint that must be connected to each of these incremental technologies represents an additional investment. As the number of endpoints has increased, so too has the cost of connectivity. This has created a challenge for healthcare IT teams, as the number of resources required to connect these new technologies and deliver on new projects has exceeded capacity. The result is an IT delivery gap between what the business needs to satisfy patient and customer demands and what IT can deliver. Given a finite amount of time and resources, and an increasing number of projects required by the business in response to healthcare industry disruption, this gap will continue to widen, putting increased pressure on IT. Without addressing the connectivity burden that has created this gap, healthcare organizations will be unable to adopt or implement the types of modern technologies that are crucial to addressing industry disruption. Traditional approaches to connectivity have outlived their ability to address this challenge, necessitating a new approach.

Healthcare enterprises have typically followed a point-to-point approach or a traditional service-oriented architecture approach to integration. Ten years ago, technology firms racked up sales by selling stand-alone solutions with point-to-point interfaces to various systems. With the recent wave of EHR implementations, health systems have indicated an increased preference for integrated and not interfaced applications. Many of the traditional technology firms are either shutting down those marginal offerings or making them interoperable through standardized APIs. The point-to-point interface approach is no longer tenable for integrations in an environment with an explosion of endpoints and an urgent need to unlock the organization's data assets.

Importantly, an API-led approach facilitates innovation through greater agility and higher developer productivity by employing standardized integration approaches. In many ways, an API-led approach is fundamental to unlocking insights from data and accelerating digital transformation across healthcare enterprises.

To understand how important integration software is, consider that Google spent $625 million[143] in 2016 to buy Apigee,[144] a company that specializes in APIs. Mulesoft, another company that has developed integration software, had a market capitalization of over $2.6 billion in May 2017. The valuation of these companies validates the API economy, estimated by research firm Forrester to be a $3 billion business by 2020.[145]

One of the real-life examples cited in Google's announcement was how drug retailer Walgreens uses Apigee's API management platform to enable consumers to order prescription refills and print photos.[146] The e-prescription use case is an excellent example of the API economy—a term that broadly refers to how APIs create value by allowing proprietary software to communicate with each other—at work in healthcare. Integration software enables the doctor's office to approve prescriptions to Walgreens electronically and the consumer to order the refills (with gentle prompting from Walgreens) by way of text messages, all in a closed loop that significantly eliminates delays, increases medication adherence and improves population health.

The API economy matters greatly for healthcare's ability to transition into the VBC era. This is because APIs are like wonder glue. Open APIs allow software applications to talk to one another using a defined set of data exchange standards and protocols. Easy interoperability between systems unleashes innovation by enabling developers to build applications using APIs to reach into underlying data on platforms. This is how technology giants such as Google, Apple, Facebook, and Amazon expand their reach and influence—by facilitating innovation through cloud-enabled mobile and digital experiences by unlocking underlying proprietary data. However, this is not the case in healthcare.

Healthcare has been relatively slow to adopt open API standards. Unlike social media and e-commerce, healthcare is mostly a closed ecosystem of proprietary software, notably EHR systems that do not permit the free exchange of data. As I mentioned earlier, the ONC has been pushing for more open standards to unlock the value of digitized medical records sitting in proprietary systems that can unleash innovation in healthcare and positively impact costs, quality, and experience (the triple aim) in healthcare.[147]

An important step in the drive toward open APIs has been the launch of the FHIR standards for data exchange in healthcare.[148] Developed by industry standards organization HL7, FHIR is a possible alternative to proprietary standards for the exchange of healthcare data between systems. Most importantly, FHIR is future-proof, and the HL7 organization has committed to making FHIR backward-compatible with earlier versions of HL7-compliant interfaces as markets transition to the newer standards.[149]

However, it is also pertinent to note that open APIs by themselves do not solve the interoperability problem. True interoperability in healthcare requires more than just the ability to exchange data; systems must also know what data to exchange under what conditions and adhere to the privacy and security aspects, including HIPAA regulations related to the exchange of PHI.[150]

Technology-led innovation is mostly about unlocking the value of data. As data becomes the new oil, integration software may be the new oil pipeline.[151] However, integration software alone doesn't solve the problem of unlocking insights from data.

Says Drew Schiller, CEO of Validic, "At Validic, we standardize and normalize data from hundreds of different sources of PGHD and provide one simple API. Now in terms of the standards such as HL7 or FHIR and getting data into the EHR, historically we have worked with our customers where they do the translation on their end. We are starting to do that on our end too and starting to make the data available via translation services that we can provide. The challenge is that some of the data cannot be standardized. For example, a blood pressure value or a glucose value can be put into an FHIR standard or an HL7 standard. However, if there is something that needs an alert to be raised, for example, the fact that maybe there was no data available for a twenty-four-hour period because the patient did not take a reading, then that is really important information. There is no standard way to put that into an FHIR resource or for entry into the EHR. That has to be raised up inside of the clinician's workflow in a different way, and so we are not just thinking about standards from a specific data flow perspective, but for delivering comprehensive patient health information, and also how to deliver all of the information."[152]

Increasingly, we are likely to see data that will live outside of a standard interface because the HL7 and FHIR standards are all based on episodes of care. They do not account for continuous streaming data, and so certain data elements can be mapped to a standard format and others cannot. Making all the data acceptable and actionable is a critical challenge to be addressed for the Big Unlock. It is not just how to shoehorn data into a standard, but how to define a data model that accepts emerging data sources.

With the explosion of data sources in healthcare, from EMRs to the IoT, unstructured data from text, images, and so on, innovation is going to be determined by how well applications can harness the data. This will require a robust API environment that permits data to be exchanged quickly, efficiently, and accurately. Digital health startups are creating entirely new experiences based on access to the EHR backbone in health systems. They are building applications that combine data from these systems in innovative ways with other data sources, such as claims data and other non-healthcare data, to create mobile experiences that are transforming healthcare. The API economy is set to play a vital role in this transformation.

Tired of the spaghetti of applications they have to deal with and their frustration with the inability to unlock insights from data, industry leaders are turning to FHIR's potential for facilitating full healthcare IT interoperability.

Under pressure, the biggest EHR vendors have built platforms on which developers can create FHIR-compliant apps. However, there is still no easy pathway for the development of apps. Health systems are having to develop their own workarounds, creating integrations to generate insights from data and using the EHR systems to deliver the insights through their regular interfaces. Other notable firms such as Salesforce have developed completely new platforms that focus on improved interfaces and workflows that create digital experiences with the patient at the center of the experience, leveraging their heritage as a CRM software company with a deep understanding of how to build customer experiences.

However, even platforms such as Salesforce's Health Cloud have to rely on integration with EHR data through APIs, and, to that extent, their progress will be determined by how fast the industry progresses toward interoperability. At best, FHIR's role as a facilitator of interoperability will continue to advance—however, not as quickly as many would like. It is also important to note that interoperability is not just a technical issue, but also a policy and business process issue.

The opportunity to transform the digital health experience is huge for enterprises and technology firms alike, and interoperability is an important aspect of unlocking insights from data to accelerate the adoption of digital and connected-health programs.

4.4 The Last Mile: Making Analytics Real-time, Invisible, Low Threshold

Data is exploding in a very nonlinear fashion. As the volume of data grows significantly, it is also changing the thought process around how data gets utilized.

The traditional methodologies of getting data through an extract, transform, and load (ETL) process and doing something with it are no longer sufficient. It used to be that enterprises would ETL the data into a warehouse and do some analytics retroactively once a month or so, mostly in the form of static reports. That methodology is no longer useful in an era of real-time decision support. Making meaningful and actionable insights available real-time at the point of care is the last mile challenge in healthcare and the area where technology solution providers have to differentiate themselves.

In many ways, the real impact can be felt when analytics become invisible; in other words, when machines have taken over much of the heavy lifting in advanced analytics, such as developing and running complex algorithms, leaving humans to deal with just the insights required at the point of care.

While advanced analytics is taking hold in healthcare technology solutions, most healthcare enterprises are concerned with the more mundane *BI*, which more often than not simply means reports. Fashionable new terms such as *AI* and *cognitive* possibly conjure up images of geeks in labs toiling away at complicated statistical models for extended periods of time and finally producing an algorithm or formula that predicts an outcome. At the same time, the terms also imply certain expectations, including that some absolute truth will be revealed that can be a panacea for a vexing problem or—more recently—that some of these new technologies will eliminate jobs and put people out of work.

The question that savvy business stakeholders ask is how to operationalize advanced analytics in an end-to-end process to improve the quality of care, save costs, and enhance patient experience. In other words, they ask to be shown the money.

With data increasingly coming in real-time, through multiple instances of EHR systems or in a clinically integrated network, the challenge is to make sure that the information is transformed in a very normalized fashion with the right codifications. This should then be made available to the clinicians with the right context of the patient in the right context of the workflow so that clinicians can take action with minimal incremental workload. Most healthcare providers are overloaded with way too much information, and, with a typical EHR system, they just want to get in and out, already spending too much time doing data entry in these systems. The last thing a clinician or provider wants is more information; they need more insights. The insights have to be relevant, actionable, and real-time in a way that makes their jobs easier or helps them meet their goals of quality or cost.

Put another way, clinicians want to see the insights, but they do not necessarily want to see the data.

Gomes describes this process in terms of one of Jefferson Health's successful analytics programs. "We do much work with medical oncology, obstetrician-gynecologist, and other areas, and many of the problems they want us to solve, involve real-time data and the whole big data thing is becoming a little old school. While you can draw many insights by looking retrospectively at data and large data sets, nowadays people want those insights in real-time. In the ER, for instance, they want insights *now* because there is an issue right now in the emergency room, and the clinician needs to decide whether to send in more staff and that type of thing. Even for population health and all of that, the space is becoming very much reliant on real-time data, and so the insights need to be happening even without warehousing the data. The insights layer has to be almost real-time. For instance, if so-and-so did not take seven thousand steps today, I want to know that *now*. But I do not want to be flooded with that information constantly either. I want specific and validated insights. I want reliable insights, but I do not want an email attachment that has five Excel files with all the data and insights because then I have to put it off for when I have two hours to go through it and realistically, I never have two hours, and nobody does anything. Instead, if I can just pick the right types of metrics—there are in most decisions about three or four different metrics I need to follow to make a decision—and put exactly those metrics into the hands of the people that make decisions, then I have something that will probably get used. That is kind of what we did in the ER."[153]

Over the past couple of years, the hype around big data and predictive models has tended to set up expectations that analytics is a silver bullet that can solve all kinds of problems faced by the industry. Even those that are effective at deploying advanced analytics admit that there is significant work to be done in measuring the fidelity of the system before an enterprise-wide dissemination and deployment can be undertaken.

At Sutter Health, a large health system based in Northern California, the R&D group looked at one of the most analyzed problems in healthcare—avoidable hospital readmissions. While Sutter Health had developed robust algorithms for predicting thirty-day readmissions, the questions they asked themselves pertained to the last-mile problem in using these models effectively, according to Dr. Josh Liberman, Executive Director for Research Development and Dissemination at Sutter Health.[154] Specifically, the questions were:

- Can you operationalize the model at scale?
- Can you deliver it to the person when they need it?
- Will they use it?
- If they use it, do they know what to do with it?

Consider transitions in care. A transition in care refers to the movement of a patient from one setting to another; for example, from the hospital to the patient's home or a post-acute care facility after a medical procedure. Transitions in care are important because patients typically need to continue to receive care in the new setting. If they do not receive appropriate and timely care, this could result in readmission, which is considered a failure at the health system level.

Developing predictive models that can identify patients at risk of readmission becomes critical in managing resource efficiencies as well as patient outcomes. This is where the operationalization of predictive models in clinical workflows becomes important. Many analytical solutions tend to be stand-alone systems, and the insights from predictive models are not available real-time to providers at the point of care. In a health system such as Sutter

Health with over 190,000 discharges every year, not only do the providers need the patient risk models in real-time at the point of care, they also need to use real-time data to determine the most effective interventions.

Several factors impact the ability to deliver real-time analytics at the point of care, including

- complex workflows and lack of interoperability between systems,
- data management and data silos,
- suitability and reliability of data, and
- HIPAA privacy requirements.

Much has been written about the poor usability of EHR interfaces, and adding a new feature on an interface already crowded with medical information can be a distraction for caregivers.[155] Also, analytics may be required by multiple stakeholders—case manager, doctor, and discharge coordinator, to name a few—and the challenge becomes a question of whether analytics can be delivered to the person who needs it when they need it.

The other aspect of making analytics effective is to make them invisible at the point of care, as I mentioned earlier. In other words, show the doctors and patients what they need to see when they need to see it and eliminate noise. In the readmissions example described above, this may mean risk profiling patients with a scoring model that highlights the higher-risk patients to doctors and care management professionals so that an appropriate treatment and discharge plan can be developed for just those patients.

This also means that user interfaces need to be improved to help caregivers receive the relevant information in an easy-to-consume format. Digital experience design becomes an important factor. At Sutter Health, Dr. Liberman and his team have done just that by radically simplifying the user interface, eliminating manual tasks and, most importantly, eliminating the need to remember. Improved user experience reduces not only medical errors brought about by cognitive overload from poorly designed interfaces but also improves patient satisfaction with the process.

Says Gomes, "Once you have figured out how to provide the right data and insights in real-time, you have to reduce the effort required to access the insights. If somebody has to go to a site, remember their login, type that in and then enter the site, try to find the page those metrics were on, then filter those metrics or do those types of things, they are never going to use it unless their job or their life depended on it. The real decision makers in a healthcare situation, the ones dealing with patients, with people's lives, are not going to sit down in the chair and say, well, let me make this big decision based on analyzing all of this data. It is very, very difficult. You have to get it out real-time, and it has to be mobile. It has to be at a touch of a button or saying a word that gets them that information. I think that is the real transformation that is needed, along with setting a low threshold for accessing data insights and things that matter."[156]

At a time when patients and doctors both complain about the loss of intimacy in doctor–patient interactions—mainly as a result of information technology overload—a well-designed user interface that simplifies advanced analytics and complex workflows and presents information in an easy-to-consume manner can greatly enhance productivity and care quality. This also enables health systems to enter risk-based contracts with a higher level of understanding of financial risks.

4.5 Unproven Data Models and Other Challenges

There are several challenges that healthcare enterprises face today in the unlocking of insights from data. Some of them are unique to healthcare, arising from the maturity level of the sector in the adoption of advanced analytics, certain fallacies, and operating model deficiencies.

Unproven data models. Healthcare data is episodic. The data models are set up to capture information that arises from discrete episodes such as a doctor–patient encounter. In the emerging world of interconnected things that transmit data continuously, these data models come up short because of their inability to harness and process the data. An example of this is patient-generated data from a continuous glucose meter or blood pressure value. If a patient takes a blood pressure reading, it is pretty simple to map that into an EHR because there is a way of storing a discrete record for blood pressure. The challenge arises because there is no great way to store a continuous stream of information that shows a trend of blood pressure data. This becomes critical in a PHM context, where the focus is increasingly on the most recent trends. For instance, if a person's morning blood pressure has been trending up over 20 percent over the last two weeks, or that person has not taken a blood pressure reading in the last forty-eight hours (important for a high-risk hypertension patient), there is important information in those readings that is not easy to bring into the current data structure in healthcare. Thus, we have one of the biggest challenges in healthcare data: the unproven data model.

Evidence base for new data models. Despite all the hype around big data, healthcare operates largely in a world of small data, limited by the structured data in EHR systems, which is often incomplete and insufficient for advanced analytical models. With significant efforts under way to unlock the 80 percent of data in EHR systems that is unstructured and integrate new data sources such as PGHD, IoT data, and genomic data, healthcare is entering the era of big data. However, healthcare looks for evidence of successful deployment for any new solution that impacts healthcare delivery and potential patient safety. For digital health solutions, creating a body of evidence based on successful deployments in production is in early stages. In some ways, this is a chicken-and-egg situation. Until we have an evidence base in place, it can be really hard to roll out large-scale programs because health systems will hesitate to extend full support to these emerging programs until the evidence is in place. We see early signs of adoption through academic medical centers and some leading health systems, but we are just not there yet.

The data scientist talent shortage. When the *Harvard Business Review* published an article in 2012 declaring data scientists to be the sexiest job of the century,[157] and, later in 2013, the McKinsey Global Institute published a report that by 2018 the United States will experience a shortage of 190,000 skilled data scientists, everyone rushed to collect and hoard data scientists.[158] Smart job applicants started including *data scientist* as a skill on their résumés (and were rewarded with exciting job offers), regardless of their actual qualifications. A 2015 study indicated the median compensation of data scientists ranged from $91,000 with one to three years of experience up to $250,000 for managers leading teams of ten or more.[159]

This rush to hire often occurred before organizations had figured out what problems to solve with these highly qualified individuals or what other investments needed to be made to make them productive and effective. To compound the problem, newly minted data scientists often worked in isolation from clinicians and administrators in an ivory tower, developing algorithms and solutions that seldom addressed the reality on the ground.

The mania has died off a bit since then as a result of several factors, the most important of which is automation. Advanced algorithms are now bundled inside analytics offerings and often within cloud service platforms. Cloud-based platforms such as Microsoft Azure's ML platform and AWS come bundled with machine-learning algorithms and a range of other advanced analytical tools. Advanced analytics platforms such as IBM Watson Health come loaded with cognitive and ML algorithms that eliminate the need for healthcare enterprises to invest in hard-to-find data scientists.

A study by IBM in early 2017 indicated that the demand for

data sciences and analytics jobs is expected to grow by 39 percent annually.[160] By 2020 the number of annual job openings for all data professionals in the United States is expected to increase by 364,000 openings to 2,720,000.[161] However, data scientists' salaries have decreased as more and more of the algorithmic functionalities have started coming in a box.

Operationalizing analytics—the need for a "plecosystem" approach. An entire community of solution providers has responded to the challenge of unlocking insights from data by developing statistical models that can identify and isolate at-risk patients for targeted interventions. For example, the LACE index emerged as a guiding framework for predictive modeling for readmissions,[162] and a research group at the Boston University Medical Center came up with a framework, Project RED, which provides protocols for post-discharge follow-up expected to minimize the chance of readmissions.[163]

There seems to be something more to implementing advanced analytics solutions than just a powerful algorithm or a robust process framework. The third leg of this stool seems to be technology or, more specifically, the ability to integrate data from disparate sources in a real-time or near real-time manner in order for the predictive models to accurately identify at-risk patients for targeted interventions. These are the basic blocking and tackling techniques that most healthcare enterprises are dealing with today. Executives at Sutter Health coined the term "plecosystem," short form for platform ecosystem, to describe this approach.

There are four components to an effective plecosystem:

- **Data integration**. Analytics is about data and an enterprise's ability to extract and integrate it from multiple sources.
- **Analytical models**. This refers to the development of predictive models that quantify the likelihood of certain outcomes through applied math and statistical methods.

- **Platform infrastructure and security.** The computing platforms and underlying infrastructure have to be robust and effective to be able to deal with large volumes of different types of data—structured and unstructured, internal and external. Information security now has to cover data at rest, in flight, and in use, given recent incidents of healthcare data breaches at Premera, Anthem, and elsewhere.[164]
- **Visualization and dissemination.** All the cool analysis and computing wizardry are of no use unless it can be presented in a visually appealing format for stakeholders to access and consume on multiple devices, anytime and anywhere.

Healthcare providers are barely scratching the surface when it comes to unlocking the inherent value of their clinical data, and analytics maturity can vary significantly across the healthcare sector. For some health systems, the big gains in the near term can come from basic blocking and tackling, such as implementing a robust reporting and BI framework that delivers timely and accurate information to stakeholders for making day-to-day operational decisions.

Florida-based Adventist Health System (AHS) is an example of a health system that does just that. Serving more than 4.7 million patients annually through forty-four hospital campuses across ten states, AHS has dedicated significant effort to laying the foundation for measurement and performance benchmarking at the facility and provider level in addition to tracking population health metrics across broader affiliations. The effort has been evolving, according to Nick Scartz, Chief Analytics Officer for AHS.[165] By using a combination of tools and platforms, including Qlik for BI and data discovery and Explorys for population health metrics, Scartz's team has set up the framework and processes for a number of clinical and financial scorecards and dashboards. An example is the monthly clinical close for the entire system, which drives accountability through a range of operational performance metrics. Scartz has started hiring data scientists with PhDs and master's degrees to develop predictive models and heuristic data mining techniques to direct more analytics toward identifying the most effective interventions for individual patients.

The journey of AHS is not atypical. By starting small and focusing on driving accountability through the tie-in of performance to operational metrics, an analytics program can demonstrate results in the short term and build an advanced analytics program over time on that foundation. Over a three-year period, AHS was able to reduce costs and length of stay for four of their highest volume and variable diagnoses by 10 percent and 4 percent respectively, controlling for case mix. AHS has also saved more than $15 million over two years by driving the adoption of disease-specific evidence-based physician order sets.

Sell your books at sellbackyourBook.com!
Go to sellbackyourBook.com
and get an instant price quote.
We even pay the shipping - see
what your old books are worth
today!

5 The Healthcare Technology Vendor Landscape: Hypercompetition, Disruption, Innovation

There are two categories of technology providers in the market—traditional enterprise health IT firms and the emerging ecosystem of startups, which are much more consumer focused. While the traditional firms have a virtually unassailable position within the enterprises they serve, startups are approaching enterprises by developing consumer experiences and applications that can be integrated into the clinical infrastructure.

"We are in a tough current environment when it comes to trying sell into hospital systems. Many hospital systems are still in the process of trying to digest their EHR systems, and so decision making in general and for new technology solutions can be slow" says Sam Brasch, Partner at Kaiser Ventures, the venture funding arm of California-based Kaiser Permanente.[166] He adds that, given all of the processes and investment challenges related to acquiring and implementing new platforms in any healthcare environment, health system executives are cautious about making investments in new and unproven technologies.

Traditional healthcare technology firms are facing hypercompetition from an emerging digital health startup ecosystem and nontraditional players who are looking to expand into healthcare. In addition, strained corporate IT budgets and the need for value creation in short timelines is forcing big-box vendors to drop prices, downsize features, or both. EHR vendors, many of which have been beneficiaries of the HITECH Act and meaningful-use incentives for setting up the national digital medical record backbone, are now aggressively moving into newer areas such as analytics and PHM. Their control over the crucial EHR data infrastructure puts them in a uniquely advantageous position in the marketplace.

IT services and consulting firms, engaged in brutal competition in the market, are vulnerable to pricing pressure in the absence of consolidation within their industry. Other forces such as automation and cloud computing will likely increase this pressure, in response to which many IT services firms are acquiring or aggressively building out capabilities to become a part of the change and evade marginalization.

However, healthcare is in the early stages of a digital transformation, and there are significant new opportunities for companies that build capabilities to help healthcare enterprises navigate this transformation. Several smaller and mid-tier companies are now beginning to take a strategic approach to healthcare. Many of them are developing specializations that make them attractive to clients as niche and nimble providers.

Global IT firms, especially those from India, continue to be in the spotlight whenever a deal is announced that results in significant job losses to offshoring. The industry has seen wake-up calls around intellectual property (IP) protection, information privacy, and security. A $940 million lawsuit by EHR vendor Epic (subsequently reduced to $220 million in punitive damages) against India-based IT services company TCS for alleged IP violation, as well as the stories of job losses related to IT outsourcing at UC San Francisco, Abbott, and other companies, are significant developments for the IT services sector. With fewer traditional multi-year service deals to go around, vendors are under tremendous pricing pressure as services get increasingly commoditized and the pressure on IT budgets continues to be relentless. As healthcare firms consolidate, they use their bulk and weight to negotiate harder with service providers.[167] A fragmented service provider community can do little to avoid the inevitable margin compression that follows.

Nontraditional players, notably Amazon with its blockbuster AWS business, are emerging as dominant players that threaten the remote infrastructure management business, which IT services firms have relied on for growth in the past few years.

There is also a burgeoning ecosystem of digital health startups, many of which are directly competing with IT consulting firms as well as traditional platform players. There is a widely held belief that traditional healthcare technology firms while enjoying the benefits of incumbency, are not necessarily investing in the kind of innovation that typically comes out of a startup ecosystem. For innovative startups, though, the challenge is to acquire new clients and expand their footprint in the market.

The technology vendor landscape is seeing a significant level of mergers and acquisitions (M&A), as vendors try to position themselves for dominance in their chosen space. Big technology firms such as IBM Watson Health have been some of the most active acquirers in recent years. Between 2015 and 2016, IBM made four major acquisitions; Truven Health, Merge Healthcare,[168] Cleveland Clinic spin-off Explorys,[169] and population health analytics company Phytel[170] (spending $2.6 billion on Truven Health alone).[171] Emerging players such as Salesforce, Google, and AWS are also making strategic technology acquisitions that fit into their healthcare market strategies.

The global IT services sector has been active in M&A as well. With large amounts of cash on their balance sheets and declining prospects for the labor arbitrage business using offshore-based service delivery models, many firms are acquiring their way into platform businesses and moving up the value chain. They are acquiring businesses with IP that not only reduces dependence on labor but also improves their standing with their client base as innovators. Just as with healthcare enterprises, M&A within the tech sector is about survival in the long term. Large recent transactions include Capgemini's acquisition of iGATE.[172] However, there is another dynamic at play. Big technology firms are spinning off their service divisions to focus on the core technology business. Examples of this are Xerox's sale of its ITO business to Atos[173] and the sale of Dell Services to NTT,[174] both of which had acquired their service businesses (ACS and Perot Systems, respectively) a few years earlier. HP has spun off HP Services (itself the result of the acquisition of EDS for $13.9 billion in 2008[175]) in a deal with CSC that has created DXC, a $26 billion IT services company.[176]

Many healthcare organizations, facing margin pressures and threats to their traditional revenue models, are reinventing themselves as technology solution providers. An example of this is Quest Diagnostics, a Fortune 500 healthcare enterprise with over $7.5 billion in revenues[177] in 2016 is aggressively monetizing its database of over twenty billion lab test records by analyzing the data sets for patterns to detect the onset of a wide variety of disease conditions.[178] By forming strategic partnerships with companies such as Inovalon and IBM Watson Health, Quest is developing innovative new product offerings that support improved care delivery and generate new revenue streams.

A common theme playing out among traditional healthcare enterprises and technology firms is the monetization of proprietary healthcare data as a vehicle to drive revenue growth. Large technology firms such as IBM have made no secret of their insatiable appetite for healthcare data.[179] But much of the data is locked up, either in proprietary EHR systems or with healthcare enterprises eager to get in on the business of data and data analytics themselves. The lines between customer, supplier, and competitor are being redrawn as these new alliances are forged and as all players recognize that they cannot do this alone.

It is logical for digital health companies to focus on the transition to VBC as the main opportunity landscape. Billions in VC money are being poured into digital health startups in the race to uncover the next Uber of healthcare.

However, all is not necessarily well in the digital health market.

Funding levels, while remaining high, are increasingly concentrated in fewer companies raising money for later rounds of financing, squeezing out new startups. As such, it is no wonder that prominent healthcare tech VC firm Venrock's prognosis suggests an impending consolidation in the digital health market.

While APMs are at the core of the transition to a VBC era, the fact is that over 75 percent of the current healthcare reimbursements are based on the traditional FFS model. While the market takes its time to shift to future state payment models, new digital health solutions have to find a way to be eligible for payment under the current dominant payment model, which requires payers to approve the use of these solutions in a clinical setting. Behavioral health startups, for instance, have been challenged to crack the code for reimbursement eligibility, despite addressing a $280 billion market that has recently received a funding commitment under the 21st Century Cures Act.[180] Digital health startups with solutions that do not qualify for reimbursement under the FFS model have to rely on demonstrating ROI for their solutions on a stand-alone basis—however, the sales cycles are long, competition is fierce, and transaction sizes are small. Many of the recently funded startups are also making a conscious shift from a B2C to a B2B model without a complete appreciation of the dynamics of healthcare B2B technology markets,[181] adding to the already crowded marketplace for technology solutions.

An additional factor that determines success rates for digital health solutions is the apparent disconnect within health systems as to the priorities for technology investments. Clinicians and C-suite executives seem to disagree on even a seemingly obvious use case such as telehealth, according to a survey by NEJM Catalyst.[182] In the near term, only those technology firms that are ready to play the long game and have deep pockets are likely to survive the long road to success with digital health solutions.

In this book, I have divided the digital health solution providers into four main categories: *custodians*, *enablers*, *arbitrageurs*, and *innovators*. In the following sections, I discuss each of them.

In my categorization, I have omitted an emerging category of competitors—the healthcare enterprises themselves. Many providers have decided to seize the opportunity to get into the business of digital health solutions. Examples include Boston Children's Hospital[183] and Mount Sinai Hospital's spin-off Responsive Health. However, many of these new initiatives are in early stages, and the long-term strategy is unclear. Healthcare enterprises are not necessarily structured to compete in the technology solution marketplace, so I imagine they will turn to strategic partnerships and joint venture arrangements to bring their solutions to a wider marketplace.

5.1 The Custodians: We Have the Data and the Workflow

The first wave of EHR implementations came thick and fast in the wake of the ACA and the companion HITECH Act, which promoted the digitization of patient medical records through a system of meaningful-use incentives that underwrote part of the costs of the digitization effort. All this was overdue for the most expensive healthcare system in the world, which was still running on paper. Some $30 billion and eight years later, EHR systems have declared victory on the digitization mandate but have left a trail of debris in the form of user dissatisfaction and increased physician workloads. These and other factors related to the transformation of the healthcare sector have led to what one study reported as burnout symptoms in some 90 percent of physicians.[184] On top of it all, the systems are closed, and data interoperability remains the single biggest challenge to unlocking the data.

EHR systems were designed for an FFS world, focused on diligently capturing encounter data primarily for billing. Since healthcare providers were getting reimbursed for the costs of the implementation of these systems by way of meaningful-use incentives, the primary focus was to ensure that the incentives were claimed and received. In the mad rush to implement systems and start qualifying for incentives, neither the technology vendor nor the healthcare institutions had any motivation to look at usability or interoperability. The most common criticism leveled against the EHR systems today (besides being very expensive and risky technology projects) is that they are not user friendly. Another important criticism is that the digitized medical records are locked up in proprietary vendor systems, inaccessible even to the patients they serve.

With the grunt work of EHR implementations behind us, the next phase of evolution for these technologies is to unlock the value of the data and improve the usability of the systems. According to one study, the biggest priority for hospital executives, who have invested tens of millions of dollars in these systems, is to optimize and enhance the systems to increase the value of the investments.[185]

Ed Marx oversaw a large EHR implementation during his tenure at Texas Health Resources. He believes that the default mode would be going to their big-box EHR vendor first for any new functionality or technology requirement. For most healthcare IT executives and leadership, if the EHR vendor had anything that could fill a need, the decision would be to go with them. If the vendor claimed to be developing a solution to meet the need, the choice would be to help build the solution and wait. Only if the EHR vendor had nothing in the immediate future would healthcare executives look to alternatives. Marx recognizes that this approach takes a while longer, but, in the long run, it is a cheaper, better-integrated solution because the EHR vendor carries all the data, and it has thus become the norm to go with them. The approach has its downsides—because there is no competitive evaluation of alternate solutions—and deepens the commitment to a single, dominant vendor. Marx thinks this is one of the reasons that healthcare is so far behind other industries, but, at the same time, he also understands the thinking from a cost and integration perspective as well as the overall ease of running a business in the near term.

Most providers have made limited progress in optimizing their EHR platforms, and few have adopted innovation programs to unlock insights from the data. Challenges include poor data quality, suboptimal configurations, and the lack of an innovation imperative. Studies indicate that, as of early 2017, only around 30 percent of health systems were analyzing their EHR data, either using the EHR system's capabilities or a combination of EHR and an external vendor's solution.[186]

The lack of a strategic imperative for health systems to pursue digital health innovation can make it harder for a startup or niche company to get in. Even those health system CIOs who are investing in innovation pilots are wary of letting too many niche companies into an environment due to the increased risk to patient safety from untested solutions introduced too quickly into the IT architecture.

Despite the preference among healthcare executives to default to a single monolithic EHR system such as Epic or Cerner and live comfortably in a world of single systems, the reality is that it is becoming harder to manage with just a single EHR system for many reasons. One reason is the formation of clinically integrated networks. A clinically integrated network essentially consists of multiple providers coming together to form a network for sharing data. Instead of a single EHR, there are multiple data sources, from small ambulatory clinics to large providers or IDNs and emerging entities such as ACO, coming together to formulate a joint plan of action and share risks. A single EHR system is not viable, and one does not exist for these situations. An additional factor is that hospital M&A activity has been growing at a fast pace, adding new EHRs to the data source ecosystem.

Says Neal Singh, "Health systems will find it increasingly hard to live by the rule that they will operate within a single EHR since that would necessarily imply that they are not part of a clinically integrated network, not part of a multi-ACO system, not doing any acquisitions, which kind of narrows you down to a very small group. Even then, if you had multiple instances of a big EHR system, those are different EHRs. An instance of Epic is an instance of Epic. Right?"[187]

The reality is that the level of commitment for EHR vendors, given the years of effort and investment dollars that have gone into implementing EHR platforms, translates into a formidable entry barrier for innovative new solutions, regardless of the merits of the case. "It is important for technology companies not to lose sight of how strong this commitment is. It is a softer aspect of the overall competitive landscape that cannot be ignored in today's context," says Sam Brasch of Kaiser Ventures.[188]

Even as healthcare transforms from FFS to VBC and a market-based system of compensation and payments, EHR systems will continue to have a dominant influence in the future of healthcare by being the electronic backbone for patient medical records nationally. Despite the challenges posed by VC-backed digital health companies and big tech firms, EHR systems will thrive and may even transform into the digital health platforms of record in the future through organic evolution or M&A activity.

EHR vendors dominate the health system landscape today because their systems control the data and the clinical workflows. For clinicians used to these systems despite all their shortcomings, the desire is to make minimal changes and instead integrate new solutions into the existing workflow for ease of use. For EHR vendors, the challenge is to innovate quickly enough to meet the latent demand for analytics and digital health solutions and find a way to hook into the data inside other proprietary EHR systems. While health systems continue to hope they can get it all from a single vendor, the reality is that no single vendor can deliver it all. However, through their ownership of the workflow and the data, big EHR companies will continue to exercise a significant influence on how data will be unlocked in the near term.

The biggest challenge for emerging technology firms is that it is tough to sell to a health system that looks at a big EHR system such as Cerner or Epic as the default option for new technology solutions. A common refrain from these emerging firms is that the incumbent EHR firms often give away their analytics solutions for free to block out the competition. Even when clients choose an innovative new stand-alone solution, EHR vendors have been accused of data blocking tactics, something that has come up repeatedly in the ONC's reports on the state of interoperability in healthcare.

The good news is that there is a small but growing segment of the market that is receptive to stand-alone digital health solutions and a large amount of white space waiting for new solutions. EHR platforms are largely transaction systems that many refer to as data hell. They do not help patients or improve their care. The ability of these platforms to use analytics to identify opportunities and target interventions in ways that are economically sustainable represents very significant untapped opportunities for emerging digital health firms. The widely held belief is that the EHR vendors are providing some level of analytics functionalities in their platforms, but not nearly enough to meet the growing needs of the market.

5.2 The Enablers: We Built it; You Can Rent it

Market wisdom is that no big traditional technology company has been able to succeed in the specialized world of healthcare IT. Anyone remember GE's Qualibria?

Notwithstanding earlier failures, many of the large technology are coming back with a new generation of technology platforms. GE has abandoned its quest for an EHR platform but has come back with GE Health Cloud which includes their Predix analytics engine. Microsoft is reviving its Health Vault platform, and Google Health has been given a new lease of life under new parent Alphabet with its Verily Life Sciences unit.

Everyone is looking for a way to drive digital health innovation by unlocking data, and several big tech firms have chosen the path of building enabling technologies for the Big Unlock.

Salesforce's Health Cloud is a cloud-based patient relationship management solution built on what Salesforce knows best:

cloud-based CRM platforms. Health Cloud translates CRM principles into the patient engagement context to give providers and patients a complete view of the care continuum with seamless workflows and slick user interfaces.

Salesforce has developed an ecosystem of technology partners to enable the implementation of its platform. Besides big consulting firms such as Accenture and Deloitte, they have also signed up smaller firms such as Mulesoft (the integration platform vendor) and Persistent Systems (a technology implementation partner) with specific expertise around system integrations, which will be crucial in orchestrating data exchange between diverse systems. According to Ross Mason, Founder and Vice President of Product Strategy at Mulesoft, the goal is ultimately to enable a digital conversation between doctors and patients.[189] Enabling this conversation requires including all data sources from EHR to x-ray images and even messages exchanged on pagers (I was informed that only doctors and drug dealers used pagers—though drug dealers have apparently moved on to more current technologies). Eventually, a technology architecture that integrates multiple systems seamlessly will unlock valuable patient information residing in disparate systems and enable advanced analytics on data that will influence diagnosis and treatment decisions.

IBM Watson Health is a cognitive computing platform that is capable of ingesting vast amounts of data and knowledge and using sophisticated algorithms to perform analytical tasks. The platform has made significant progress in oncology and medicine with strategic partnerships with leading health systems such as Memorial Sloan Kettering of New York. As mentioned earlier, IBM has splurged on several acquisitions in the past couple of years to build platform capabilities for the healthcare provider markets. In many ways, these acquisitions feed the Watson engine with data that improves the platform and its algorithms. However, IBM and other major technology firms such as Salesforce have limited access to patient medical records which are the main form of healthcare data today. Patient data sits inside proprietary EHR systems such as Epic, Cerner, and Allscripts which are independent stand-alone companies at the time of writing.

Apple's CareKit takes an innovative approach to data gathering for clinical studies.[190] The CareKit open-source framework enables developers to build mobile applications for clinical studies by gaining access to iOS device owners. An example of this in action is One Drop, the diabetes management app that has intuitive workflows and interfaces designed to help consumers self-manage their condition and maintain contact with their primary caregiver. Given that most consumers have sporadic interactions with their primary care physicians, this would seem like a good way to improve the frequency of interaction, especially for chronic conditions that require constant monitoring. Anyone who has dealt with the user interface design of leading EHR systems will welcome the slick and friendly look of these new mobile apps.

Platforms such as IBM Watson Health and Apple's CareKit represent an incredible opportunity for CIOs and technology professionals to innovate and create value in areas such as advanced analytics and clinical trials. The last mile in healthcare, the place where healthcare consumers meet healthcare providers, is a cauldron of technology-led innovation, led not just by VC-funded digital health startups but also by traditional technology firms and innovative health systems with mature technology capabilities and deep knowledge of healthcare IT. All emerging platforms and solutions in the digital health space are addressing market opportunities through the three Cs of success: consumer orientation, clinical workflow integration, and collaborative partnerships.

Salesforce, IBM, Apple, GE Healthcare, and Siemens Healthcare, along with many other large technology firms, have pumped vast amounts of money into building enabling platforms. The logic seems to be: if we build it, they will come. The long-term strategy for these companies is to gain access to all the data that they can, which in turn helps improve the platforms and makes them indispensable to users at the same time. However, not all platform companies are approaching the markets in the same way.

Singh describes Caradigm's PHM platform, which is focused on time to value for customers, "We try to remain neutral for a very simple reason; we are focused on the end outcomes the customer is trying to achieve. The typical outcome of a go-to-one-system approach is simply to keep spending more money on the system versus our outcome focus, which is how to drive faster time to value. Notice I did not say the total cost of ownership, I said time to value. We are very singularly focused on driving time to value for our customers, so we look at specific outcomes and then focus on how in a very timely fashion we drive an outcome-based value for our customer. I think it becomes a very straightforward conversation in terms of an ROI for the customer because the customer can then make the right choices."[191]

Other companies such as Health Catalyst that have established a relatively large footprint among health systems have reached a point where they are taken seriously as independent and viable alternatives to the big-box EHR systems. For the more recent entrants, including some of the large global technology firms, building that kind of footprint is in early stages. Their size, scale, and ability to access C-suite executives to create opportunities for a dialog are favorable factors for them.

It is not just big technology firms that are developing enabling platforms. Smaller firms such as Validic enable users to build digital health experiences based on the underlying data in the platform. The Validic platform integrates PGHD from hundreds of device types, including blood glucose meters, blood pressure meters, and the like, then normalizes and standardizes it in a ready-to-use form for building patient engagement applications.

Many health systems are also getting into the act. The highly successful Health Catalyst came out of Intermountain Healthcare, and Explorys started as an offshoot of Cleveland Clinic. Health systems can provide much-needed data and initial use cases for these startups and, in some cases, use innovation funds to acquire equity positions in these companies.

The big challenges that enablers face today are the same faced by and large by health systems—data lock-in by the big EHR vendors and lack of interoperability. Considering that the majority of treatment decisions still rely heavily on EHR data, it becomes imperative to make this a part of the digital conversation. What the enabling platforms need most is a supportive sponsor in a health system who champions the use of the platform to leverage its potential. Often, the hardest part is finding that one champion.

Even though many technology companies failed when they tried to get into healthcare, the second generation's attempt could be more successful than the first foray into healthcare, according to Ed Marx of Cleveland Clinic. Because there is more motivation on the provider side than in the past and more pressure on cost reduction under the VBC model, Marx believes this works to the advantage of big technology firms. Despite the tailwinds from VBC, for big technology brands, the best way to accelerate market growth may be to acquire an EHR vendor that gives them instant access to the provider relationships. It gives them the integrations they need and eliminates interoperability challenges. Despite the sound logic, we have not seen any of the major EHR vendors acquired by a big technology firm as of writing.

5.3 The Arbitrageurs: We Will Do it For You (and For Less)

Big global consulting firms such as Accenture and Deloitte have had a long history of deploying skilled technologists and analysts to help enterprises with their most complex technology-led transformation initiatives. Bringing a combination of business domain knowledge and technology capabilities, these firms dominated the landscape for many years, first by riding the ERP wave of the '90s and early '00s and later replicating the model with other technologies such as CRM. Notably, these firms have had limited success in the EHR implementation space, largely due to the tight control exercised by the dominant EHR platform vendors. These firms have experiential and informational advantage over their end-user clients, by having executed complex projects in similar environments, and can bring to bear best practices from their vast body of work. Also, many of these firms leverage global resource pools that provide labor cost advantage as well. This combination of experience, talent, and cost structures can be used as arbitrage with clients who are looking for help to execute technology initiatives reliably, within budget, and on time.

As the innovation and digital transformation agenda takes hold across industry sectors, big consulting firms are trying to become strategic partners with large healthcare enterprises to enable the transition to a digital future. Recognizing that providing expensive consultants alone will not sell, the firms are investing in augmenting their consulting services with a certain amount of intellectual capital in the form of acquisitions and partnerships. The models include embedding innovative new technologies from startups, partnering with larger technology platform firms such as Salesforce, through system integrator relationships, and outright acquisitions of niche technology or consulting firms, especially in emerging areas such as digital.

Most consulting firms do not position themselves as product or platform companies to avoid being seen as competition to the technology firms with whom they partner. They also do not have the corporate DNA to run their businesses like technology product companies. When the two mix, it produces mixed results. While IBM has managed to operate as a consulting firm as well as a product company, most technology companies such as Microsoft, Oracle, and SAP prefer to work with consulting partners and maintain relatively small in-house consulting teams. One of the most visible combinations of technology product and consulting services in recent times was the merger of the former EDS with HP in 2008.[192] Billed as a combination that was expected to "create a leading force in global IT services," the merger did not deliver on the promise and EDS (renamed HP Services) was spun off eventually as a separate entity to merge with CSC and form a new company, DXC, in 2017.

When the Y2K scare took hold in the '90s, American corporations racing to beat the clock found a solution in offshore companies that were able to supply cheap labor to fix and maintain code in aging mainframe and legacy systems. As the dot-com boom came and went, followed quickly by 9/11 and its aftermath, offshoring started ripping through corporate IT functions looking to shed costs and get out of legacy system management.

Indian IT firms such as TCS, Infosys, and Wipro and American firms, notably Cognizant, rode this wave and became highly valued global corporations, climbing quickly up the value chain in the years following Y2K to become strategic IT partners with the companies they were serving. The business model was based on a cheap and abundant labor pool of software programmers and engineers in India and subsequently in other locations such as the Philippines. For a long while, the offshoring boom continued unabated, spawning entirely new industries on both sides, including advisory firms, research groups, vocational IT training, and engineering schools, all rushing to cash in. Big global consulting firms such as Accenture, feeling their hold on corporate IT slipping, decided to get on the offshoring bandwagon, eventually setting up global delivery centers that paralleled the largest Indian multinationals in their scale of operations.

While corporations were reducing their legacy system footprint, the ERP wave rolled in, dominated by SAP and Oracle who between them spawned an entire industry of implementation and integration partners. The biggest of them, such as Deloitte, Accenture, TCS, and a few others, took on end-to-end responsibility for executing these massive programs for their clients, sometimes running up hundreds of millions of dollars in implementation costs. In effect, they traded their knowledge of business processes and ERP platforms for long-term lucrative implementation contracts. Many technology consultants built successful careers on the ERP wave, even as many corporate CIOs lost their jobs due to failed implementations and unexpected cost overruns.

The years between 2000 and 2010 belonged to *the arbitrageurs*.

As an insider in that world, I had a ring-side view of everything that was happening. For most of the first decade of this century, the arbitrageurs saw nothing but growth on the horizon for technology consulting, implementation, and maintenance. As the decade started turning the corner, talent shortages started pushing up wage levels just as the quality of talent started dropping. Many early adopters of offshoring, such as the banking industry, started to get in on the act themselves by setting up captive centers in India under direct management control. Others started looking to different solutions and were helped by the emergence of new technologies such as cloud computing and RPA. Today, these technologies threaten to disrupt the $300 billion Indian IT and IT-enabled services industry.

In the four quarters leading up to Q1 2017, healthcare IT service growth rates declined quarter after quarter for the top five publicly held global IT services firms, according to research by my company Damo Consulting.[193] By Q1 2017, many slipped from double-digit growth rates into negative territory, buffeted by the uncertain policy environment and automation technologies that eliminated the need for labor across the board. Aggressive acquisitions for growth—notably Cognizant's $2.7 billion acquisition of Trizetto in 2014,[194] and Wipro's $460 million acquisition of Health Plan Services in 2016[195]—gave way to aggressive share buybacks, with around $9 billion in buybacks announced in Q4 2016 and Q1 2017.

During this time, the nature of enterprise technology buying changed for IT services. In the early '00s, it was all about setting up extended teams in India and taking advantage of labor arbitrage. IT was purely a supply-side business with Indian firms scrambling to hire as fast as they could to meet the seemingly endless demand. In the second wave, the pure time and materials model of billing for resources gave way to managed service agreements with the vendor taking most of the responsibility and risk for outcomes, often based on fixed price contracts. In the current wave, the labor arbitrage model is almost extinct. Automation is eliminating the need for labor, and innovation-led deals are increasingly the norm.

In a hard-hitting article in April 2017, *Knowledge@Wharton* asked a simple question: "Has the 'Dream Run' of Indian IT Ended?"[196] At the time of writing, Indian IT firms had posted declining revenue growth rates for four quarters in a row, and major firms were announcing share buybacks to reduce the huge cash stockpiles and improve returns to shareholders. However, many saw these share buybacks as indicators of declining confidence by the companies themselves in the prospects of the industry (and a preemptive measure against hostile takeover attempts).

Faced with declining growth rates for traditional IT services, large firms with cash on hand have also been aggressively pursuing M&A. Notable deals, in addition to Cognizant's acquisition of Trizetto and Wipro's acquisition of Health Plan Services (HPS), include NTT Data's $3.1 billion acquisition of Dell Services in 2016. However, M&A can be a double-edged sword; Wipro's HPS acquisition has been at the cost of margins, and the outlook for HPS has been uncertain due to its reliance on the Obamacare/ACA exchange markets. In contrast to the big firms that are focusing on M&A deals to build horizontal capabilities in cloud and automation, tier-2 firms seem to be belatedly buying their way into the healthcare markets by acquiring niche firms with healthcare specialization. Tech Mahindra's acquisition of EHR consulting firm HCI and business process management company WNS's acquisition of care management services provider HealthHelp, both for around $100 million in Q1 2017, are aggressive plays to gain a meaningful footprint in the healthcare space. Besides the questions on the price paid for these acquisitions for market entry, India-heritage firms have also traditionally struggled to integrate specialized firms due to DNA mismatches - fundamental cultural differences - at various levels, and it will be interesting to watch how these acquisitions unfold.

Damo Consulting's annual survey of healthcare technology vendor executives in 2016 indicated that over 90 percent of the respondents planned to increase investments in market expansion in 2017.[197] As healthcare undergoes a digital transformation and a shift to VBC, it remains an attractive sector for technology firms. Besides traditional offshore-based IT players such as Wipro, Infosys, TCS, Cognizant, and HCL, a host of large incumbents like IBM, Accenture, Deloitte, and NTT Data (formerly Dell Services) are aggressively pursuing growth in healthcare. At the same time, nontraditional players such as AWS, digital health startups, and mid-tier companies with a strategic approach to healthcare are redefining the healthcare IT services market. The survey indicated that the top three areas for growth are digital transformation, analytics, and cloud. Cybersecurity and data privacy concerns were the biggest obstacles to top-line growth for healthcare IT spend, along with a reduction in IT spend.

IT spend reductions are exerting pricing pressure on IT services firms, as is the rise of nontraditional players such as AWS, which has made tremendous gains in migrating IT infrastructure to the cloud. Healthcare has been relatively slow to adopt the cloud; however, the new wave of digital health solutions are almost entirely cloud based, which means a steady transition of enterprise IT workloads toward platform solutions with a light on-premises footprint.

In this hypercompetitive environment, the arbitrageurs are at very high risk of a slowdown in revenue growth and are turning to a variety of strategic options to remain relevant. Tier-1 companies are building new competencies (e.g. Wipro with Appirio Cloud enablement), and building automation and AI technology in house (e.g. Infosys with Nia). Pure-play analytics service providers such as Mu Sigma that have built their business models almost entirely on labor arbitrage may see revenue decline as advanced analytics platforms such as IBM Watson Health eliminate the need for expensive data scientists. For the arbitrageurs, the tightening rules around H-1B work visas create further urgency to reduce the dependency on offshore-sourced labor pools.

The one thing that arbitrageurs have in their favor is the huge amount of cash on their balance sheets (though some of it is being taken off the table through share buybacks), which can be used to acquire their way into new markets. Some of this is also being invested in client relationships to defend existing books of business and in recruiting high-cost, high-skill talent to enable a successful transition to the next stage of market evolution.

5.4 The Innovators: We Have a Whole New Way of Doing it

In 2016, the president of the American Medical Association (AMA), Dr. James Madara, declared that digital health was the "snake oil" of the twenty-first century.[198]

He was referring to the rash of consumer health applications developed without an evidence base to support their claims to deliver improved health outcomes, but often ended up confusing clinicians and were impediments to care quality. A 2015 study by the IMS Institute of Health indicated that over 165,000 consumer health mobile apps were available on iOS and Android, though only a small number were clinical-grade from a physician's perspective.[199]

A study conducted the same year by the AMA indicated that physicians were enthusiastic about adopting digital health tools subject to some important requirements.[200] These requirements included, among other things, liability insurance coverage for the use of the solution, the ability to integrate with hospital EHR systems, data privacy, and billing and reimbursement eligibilities. It also went without saying that the digital health tools had to improve physician efficiency, patient safety, and physician–patient engagement levels.

However, this has not stopped or slowed the growth of digital health startups, which have continued to raise billions of dollars in venture capital over the past few years. Lately, it has started showing signs of slowing amid growing rumblings and dire predictions that most of them would disappear due to a lack of traction and funding or would become victims of industry consolidation.

The digital health revolution is driven partly by a need for more consumer-oriented health solutions. Healthcare technology has traditionally provided poor user experience to patients. Large purveyors of EHR systems have provided rudimentary digital capabilities with suboptimal user interfaces (which, among other things, has led to physician work overload and burnout), choosing instead to focus on functionalities designed to maximize federal incentives. In some sense, there was a giant vacuum simply waiting for new companies to rush in to fill. Thus we now have a slew of digital health startups who are trying to provide consumers with a superior healthcare experience and a semblance of control over their health data.

The healthcare sector is awash with data, with more and more new sources being integrated into PHM and VBC initiatives. Advanced analytics is expected to unlock insights from all of this data—structured and unstructured, internal and external, clinical and nonclinical.

While this is true, the healthcare sector also varies widely in adoption rates when it comes to analytics. A vast majority of the over 5,500 hospitals in the United States are low-margin operations that are nowhere near ready for the kind of investments and levels of preparedness required for new digital health and advanced analytics solutions, presenting a challenge for the hundreds of VC-funded startups looking to gain traction.

As of late 2016, the FFS model covered 86 percent of US physician healthcare payments, according to a survey by consulting firm Deloitte.[201] New solutions that are not eligible for reimbursements under the current structure will need to convince health systems about the ROI from these investments—which could be a long and expensive process. It is no surprise that industry observers predict a consolidation among VC-funded startups.

A common challenge for health systems and digital health companies is the access to large data sets that are interoperable. Healthcare providers do not share data freely among themselves, and technology providers, especially the vendors of EHR, prefer to keep it locked up in proprietary databases. Emerging interoperability standards such as FHIR could eliminate these bottlenecks in the coming years.[202]

In the meantime, large technology firms such as IBM Watson Health have chosen the M&A path to gain access to large data sets such as Truven, Phytel, and Explorys to feed Watson's cognitive platform and increase affordability, access, and performance. Others, such as GE Healthcare and Salesforce Health Cloud, are pursuing similar strategies of creating partner ecosystems that will bring data to their platforms and develop innovative digital health solutions.

Healthcare enterprises, technology firms, and investors recognize that harnessing data and unlocking insights to generate immediate value is the key to driving healthcare transformation.

A new category of startups is emerging to provide less expensive (and often more convenient) alternatives to traditional healthcare technology offerings. In addition to a new whole category of price and quality comparison platforms such as Leapfrog, Castlight, and Healthgrades —often referred to as *navigators*—even large health plans such as Aetna and Cigna have gotten into the act and have begun to offer monetary incentives in some cases to nudge consumers toward cheaper alternatives.[203]

How do startups and early-stage companies compete with established tech firms in this market? There are several reasons why startups may be better positioned than big tech firms to address the digital health and big data analytics opportunity. Here are just a few:

- Traditional healthcare technology firms have huge investments in existing products and platforms and would prefer not to do anything that would disrupt existing revenue streams.

- Big tech firms are not structurally set up for the kind of rapid, technology-led innovation that is required to navigate the fast-changing technology landscape and successfully transition to VBC.
- Unburdened by legacy environments and traditional thinking and approaches, startups can demonstrate speed, agility, and efficiency to bring innovation to legacy health IT. Startups bring a fresh perspective to old and new problems in healthcare, infuse more optimism and enthusiasm, and are willing to take more risks than traditional healthcare enterprises and even many traditional technology firms.

Anand Shroff, CTO and Cofounder of Health Fidelity, a Silicon Valley startup that has developed a unique analytics platform for risk adjustments using NLP technology licensed from Columbia University, says, "Startups looking to break into healthcare enterprise IT will need to consider the dynamics of B2B technology business, which are quite different from consumer-facing applications."[204]

The shifting burden of financial responsibility toward consumers is driving a whole new set of behaviors among consumers and the healthcare system alike.[205] The increased responsibility, along with rising costs of healthcare, are compelling consumers to focus on stretching the available dollars for maximum benefit through price comparisons for a range of healthcare services. Health savings accounts or HSAs are an example of this.

"Consumers are paying attention to their money," says Steve Auerbach, CEO of Alegeus, a company that uses technology to help consumers manage their HSAs.[206] HSAs have been around since 2003 and were created so that individuals covered by high-deductible health plans could receive tax-preferred treatment of money saved for medical expenses.[207] Given the caps on HSA contributions and with deductibles now going through the roof, the need to stretch HSA dollars is even more critical for healthcare consumers. HSAs (and the related FSAs) allow consumers a degree of flexibility in how they spend the funds set aside in these accounts, in addition to tax benefits.[208]

Companies like Alegeus are stepping in to help consumers maximize the value from their existing options and make the best possible decisions with their HSA and FSA dollars. They are doing this by integrating a range of partner offerings into a single platform. Using the Alegeus platform, a consumer can shop for affordable care using a service such as Healthcare Blue Book, consult a doctor via phone on Teladoc, and use Copatient to consolidate all bills and negotiate for fair prices. This last piece has been a topic of much attention, with many healthcare consumers facing unexpected bills for hospital procedures.[209]

Insurance companies and third-party administrators are increasingly embedding platforms such as Alegeus into the overall package so that consumers have the necessary tools and enablers from a wide range of providers to make informed choices.

While VCs and technology firms remain understandably optimistic about digital health startups, an alternative view comes from the study by NEJM Catalyst, discussed earlier in this chapter, that explores the disconnect between the potential and the reality for many of these initiatives, especially between clinical and executive staff in healthcare organizations. The study highlights stark differences between clinicians and the executive suite on the benefits of VBC, APMs, and new delivery models such as telehealth—all of which are important drivers for the growth and adoption of digital health solutions.[210] Clinicians see many of these as unwelcome burdens that increase the costs of care, while the executive suite sees them as necessary to navigate the transition to VBC.

Some of the biggest disconnects are also the most telling indicators of what the C-suite considers important and effective. Executives find APMs to be the most important driver of change and place the most value on big data and analytics as necessary tools for enabling changes. At the same time, patient engagement tools, one of the most important digital health tools, were seen as less effective by executives and clinicians compared to clinical leaders.

For technology firms trying to parse all this, the overall picture looks confusing and contradictory. However, the one common theme that all groups agree on is the importance of big data and analytics.

In the past several years, healthcare enterprises have made significant investments in implementing EHR platforms claiming the meaningful-use incentive dollars. What does this mean for innovative startups in an environment where the entire transactional system landscape is dominated by the big EHR vendors? What is the implication for innovative new startups that are trying to unlock the database sitting inside these systems?

"I would agree that startups are going to be much more innovative. That is just in their nature. They have a couple of years of advantage before others try to emulate them, or till one of the big-box companies try to acquire them," says Ed Marx of Cleveland Clinic.[211]

One of the biggest questions for digital health startups is how to acquire new clients. Most health systems are not looking for point solutions (solutions that address a specific and narrowly defined problem), according to Sam Brasch of Kaiser Ventures.[212] The cost and effort involved in evaluating new solutions, which dictates the required payoff from new technology investments is often prohibitive. Health systems' willingness to engage with startups that have developed point solutions is thus limited. However, technology firms that can present these solutions in the context of a broader vision for what the platforms can achieve will potentially get more attention, justifying the organizational effort involved in bringing in these new platforms. According to Brasch, very few startups have crossed the chasm to achieve a level of adoption, not necessarily at an industry level, but even on a smaller scale to demonstrate a viable business model.

One solution for digital health innovators, especially smaller firms, is to consider partnering with larger consulting and services firms. Smaller firms and digital health startups consider the entry of big consulting firms in this market a boon in many ways. Big consulting firms educate clients and invest in evangelization programs that move the market in the direction of new and innovative approaches to solving problems. They have the ear of the client's C-suite, especially in the larger enterprises, who in turn are being watched by the smaller enterprises who will follow the direction of the larger enterprises. Also, big consulting firms have the resources and ability to cover a wide range of stakeholder interests and remain invested in the relationship for the long haul, something that small, resource-constrained innovators are unable to do. For these reasons, these partnerships make sense.

However, the underlying revenue model for all consulting companies is based on consultants being billed for their hours and remaining as fully utilized as possible. Services companies and consulting firms are used to selling in a certain way to a set of stakeholders and products; platform companies are used to selling differently to different groups of stakeholders. Other issues such as ticket sizes come into play. Big consulting firms are looking for big-ticket transactions, and niche technology companies are not necessarily big-ticket transactions; they are high value in terms of visibility and brand image for creating a beachhead, but not much more. Because of this DNA mismatch, many big consulting firms can take smaller, innovative solution partners to the point of consideration but struggle to convert the consideration to a recommendation or an adoption, leaving the smaller firms to take the transaction across the finish line by themselves.

Brasch of Kaiser Ventures offers a pathway for consumer-focused digital health companies: align with employer groups and large health insurance companies. While there is recent evidence that many digital health startups are doing just that, large healthcare enterprises have been reticent to promote innovative new solutions, given the challenges and costs of integrating them into existing workflows and the questions around expected returns and timelines.[213] In the following chapters, I will discuss several approaches that startups and innovators can apply for market development and growth.

6 Strategic Positioning, Market Entry, and Expansion

The goal of the 2009 ACA was to achieve the triple aim—reduce costs of care, improve the quality of care, and improve healthcare outcomes. Over the next seven years, the ACA and its companion HITECH Act, which aimed to digitize patient medical records, consumed over $30 billion of taxpayer money on meaningful-use incentives, creating a once-in-a-lifetime opportunity for EHR companies, which would go on to become dominant players in healthcare IT.[214]

With a national digital health record backbone in place, a new wave of innovation is looking to unlock insights from data to develop new digital health experiences, increase patient engagement, improve care management, and reduce costs of care through targeted actions driven by analytical insights.

As the demography of our population changes and millennials come of age, they are no longer going to tolerate the poor service and opaque transactions of traditional healthcare providers. Moreover, they are unwilling to pay the high costs of traditional health insurance coverage and healthcare. The healthcare system will need to transform by adopting digital platforms that improve user experiences, enable scalability, and enhance responsiveness to patient needs.

An indicator of the progress on this front is the amount of funding for digital health startups, which has averaged over $4.5 billion in the last couple of years, according to data from San Francisco-based Rock Health.[215]

How successful will these new digital health technologies be? In my work with healthcare tech companies, I hear excitement about the opportunities for slaying dragons like the dreaded diabetes with big data analytics, improving patient engagement with smartphone apps, and unlocking insights from a vast array of connected IoT devices as healthcare transitions from an FFS to a VBC model.

Diabetes is a case in point. As a high-profile chronic condition, it has attracted the attention of big technology firms such as Google (which developed contact lenses that sense glucose in teardrops) and IBM Watson Health/Medtronic (SugarIQ), as well as many Silicon Valley VC-funded startups. Some of these startups focus on a single aspect of treating and managing diabetes (such as remote monitoring); others have developed mobile apps that aim to improve patient engagement and compliance with treatment protocols to keep their diabetic condition in check. Others offer technology stacks and frameworks that provide intelligent devices that can be implanted or worn to collect continuous data that can be analyzed with advanced algorithms for real-time insights and interventions.

The question is whether healthcare as a whole is ready for the slew of innovative new products and platforms that are emerging from VC-funded startups as well as established technology firms. For early-stage digital health companies looking to establish a footprint in the complex and highly competitive healthcare IT markets, it is important to understand the industry structure before getting too far ahead of market readiness.

The biggest challenge right now in healthcare is that incentives are not aligned to keep a patient healthy and reduce the cost of care. Despite the talk about waste, cost, and preventive measures, most incentives are not aligned. Technology providers trying to help patients and use data, predictive analytics, and new technologies to improve healthcare outcomes are unable to do as well as they could because buyers of these solutions do not have their incentives aligned to these objectives. Indeed, in some cases, there are perverse incentives that encourage rational hospital executives to act in an entirely irrational manner.

A good example of one of these incentives is a system-wide effort to reduce hospital readmissions. Readmissions imply that the hospital has not taken care of the patient adequately the first time around. To bring readmissions under control, the CMS set up a system of penalties, started publishing lists of hospitals with readmission levels above permissible thresholds, and made readmissions reduction a priority for hospitals and clinicians.[216]

Shantanu Nigam, CEO of Jvion, a provider of predictive analytics solutions for clinical performance improvement says, "You would imagine that if a hospital was provided with a predictive modeling solution that identified who would get readmitted and possibly the reasons for the same, along with recommendations for preventive measures that cost a fraction of the cost of treating that patient if they are readmitted, the hospital would want to adopt it. Some hospitals indeed like that idea and do exactly that. Others, however, will resist the idea, without saying why. The reason is that if a hospital is running on a very thin margin and 30 percent of its beds are empty, it is likely not getting penalized for readmissions, and has no incentive to prevent patients from coming back. In fact, the hospital has a negative incentive because when patients stop coming back, it loses revenue and when that happens, the 30 percent vacancy may become 35 percent, which is going to hurt that hospital's top line and bottom line and its ability to sustain because it is running on a thin margin. This is just one of the many examples of perverse incentives that get in the way of adopting emerging technology solutions that unlock data and make healthcare more efficient and cost effective."[217]

The CMS has prescribed readmission penalties that are risk adjusted, with the result that some hospitals get penalized, while others gain an advantage. For hospitals that are not exposed to penalties—and there are many—there is no incentive to change. On the flip side, the ones that are likely to be penalized may look at the penalty amounts (2 percent or 3 percent of Medicare payments) and decide to absorb the losses since the upsides from patient readmissions are higher on the whole. Companies like Jvion routinely run a few numbers to understand if there is going to be a negative or positive financial incentive for a hospital to adopt a predictive analytics solution. Nigam believes that there is a lot that technology can do to improve patient outcomes and eliminate the costs that go into taking care of those patients if the incentives are aligned correctly. As long as the incentive structures are misaligned, he feels there is not a whole lot any analytics solution provider can do to change the status quo.

The reality is that only when the cost is higher than the reimbursement for a certain type of situation will advanced analytical solutions bring financial value to a hospital. If that equation does not match, then very few hospitals are willing to go down a new path.

Incentive alignment is therefore at the heart of the reason why healthcare is the way it is in the United States, and because FFS still dominates the payment model, APMs represent no more than 25 percent of the dollars that flow through the system by way of reimbursements. We still have a system that is very heavily incentivized to do business the way business has been done all these years, simply because the FFS model dominates. The needle is shifting, but is it shifting fast enough? Out of the 5,500 hospitals in the country, a relatively small number have adopted APMs and outcome-based measures, though more and more are experimenting with it. The vast majority of community hospitals and small hospitals are still operating in the same system that healthcare has operated on for decades. The good news is that most health systems are experimenting with APMs and value-based incentives for at least some part of their income.

The progress of digital health is driven by financial incentives, and, to the extent that healthcare enterprises and solution providers are aligned to those incentives, digital health adoption will continue to progress. However, there is a human side to adoption as well— specifically the question of the patient's point of view, which has pretty much been ignored by most solutions. We may be three or four years away from greater mainstream adoption, when hospitals no longer have to justify technology investments in digital health solutions. However, decision cycles typically take eighteen to twenty-four months to push something through a budget cycle before deciding to shop for a new solution and buy it. Even if the change were to begin today, it would be about three to four years before it takes hold.

Despite the noise and hype in the marketplace, the adoption of newer technologies, especially advanced analytical tools and digital health solutions, will coincide with an increase in the adoption of APMs. In other words, the adoption curve of VBC models and new technology solutions will intersect when APMs reach a certain inflection point, and that point could be three or four years away.

The good news is that, while the penetration of alternate payment models is relatively low, it is also difficult to find a health system that does not have some component of its revenue tied to an APM. The slow but steady growth of APMs is probably the single biggest indicator of a sector in unison, as it marches forward to a VBC era.

6.1 Understanding the Structure of the US Healthcare Industry

Understanding the changing structure of the healthcare industry is probably the most important aspect of a marketing strategy for technology firms. The changes in the industry have direct implications for the success of growth strategies for both startups and well-established global tech firms. As we have discussed in the course of this book, the shift toward VBC represents the biggest growth opportunity for technology firms, especially those that are focused on unlocking insights from data to drive performance improvements and patient engagement.

The major components of the US healthcare system can be broadly classified as providers, payers, and life sciences companies. Life sciences companies include multinational pharmaceutical companies, medical device companies, and newly emerging "-omics" companies, such as genomics and proteomics. This book is focused mostly on providers and payers.

Providers. This broad category refers to enterprises that deliver healthcare services: hospitals, clinics, physician practices, long-term care facilities, and others. The American Hospital Association tells us that there were 5,564 registered hospitals in the United States at the beginning of 2017.[218] Before proceeding, it is important to understand that this is a highly fragmented market segment.

Out of the total registered hospitals, about 20.2 percent are state owned, 58.5 percent are nonprofit, and 21.3 percent are for-profit. Of the 5,564 hospitals in the United States, 4,862 are considered community hospitals, representing around 85 percent of all hospitals in the United States. Many of these hospitals are in poor financial condition, especially the rural hospitals, and at risk of closing, not least because of underpayment by the government for healthcare services (in 2015, these underpayments amounted to $58 billion).[219]

Why is all this important? Some hospitals may not be ready for technology companies trying to sell advanced analytics and digital health solutions. These are entities with low revenues, low margins, and highly centralized decision making, and they are two steps behind the rest of the industry in technology and analytical maturity. These hospitals may be a viable target market for larger technology firms with the resources and reach to serve them with minimal marginal cost on their established sales and marketing infrastructure. On the flip side, decision making tends to be relatively less bureaucratic and time consuming in smaller hospitals, especially for solutions that have immediate payback.

At the high end of the provider segment, academic medical centers (AMCs) are highly sought after. AMCs are hospitals affiliated with a medical school and pursue clinical research in addition to direct patient care. They are also referred to as tertiary care centers, because of their ability to treat a full range of complex conditions. UC San Francisco, Johns Hopkins, and Cleveland Clinic are examples of AMCs that command a high level of prestige in the healthcare and medical communities. AMCs are pioneers in adopting new technologies and approaches to improving healthcare and medicine.

In 2015, approximately four hundred US hospitals were affiliated with a medical school. Then you have other categories: for-profits (such as HCA and Tenet Healthcare) and faith-based systems (such as Catholic Healthcare Initiatives and Ascension Health), to name a couple.

Most technology firms, especially those trying to sell analytics solutions, are looking at an addressable market that is between five hundred and six hundred hospitals.

The structure of many of these health systems can be very complex, with multiple layers of decision making at departmental and functional levels. It is no wonder that hospital IT environments have hundreds of applications from technology vendors, accumulated over a long period. However, over the past few years, much of the legacy technology footprint has been replaced by EHR systems, with implications for legacy as well as emerging technology solution firms.

Payers. The total national health expenditure stood at $3.24 trillion in 2015, while the overall spending toward health insurance was $2.38 trillion, growing at 7.02 percent.[220] The total national expenditure toward health insurance accounted for 13.24 percent of the total GDP. In 2015, private health insurance accounted for 44.1 percent of the total expenditure toward health insurance. Government-sponsored health insurance—Medicare and Medicaid—together accounted for 49 percent of the total health plan expenditure. If we combine the Children's Health Insurance Program (CHIP) with Medicare and Medicaid for adults, the total share of government-sponsored health insurance stood at 49.6 percent of overall payments for healthcare.

By 2025, overall spending toward health insurance will touch $5 trillion.[221] A significant rise in the share of third-party insurance is expected, rising from a mere 2 percent in 2015 to 15 percent in 2025, indicating a growing popularity of employer-funded health insurance.[222] Third-party insurance comprises worksite healthcare, Indian Health Service, workers' compensation, general assistance, maternal and child health, vocational rehabilitation, Substance Abuse and Mental Health Services Administration, school health, and other private, federal, state, and local programs. The highest growth segment is Medicare, which was expected to grow at a rate of 88.3 percent between 2015 and 2016.

Employer-sponsored insurance covers over half of the non-elderly population, approximately 150 million people in total. As employers get more involved in managing healthcare costs, they are emerging as an entirely new target segment for digital health companies. If healthcare providers are fragmented, the opposite may be true for payers. A small number of large commercial health plans (such as United Healthcare, Aetna, and Cigna, which operate nationally and are public companies) dominate the market, followed by large Blue Cross Blue Shield plans, which are more regional in structure and tend to be not-for-profit corporations.

As margins erode and market participants try to improve their negotiating power, the market for payers and providers may consolidate further under a wave of ongoing M&As. For technology firms, it becomes imperative to be on the right side of consolidation or risk being squeezed out.

The reason why all technology firms need to do go through the exercise of understanding the different sub-sectors in healthcare and the multiple segments within each sector is to understand where the money is and follow it. Many technology firms start with an inside-out view of the marketplace, usually from a product idea that solves a problem, that fails to recognize the specific characteristics and needs of a target segment. Tech firms are also known for identifying and solving unknown problems (generally influenced by the widely attributed quote to Steve Jobs, Apple's late founder and CEO, that consumers do not always know what they want, which also became the driving force behind breakthrough product innovations such as the iPhone and the iPad). However, the healthcare sector operates within a set framework of evidence-based medicine and a reimbursement model that requires large payers, including the government, to pay for new technologies used in healthcare.

As of early 2017, many technology firms and their VC backers realized that the path to growth and profits in healthcare is not as straightforward as developing a new mobile app and getting users to pay for downloads. Recent VC funding data indicates that new funding is concentrated in fewer firms that are in later rounds of financing for market expansion.

6.2 Competitive Strategy and Revenue Models: Following the Money

The transition to VBC is driving healthcare enterprises to experiment with alternative healthcare delivery and payment models such as ACOs and bundled payments. These payment models require them to build advanced analytic capabilities and adopt digital health models for improved patient engagement and care management.

Recognizing this, analytics and digital health startups have mushroomed. The first generation of these startups were acquired and are now building advanced capabilities; for example, Explorys, a spin-off of Cleveland Clinic, was acquired by IBM Watson Health in 2015 and is now integrating IBM Watson Health's cognitive and AI capabilities into its product offerings. Others, such as Optum, part of the giant United Health Group, had a head start and expanded through acquisitions (such as Humedica) to strengthen product portfolios. There has been a rapid growth of analytics and digital health startups recently, essentially building businesses on the foundation of data. They are unlocking data insights from existing EHR data and bringing in new forms of data, such as PGHD, social determinant data, and IoT data. Many of these startups are better positioned to be innovative than either the traditional technology platform companies or the transactional EHR companies. They are certainly more innovative than most healthcare enterprises. However, they also have some challenges.

The key question for established technology firms and early-stage digital health companies is: what are we trying to offer and how does it align with the institution's priorities and funding availability?

Healthcare organizations are looking for advanced technology and analytics capabilities that were not found in EHR systems three or four years ago. Since then, the market for stand-alone digital health and analytics companies has grown. The big EHR vendors have an incumbent advantage in keeping their clients from going external and spending money with a different company. However, as we have seen, innovative startups and technology firms have established a market share for themselves. Solutions that align themselves to the transition to VBC are considered disruptive, transformative, and winning bets; hence, the billions in VC money poured into digital health startups.[223]

However, while the markets evolve rapidly, the window of opportunity for new solutions to establish a foothold is getting smaller and innovation cycles are getting shorter. Big data analytics, which primarily referred to applying retrospective and predictive analytics models on large data sets, was a dominant category a couple of years ago. The more commonly used terms today are cognitive and AI, which refer to current analytical techniques as well as more advanced technology architectures. Emerging and disruptive technologies such as blockchain are registering their presence in the market.

As of the time of writing this, the healthcare policy environment is in a state of flux, which could influence the direction of healthcare technology investments. However, standing still is not an option, and technology firms, as well as enterprises, will need to continue to make bets. For now, solutions based on data and analytics that improve the top or bottom line seem to be the safest bet to make.

In this environment, the path to success looks different for different kinds of technology firms. Digital health and data analytics solution companies, especially startups, have to address several challenges and answer strategic positioning questions to build and sustain their businesses.

Barriers to entry for enterprise healthcare IT. Unlike consumer-facing technologies, barriers to entry for enterprise IT solutions are high. For enterprise IT, developing healthcare solutions demands compliance with several regulatory requirements. Healthcare enterprises require rigorous compliance with regulations such as HIPAA and stringent BAAs that are getting tighter by the day in light of industry-wide data breaches and ransomware incidents. Enterprises tend to be cautious about startups because of risk considerations. Ways to overcome this include raising funds from well-known investors whose reputation can act as risk mitigation or partnering with incumbent technology vendors to provide solutions under subcontracting arrangements.

Customer acquisition. Customer acquisition in enterprise healthcare IT is, without question, the single biggest challenge for a startup. No matter how innovative the technology or solution, getting through to healthcare IT buyers who are bombarded incessantly by vendors is incredibly difficult. Sales cycles tend to be long (nine to twelve months), which can create financial hardship for underfunded startups with limited resources and market reach, relative to established vendors. Big tech firms also have limited runways for product failures and tend to be cautious with investments, preferring at times to go the M&A route. On the flip side, enterprise IT buyers seldom switch from incumbent vendors, and this makes it easier to keep customers once a solution provider has established itself as a useful partner.

Implementation cycles and ROI. Due to the extraordinary investments healthcare organizations have made over the past few years in large-scale programs such as EHRs, advanced analytics, and now PHM systems, there is very little funding available for discretionary projects, especially those that do not qualify for reimbursement under an FFS payment model. Even for highly innovative solutions, healthcare IT buyers are looking to acquire solutions that can quickly demonstrate results, even if at a small scale, before making commitments to enterprise-wide rollouts.

Additionally, due to significant concerns around security and privacy, healthcare organizations have been slow to adopt cloud technologies, although this is changing rapidly. One way to overcome this barrier is to recruit early adopters to become champions for the product and the company. Often, big health systems or health plans become strategic investors in innovative startups and provide a quick start by becoming early adopters of the technology. Reputed early adopters can impart credibility to the product/solution and also make important introductions that can accelerate client acquisition and initial traction.

Compliance, security, and privacy. Healthcare is a highly regulated industry. Most enterprises and technology firms have robust compliance processes in place, and startups that are looking to build a market in this space will need to become familiar with the regulations. Recent high-profile instances of startups running afoul of regulators and putting their entire business and investors at risk (e.g. Zenefits and Theranos) are cautionary tales to digital health startups looking to avoid a similar fate. The good news is that, with the growing adoption of cloud-based technologies, CSPs such as AWS and Azure have built robust HIPAA-compliant environments that can be used as platforms for developing new solutions and applications. However, HIPAA goes beyond just IT compliance, and startups will need to ensure they are compliant in all aspects. Healthcare has also been in the news for massive data breaches and ransomware. A combination of aging technology environments, security vulnerabilities among healthcare enterprises as well as their BAs, and a lucrative market for stolen personal information has made healthcare a target for cyberattackers. Startups building solutions for healthcare enterprises will need to sign agreements that require compliance with HIPAA regulations and carry significant penalties for data breaches.

Technology firms have to look at the addressable market for tech firms and assess their competitive strengths in the healthcare landscape. In the provider market, for instance, most hospitals in the United States are not-for-profit operations, including community hospitals that run on outdated information technologies and rarely even have a dedicated IT function. After eliminating this cohort of hospitals from consideration, the addressable market shrinks to under five hundred hospitals, comprising large health systems, AMCs, and for-profit institutions. Every healthcare B2B tech firm is addressing this market, which makes AMCs highly sought after and competitive target markets for incumbents and new entrants alike.

Ed Marx of Cleveland Clinic says that one way for digital health companies to get a foot in the door is to go "at risk," or, in other words, be willing to enter into contractual arrangements by which technology vendors are willing to link some part of their fees to demonstrating agreed outcomes. Marx has implemented a few arrangements in which the technology vendors have used this contracting model as a means to gain traction for their solutions in the market.[224] The resultant symbiotic relationship could benefit both parties and build a pathway for a startup willing to work with innovative payment structures based on shared gains (just like the VBC programs that healthcare enterprises are signing up for). Health systems are more open to these arrangements now and aware that, if they can save money, they will have a benchmark for similar arrangements in the future. The downside for startups is that, if they do not do well, the client does not do well. Hospitals are also acutely aware that, if the value-based contract structure loses money, they will have to participate in the downside as well, implying that VBC contracts may lose money if performance thresholds are not met. Either way, these are complex arrangements, but this is what VBC is about; there are risks, but organizations are increasingly accepting them and learning a new style of business.

Marx cautions that sales cycles in a large complex health system are typically twelve to eighteen months. In a stand-alone community hospital, the cycle is comparatively shorter due to less politics and fewer stakeholders; however, it is still likely to be a six- to nine-month cycle. In the emerging VBC era, sales cycles could accelerate as healthcare enterprises try to get results more quickly and become a little bit more nimble and entrepreneurial. The challenge for smaller firms with stand-alone solutions is to transition from initial engagement to a long-term strategic relationship.

Most health systems operate on wafer-thin margins, typically in the low single digits. For innovation to take hold, there has to be a payment model. For digital health and analytics firms, this translates not just to a business model problem but also to a revenue model problem. Many businesses start off with a strong business case, with performance assurances that translate to a positive ROI. However, the payment model may vary across entities depending on their arrangements in the healthcare marketplace. Multiple buying centers exist within these institutions, in addition to a centralized technology function, adding to the complexity and making it that much more difficult to target and navigate the environment for smaller, resource-constrained tech firms trying to find a toehold.

Drew Schiller also sounds a note of caution about likely conflicts between these emerging payment models and the dominant FFS model. "At-risk models may sound appealing, but on the other side you have the CEO and the CFO saying, 'We need to reduce our IT budget, we need to reduce the number of vendor interactions and contracts we have, and we need to focus our efforts on how we can provide a simpler path for FFS reimbursement for our providers so that they can see more patients and get reimbursed faster.' It's a sort of duality we have to live in the short term."[225]

Assuming that digital health companies successfully find an entry point, the question is: how does the solution align with the institution's priorities and funding availability?

Says Neil Gomes of Jefferson Health, "We are a not-for-profit institution and so we do not have the luxury of failing multiple times or losing much money. In fact, we rarely ever do that on the technology innovation side because we focus on real problems, and we attach technology investments to value that we will deliver. We, therefore, want to be sure that we are addressing the right problems and developing the right solutions to achieve the outcomes. The outcomes have to generate value, not just for the institution, but also for the patient. We did a project in the ER where we reduced the total time in the ER, and the time to discharge, which increases revenues because now fewer people wait and stay in the ER because you have increased the throughput and revenues. You need to be able to address the overall value equation."[226]

A workforce survey by the Healthcare Information and Management Systems Society in 2017 offers some clues for finding the value equation in healthcare enterprises.[227] The survey, which covered healthcare executives as well as IT vendors, highlights interesting contrasts in views between the two communities representing opposite sides of the table on a range of issues, starting with whether IT budgets are going up or not (vendors believe they are; hospital execs are not so sure). While there is broad alignment on the top three priorities (patient safety and quality; privacy and security; and care coordination and population health), there are starkly divergent views on many other important themes. Hospitals considered EHRs to be a much higher priority than vendors did, and they considered APMs to be a much lower priority compared to vendors' assessments.

The head-scratching discrepancies between what IT vendors and their clients think have some basis in findings from other surveys. An NEJM Catalyst survey conducted around the same time states that EHR data will remain the primary data source in a clinical context over the next five years.[228] Another survey by Premier Inc., a company representing nearly four thousand hospitals, places the move from "meaningful use to meaningful insights" as a top priority in the C-suite.

The message is simple: most health systems are focused on extracting value from the millions of dollars invested in implementing EHR systems over the past several years, and this is where most IT budget dollars are likely being allocated.

The EHR market is dominated by a handful of companies, so the strategic choice for emerging tech firms is to find a viable space that aligns with spending priorities to increase value from EHR investments and avoid being crowded out for scarce investment dollars.

From a strategic positioning standpoint, the question for digital health tech firms becomes: is the product or service we are bringing to market sufficiently distinctive to stand out or is it just going to add to the noise?

Lidia Fonseca, CIO of Quest Diagnostics, has some advice. "I think what will accelerate adoption is being able to show that these solutions help meet clinical and financial goals. You have to connect the solutions to the value that they bring to that provider." She adds, "At the end of the day it goes back to 'what is in it for me'?"[229]

Just as there are unproven data models, there are few strong reimbursement models in place around many emerging digital health solutions. We now have emerging APMs for a limited set of procedures, such as bundled payments for orthopedic surgeries or transplants. However, these bundled payments do not include strong incentives or opportunities to bring in new data solutions to improve outcomes and care and keep people healthy post-surgery. While there are financial incentives to reduce readmissions, in the broader picture there are no strong reimbursement models for monitoring high-risk cases, such as comorbid patients or patients with pre-diabetes conditions, to prevent disease progression. The entire healthcare system is still focused on managing risks as opposed to preventing them. This approach goes back partly to the perverse incentives that we discussed earlier in this chapter and partly to predictive model paradoxes where it is hard to put a value on prevention. The fact remains that, while a lot of the preventive care today would likely yield better patient outcomes, it would also yield less revenue for physicians' practices or health systems. The paradox in the current payment models is that clinicians may have effectively worked without pay to prevent disease and manage health and wellness.

6.3 Thought Leadership: The Emerging Model for Engaging with Clients and Prospects

In the last five to six years, there has been a significant shift in the types of marketing adopted in the B2B technology space to attract and retain customers. A big part of that shift ties to content marketing and more specifically thought leadership content marketing, which is a long-term branding and awareness exercise actively pursued by leading B2B technology companies.

Technology buyers are increasingly doing most of their research themselves online. They are more than halfway past an evaluation cycle before they have an in-person interaction or even a phone call with a sales person. According to marketing automation software company HubSpot, 47 percent of buyers viewed three to five pieces of content before engaging with a sales rep. As buyers increasingly look for self-service options to evaluate technology solutions and vendors, they are faced with the challenge of going through hundreds of content pieces. Between industry publications, social media, and email, there are thousands of contact points for potential buyers to learn about a company and its offerings. The sheer volume of content published, low attention spans, and fleeting media visibility mean that getting noticed is harder than before.

B2B technology organizations need to break through this clutter of content to gain their target audience's attention and position themselves as thought leaders in their chosen space. The good news is that high-quality content gets disproportionately more visibility, and it is worth the effort to produce content that informs and educates buyers in value-added ways. Tech firms are therefore shifting their marketing budgets to focus on thought leadership marketing, investing heavily in developing content that engages and educates their target audience and enables them to make critical decisions in a formal buying process.

Damo Consulting's 2017 annual survey of content marketing trends for B2B healthcare technology marketers indicated that

- technology vendors spend between 10 percent and 30 percent of their overall marketing budgets on content;
- content marketing budgets are increasing; and
- thought leadership content is the single biggest spend category.

However, the going is not easy. The trade publications are awash in sponsored white papers and blogs that fail to make the required impact. Many organizations develop white paper elephants in the name of developing thought leadership, wasting resources and efforts.

The primary issue with thought leadership marketing is that many firms put out content that is nothing but thinly veiled sales collateral. Thought leadership is about engaging an organization's customers and prospects with their topics of interest and providing new information that educates the audience and helps them perform their jobs better. It is an indirect way to drive interest in an organization and its offerings, though the structure of the content may change significantly based on the stage of the buying cycle. Regardless of the buying stage, it is important to develop and maintain a connection with buyers through a sales cycle that may last months if not years.

As Guy Mansueto, Vice President of Portfolio Marketing at IBM Watson Health puts it, "Thought leadership is one component of a content marketing strategy focused on adding value and engaging your audience in topics that are of interest to your customers while building relationships with key stakeholders."[230]

In my company's experience working with B2B technology firms on their growth strategies, we identified several common challenges with their thought leadership marketing strategies:

Lack of leadership buy-in for a thought leadership (content) marketing strategy. B2B technology firms are primarily sales-focused organizations. Everyone in the firm is primed for any activity that involves a tangible lead and a specific opportunity. Early engagement with buyers is seen as a secondary activity, with intangible short-term outcomes in lead generation. Our studies tell us that thought leadership content marketing takes six months or more to show any results; that can be too long for impatient business leaders with quarterly quotas. Without leadership buy-in, it becomes difficult for marketing teams to secure the necessary budget, launch new thought leadership initiatives, hire people to develop content, run campaigns, and ensure leadership participation.

There is no content strategy. Content strategy is about the right content at the right time in the right place. It is about matching an organization's target audience's needs and preferences to its business objectives, defining personalized goals and metrics for the organization, experimenting with new content initiatives, and staying committed to the plan. Unfortunately, many B2B tech firms, including big firms, operate without a documented content strategy. Content is very often developed from an ad-hoc editorial plan that focuses on meeting output volumes and deadlines as opposed to quality and relevance. Typically, such content has little or no alignment with the overall business and market strategy of the organization or with their buyers' pain points.

Content is unfocused and of poor quality. In a quarter-to-quarter sales quota-driven environment, the main focus of organizational resources is on meeting the numbers. Tech firms tend to use most of their digital real estate on selling. For a large number of technology firms, every page on the website seems to be about products and offerings, and every email campaign is a call to action requesting a meeting to pitch a product. The content that hangs off of these pages and emails is mostly sales collateral. Content creation is uncoordinated and assigned to junior-level resources, does not address the audience/buyer's pain points, and is often misaligned to its overall business goals.

There is no strategy for content distribution. If a tree falls in a forest and no one hears it, did it happen? Often, good content tends to be buried deep inside a site somewhere, with limited or no visibility to an organization's target audience. Multiple content development programs often overlap even within a particular department or function, with conflicting timelines and objectives and no thematic connection. In the absence of a content distribution strategy, social media engagement tends to be spotty and uncoordinated, with no alignment to a higher-level strategy. It is important for technology marketers to find out where and when their target audience likes to look for information and plan their content distribution strategy accordingly.

There are no metrics. Many B2B technology organizations consider lead generation to be the only metric for measuring their content marketing success. However, marketers should also be able to measure other types of the content's impact such as brand value, audience engagement, and cost of customer acquisition. Research by the Content Marketing Institute indicates that the highest performers in content marketing are also the ones that have a robust metrics program and are realistic about their goals.[231] Currently, however, only 6 percent of B2B marketers can provide accurate metrics to measure their content marketing ROI across the organization, which explains why so many technology firms fail to see value from their content development efforts.

The volume vs. quality conundrum. Achieving a balance between content volume vs. quality has always been a challenge for content marketers. The volume–value matrix depends on the number of products or solutions an organization tries to market, the types of buyers they are trying to reach, and the duration of the campaigns. If an organization is trying to address three different personas in a target company, it may have to produce three different versions of a piece of content. Depending on the stage of the buying cycle, alternate versions of content may need to be produced. All of this can add up very quickly, and, without a clear content strategy and an awareness of buyer personas and their roles in the buying cycle, content development efforts could be a waste of time and, in extreme cases, detrimental to the sales process.

Consistency and continuity are important as well. Content marketing is as much about long-term brand building as about generating short-term sales interest. Creating a single piece of content for a buyer in a year is rarely enough to gain sustained attention or brand positioning in the market. At the same time, reusing the same piece of content repeatedly during the year will not help to get the buyer's attention either. Instead, a single piece of comprehensive and relevant thought leadership content, which can be repurposed into multiple subtopics, will help to get the buyer's attention over the course of the year.

Thought leadership marketing is a part of the bigger content marketing strategy of an organization. It is about trying to influence the discussions and buying decisions of the organization's target audience. To make thought leadership marketing fully effective, it needs to be part of a range of content, including sales and marketing collateral that is purposed toward generating interest in a company's offerings.

Through my firm Damo Consulting's work with global technology brands, Silicon Valley startups, healthcare enterprises, and consulting firms, we have identified a set of best practices and benchmarks for thought leadership marketing strategies.

Align content strategy with business strategy. A robust thought leadership content strategy begins with strategic positioning and market segmentation for a company's offerings. Best-in-class content marketing organizations develop a thought leadership content strategy that aligns with the overall business strategy and addresses their audience's needs with a high degree of relevance and timeliness. White papers and blogs are by far the most widely used forms of thought leadership today for technology firms. Research papers, market surveys, e-books, videos, and webinars are other forms of content being produced.

Develop content with industry context. B2B tech marketers need to create a point of view to establish a differentiated position in the minds of their clients and prospects. They need to increase the perceptual distance between their solutions and those of their competitors. One way to differentiate is by creating a point of view using subject matter experts within and outside the organization to build credibility with buyers. The objective is to help buyers see the delineation between an organization's strategy or solution and their competitor's. In the context of a specialized industry such as healthcare, an example of this could be developing evidence-based research in collaboration with reputed clinicians or health systems that are clinically relevant, credible, and promotes a level of confidence among the organization's target audience and buyers.

Allocate adequate, qualified resources. There is a big conundrum many tech firms struggle with; thought leadership content gets the most attention and spend, yet most organizations struggle to produce good content consistently at scale. Some firms recruit the services of internal technology executives to develop content; however, it does not always produce the best content. Organizations with significant content development needs outsource at least a part of their content development, in some cases engaging freelance writers on a long-term retainer (this is preferable to random or constantly shifting writing resources). The best-in-class firms hire writers who also bring industry knowledge and experience to the table, so they can appreciate the context in which content is being created and work with minimal supervision to deliver content assets within short timelines. The best thought leadership content creators have the following in common: industry knowledge, experience with technology and the tech sector, and writing skills.

Multipurpose all content. Much of B2B technology thought leadership content is developed as a use-once-and-throw-away asset. One-time effort that cannot be leveraged is a waste of an organization's resources. We are also increasingly moving to a buying environment where individuals want quick answers and easily consumable content. A twenty-page white paper is not easily consumable, and the ideal approach is to develop comprehensive thought leadership content assets that can spin off several other content assets that can be easily consumed. Content assets that are thematically linked and easily cross-referenced and back-linked also improve engagement rates among audiences. For example, a survey can be used to gather inputs from a target audience on a topic that is of interest to the entire audience. The findings can be converted into an e-book or infographic or disseminated through a medium such as a webinar featuring an industry expert. The idea is to emphasize thought leadership and establish the organization as the problem solver for a specific issue through the content assets. One way to achieve this is by communicating the same message packaged in different formats and served to the recipients in ways in which they are used to consuming content.

Have a content distribution strategy. B2B technology vendors should have a well-thought-out content distribution and amplification strategy in place that is relevant to their products and markets. Delivering content to the right audiences at the right time on the right medium—whether it is webinars, videos, newsletters, or any other channel—is crucial. LinkedIn and Twitter are widely considered the most effective social media channels for B2B technology marketers; direct marketing campaigns tend to rely more on newsletters and email campaigns. Content marketers should carefully monitor distribution channels and ensure content is reaching the right personas at the right stages of buying cycles. A related topic that comes up in this context is the amount spent for paid promotions. Making sure that the content goes to the right buyers, especially new contacts or leads that an organization might not otherwise have reached through its traditional channels, may require a portion of the content spend to be set aside for paid promotions. The spend on paid promotions depends on how big the market is and whom content marketers are trying to target within the segments they are servicing.

Dig in for the long haul. Content cannot deliver results in a vacuum, and the success of content marketing depends on a variety of factors. Thought leadership marketing hinges on trust and the ability to connect with an audience, ultimately driving customer action and business growth. An organization's thought leadership initiative must add value to its customers and prospects to build this trust. Technology marketers should continuously look for ways to stay relevant to their audience or buyers, to the point of becoming an indispensable source of information in the area in which they are trying to market. All this requires strong planning and commitment. Content marketers must spend time analyzing and thinking about what is at the top of their audience's mind. They should cover the entire spectrum, providing every target persona with the right type of information they need to make a decision during their buying journey.

Damo Consulting's annual survey of content marketing in 2017 found that in technology firms content budgets vary between 10 percent and 30 percent of marketing budgets.[232] The number varies based on the stage of a firm in the marketplace. For an early-stage technology solution firm just starting with content, moving a third of the total budget into content marketing may not be a realistic strategy. However, B2B marketers must also resist pressure from sales leaders who think that a single piece of good content will deliver immediate results.

There is a growing awareness that content marketing is an essential part of a B2B tech marketer's toolkit, and it is early days yet. Ongoing acquisitions of digital strategy and marketing firms across the globe by big technology and consulting firms point to the growing importance these businesses are attaching to building content development capabilities. These very same firms are also best in class when it comes to their digital and content marketing strategies. Content marketing is now beginning to separate the leaders from the laggards in the sweepstakes for market share and growth.

6.4 The Digital Health Funding Environment

Digital health startups received $5.1 billion in VC funding across 622 deals in 2016, up from $4.6 billion in 2015 and accounting for over $8.5 billion across 2,672 deals since 2010.[233]

Digital health represents multiple categories, including telemedicine, wearables, genomics, and population health, that are distinct yet interconnected. Analytics and big data is a fairly broad category with a loose definition that cuts across all other segments; data-generated insights power almost every new digital health application. Some of the other prominent funding categories, such as population health and genomics technologies, embed analytics at the core of the platform so analytics could be even more pervasive than is indicated by a single category.

Jim Pavlik, a partner at Baird Capital, a VC firm that has made several digital health investments, says that the environment is robust for digital health investment. With most health systems having completed their major EHR implementation projects, it is now time for digital health innovation, for which healthcare enterprises have to look beyond their EHR platform vendors. However, he adds that, after the flood of angel and series A funding a couple of years ago, startups are facing an uphill struggle trying to compete in a crowded marketplace. He believes VC investors may be taking a pause, and there could be a period of rationalization ahead during which several startups could go out of business due to lack of funding, clients, or both.[234]

One way to gauge the market is by tracking specific funding categories for VC investments. By this measure, the one category that stands out is analytics and big data, which was the second-most-funded category for VC investments in 2016[235] and the most-funded category in Q1 2017.[236] Additional confirmation of this trend came from a broad-based survey of healthcare executives in early 2017 by VC firm Venrock, a prominent digital health investor, which indicated that the industry overwhelmingly thinks analytics and big data is the subsegment that will see the most growth in the next twelve months.[237]

A closer look at the numbers reveals that funding activity is concentrated in a relatively small number of firms, all of which were raising their second, third, or later round of funding. Just one company, Grail, accounted for nearly $1 billion in funding in Q1 2017, and, after adjusting for this and a few other transactions, the overall picture seems to indicate a modest quarter in line with the trends from the last quarter of 2016.

A separate report on digital health funding by Rock Health indicates that 2016 was a tipping point for consumer adoption of digital health tools, with 46 percent of consumers now considered active adopters.[238] Increasing smartphone penetration and novel technologies, specifically mHealth apps, are contributing to this trend. The Quantified Self movement, growth of wearables and sensors, and increasing need for cohorts to engage remotely with their care providers have all contributed to the growth in consumer-oriented health apps. While the Rock Health report remains optimistic about how digital health firms are positioned in the market, the Q1 2017 report also quietly acknowledges that providers and health plans are delaying spend due to the uncertainty in the environment.

A significant amount of funding has gone into the digital health startup space in the past five to seven years. However, according to Sam Brasch of Kaiser Ventures, "The promise of these digital health startups has been exciting, but the growth of these firms has been relatively slow. A lot of us are just pausing and asking ourselves why the growth has been so slow, and why so many of these companies are failing to cross the chasm." He adds, "We have all put in a significant amount of investment in these early-stage companies based on their promises. However, the exits are not happening as quickly as we would like them to."[239] Since they are maturing slowly, the funding is directed to the few companies that are showing promise and have a better chance of success.

VC firms' digital health funding categories do not necessarily take into account the role that analytics plays across other solution categories such as PHM. The transition to VBC and APMs will require health systems and health plans to look beyond their transactional systems, which are designed for documenting and billing for healthcare services. Transition to VBC requires advanced analytics to be embedded in all manner of applications to enable the optimization of care delivery processes, eliminate waste, and increase healthcare outcomes to maximize performance and earnings.

In some ways, the space is maturing, and many VCs do not see digital health as a category anymore. They are seeing digital health startups merely as companies that solve discrete problems in the healthcare space. Many of these companies are a combination of technology and services bundled in a way that goes after a need, such as behavioral health or diabetes prevention. However, the innovation ecosystem that will bring new solutions to the healthcare sector requires healthy funding for digital health entrepreneurs. "Generating the hard data that generates a value proposition remains the price of entry," says Sam Brasch.

Entrepreneurs can look at four main sources of funding today:

Angel funding and startup accelerators. There are seed capital funding options available to digital health entrepreneurs coming up all across the country, with major hubs in the San Francisco Bay Area, Chicago, Boston, and Nashville. Healthcare-focused accelerator programs across the country (e.g. Rock Health, Healthbox, and Matter Chicago) provide seed capital and angel funding to very early-stage startups. Many of these are platforms and stepping stones for series A funding rounds with established VC firms. Some VC funds and incubators provide innovation development resources that help accelerate technology development under the right circumstances and structure. An example of this is Accenture's partnership with Matter Chicago.

Traditional VC/PE firms. These include top-tier venture funds such as Sequoia, Andreessen Horowitz, KPCB, and Khosla Ventures and specialist firms such as Venrock that invest in healthcare. Private equity firms such as Bain Capital are also making bets in the enterprise healthcare space. These firms bring enormous experience to the VC world and can help founders accelerate growth with capital and management advice. They are also very comfortable with risk and are best-suited to provide a range of exit options.

Corporate venture capital. Many healthcare organizations have created investment arms to take advantage of innovation in the startup ecosystem; they do this partly to gain access to innovation capabilities that they cannot build in house and partly to cash in on potential upsides in the event of a successful exit by the startups. Examples of this include Ascension Health Ventures, Kaiser Ventures, and UPMC Enterprises (part of the UPMC) in the health system space and Blue Cross Blue Shield Ventures (a consortium of Blue Cross Blue Shield health plans) in the health plan space.

Technology firms. Venture arms of technology giants such as GV (formerly Google Ventures) and GE Ventures acquired several important healthcare businesses. Several technology services firms such as Accenture have been actively integrating innovative startup solutions into their offering stacks for healthcare customers. While this may or may not involve equity participation, the instant credibility by association with a globally recognized brand and the facilitated customer acquisition process can accelerate growth for digital health startups, albeit indirectly.

An important consideration on growth strategy and strategic positioning is the startup's eventual exit, whether it is through an acquisition or an initial public offering (IPO). Most VC-funded startups are forced to consider exit strategies as an integral part of their business and revenue models. Acquisitions could involve other VC-funded firms or large healthcare technology vendors. While the number of acquirers may not be large, the companies have sold at healthy multiples of earnings and revenues, suggesting that the acquirers are interested in the strategic acceleration that the innovative technologies provide in their existing businesses or help them enter new markets. A recent report by VC firm Healthcare Growth Partners analyzed the healthcare tech exits during the 2010–2016 period and indicated that population health topped the list with a median revenue multiple of 5.1 times across twenty reported transactions.[240]

The IPO market, while less frequently used as an exit option, has been quite rewarding for the businesses that have taken on a broad mandate and demonstrated the capability to be a strategic partner to customers in achieving operational transformation. Some examples include Nant Health (2016), iRhythm (2016), Evolent Health (2015), Inovalon (2014), and Castlight Health (2014).

Ultimately, fundamental principles will drive value creation in healthcare enterprise IT. Startups that align with the organizational priorities of the future, such as VBC, will have a better chance of success.

Says Schiller, "What I am seeing is fewer investments for bigger dollars and sort of a consolidation of funding. I think we are going to start to see some more strategic mergers where some companies may scoop up competitors or individual complementary startups who have strong funding. It may be a case of one plus one could equal a little bit more than two, and it is a lot easier to play in healthcare when you are a bigger entity yourself, and so I think that we could start to see some of that."[241]

Jim Pavlik of Baird Capital feels that the keys to success are differentiation and traction through market validation. He recognizes that healthcare investors have to hold their investments for longer periods and advises startups not to get ahead of themselves on funding or product development before validating the business model.[242]

The broad view across the startup and investor community is that solutions that address costs or quality will continue to gain traction, regardless of the policy environment. However, the bar for investments may be raised as investors start looking for additional validations from the marketplace before making significant funding commitments. Startups may, in turn, need to be more nimble and ready to pivot on new markets or new solution features without burning up too much cash to stay afloat in order to get to the next stage of growth.

7 Universal Themes and General Principles

In the concluding chapters of this book, I have identified a set of universal themes required for the success of the Big Unlock in the emerging VBC era.

Universal theme #1: Ensure alignment of incentives.

The central issue for a digital health solution provider is: how well is the solution aligned with the incentives of the prospective buyer? Do they get paid for what you are trying to sell them? Even if your solution can do a great job for patients and reduce costs, will the provider system get paid for what you are selling?

Despite the growing share of APMs and performance-based incentives, these are still a relatively small—but growing—percentage of health system revenues. "We spend a lot of our time understanding how people get paid and being able to articulate in terms that make sense to them. We try to understand where they are now and why it makes sense for them to use analytics to connect data across care settings to help them be more successful in business" says Neil Smiley, CEO of Loopback Analytics, a population health analytics company. Smiley, who was a founder of Phytel, an analytics company that was bought by IBM in 2015, knows a thing or two about serving healthcare enterprises. "The number one challenge is making sure that we can appeal to some current economic imperative. If you do not have an economic imperative that makes sense, then you are not going to penetrate the account. Other priorities will overwhelm it," he adds.[243]

The EHR boom was fed by federal meaningful-use incentives. However, the term is a little bit of a misnomer since *meaningful use* was primarily a driver to claim incentive payments and can be disconnected from improving care. Having made these huge investments, leadership in healthcare enterprises are focusing their IT groups on optimizing their EHR systems. For new solutions and services trying to penetrate, it can be hard to fight through the noise. The key is, therefore, to understand how current payment models work; pay attention to the new ones that are coming along; and find intersections where providers can make more money, patients benefit, and costs are reduced. Most of the time spent in a sales cycle goes toward trying to identify those little pockets where the value proposition can be constructed.

Says Drew Schiller of Validic, "My advice to entrepreneurs who get into healthcare for the first time is to understand that it is important for them to solve the business model problem at the beginning and not focus solely on the technology."[244] The bottom line is that, if you are not solving a problem that clinicians broadly care about, it is going to be a hard climb.

While seasoned technology industry executives understand this, startups, especially from Silicon Valley, look at what works in other industries and don't always understand the peculiar dysfunction of healthcare. Healthcare's perverse incentives and myriad regulations can be bewildering to entrepreneurs who see opportunities galore in a complex and broken value chain that is unique to healthcare. The good news is that, with emerging payment models, new digital health and technology firms are finding success being able to sell on an ROI basis.

Says Schiller, "There is a phase that every startup healthcare entrepreneur goes through very early on, and they think, 'Everyone is so stupid in healthcare. This is so easy, and I do not see why people are not doing this,' and they try to create a business around that. A year and a half later, they realize that was never going to work, and there's a reason why no one was doing it that way because you cannot do it that way. It seems like there is a certain amount of hubris among certain startups, and that is healthy, but it is also dangerous. You have to be willing not just to think you know how healthcare should work; you have to take the time to understand why it does not work that way and start working on solutions from that perspective. You also have to be aware that you can have a great business case, but there may still be no money there for it."[245]

In most cases, a new solution provider has to establish the ROI and understand the scenarios that ensure alignment between reimbursement and costs of the program. Most business cases are straightforward. The path to success is to devise a way to calculate the ROI with the cost and reimbursement metrics for the particular hospital and use case in question.

The ROI can become tricky for advanced analytics solutions, in what Shantanu Nigam of Jvion describes as a "predictive paradox." "Let us say you give flu shots to the population in a zip code, and you come back and report that fewer people had flu that season. Over time, the zip code reports such a low occurrence of flu that it becomes hard to argue that the population in that zip code has a low occurrence of flu because they have been getting flu shots. So the paradox becomes whether the incidence of flu is lower because of the flu shots, or because they were never at risk of getting the flu and we wasted all our flu shots. You will never know the answer."[246] Calculating the ROI in a predictive system is challenging because that flu shot scenario describes the same methodology that gets administered across various diseases in every hospital in every situation. Every patient and every department want to know those answers, but those answers are tough to calculate because of this predictive solution paradox. Once you touch a system, you do not know if the outcome changed because you touched it, or if the outcome was never going to be what you expected and you were wrong in your prediction.

Adds Neil Gomes of Jefferson Health, "Just addressing a problem and solving it is not sufficient. You have to think about incentives in both directions, for the patient as well as the hospital. Technology providers often focus too much on the value to the institution and not enough on the value for the patient. The institution will eventually realize that if the patient is not asking for a solution or if the solution is not delivering them any value, it is challenging to sustain the solution into the future because it does not drive more patients to the hospital which is ultimately what the institution is concerned about. There is a fine balance between the two. There are valid solutions that bring about cost reduction to the institution, and even if they have nothing to do with delivering value to the patient, they could still be of value to an organization. It is difficult to generalize, but I think the simple rule is that you have to build the incentive into the solution, especially when a solution is directed to a third party such as a patien that does not participate in how the platform is deployed for a hospital's benefit. At other times, the benefits of a solution do not go to the person who is using it, such as a nurse or a care coordinator, but to the patient. In such cases, you have to create incentives for the person who is using it to deliver care to the patient. Otherwise, it will not succeed."[247]

Universal theme #2: Build it with them, not for them.

Digital health innovation is a scattershot process today, with startups building solutions wherever they see a gap in the market. In an era of profit margin pressures and cost reductions, digital health solutions have to get it right the first time. Neil Gomes makes a nuanced observation about the approaches that digital health companies, especially startups, take to launch an offering in the market. "Many early-stage companies make the mistake of developing products in isolation and approach us to help validate it. However, they have already made decisions about what they want the tool to do and how it is going to help us when ideally, they should have partnered with us soon after the inception of the idea. Often, we tell them the hard facts, and then they do not like it. They refuse to pivot, and they just continue on their path, but we are close to the problem and can help develop solutions that deliver an outcome in a short time instead of the usual three or eight or twelve months. We are seeing this starting to happen and not just with Jefferson Health but also other healthcare institutions that are investing in innovation and digital innovation, focused on the consumer experience."[248]

The digital health ecosystem needs to adopt a co-development approach to avoid making early mistakes that could be fatal to a startup. Gomes suggests approaching institutions with a proposition to build a solution along with them. With health IT solutions, each institution is very different, so trying to sell something that has already been built can be a challenge. This is a standard approach by large tech firms who spend time co-developing solutions, usually with a client who is willing to share their domain knowledge, data, and other resources in exchange for the benefits of being the first client for a new product or solution. It is also important to note the difference between co-development and a pilot project; a pilot is usually a trial for a fully developed product, whereas co-development implies a long-term commitment to the product and the relationship from the outset. Gomes thinks that most startups are afraid of the co-development approach because they worry they will never be able to scale up to ten to fifteen organizations using their product. Gomes advises patience and the belief that the co-development approach eventually delivers a set of common features that will resonate with the larger market.

Schiller of Validic concurs with this approach. "I think that you should probably be asking those stakeholders first what they need and solve a problem for them from a financial perspective. It might be that you need to modify your product to meet their needs, and it could be a lot better if you are not selling them on a finished solution but getting your thoughts and your idea on the table first. At Validic, we were lucky we got solid feedback early on from a client in the development process that resulted in a strong pivot for us. If we had not been focused on following the money and having those conversations before the product was built, we never would have gotten off the ground because we would have been trying to sell what we had rather than listening to what the market needed."[249]

Neil Smiley also understands this well. His company Loopback Analytics has focused on a specific problem that relates to medication non-adherence, a $100 billion healthcare problem and one that can impact readmission rates for hospitals due to unfilled prescriptions during the time a patient is discharged from a hospital. Recent studies show that 20–30 percent of new prescriptions go unfilled, and 50 percent of chronic disease medications are not taken as prescribed. Loopback Analytics looked at patients who are late in starting therapy due to delays in getting their medications from a retail pharmacy in their community after hospitalization. When that patient is at high risk, the result is often an avoidable readmission. Using advanced analytical models to design a solution targeted at high-risk patients, the solution alerts administrators and care coordinators to follow up with the patient and ensure that he/she is provided with the right medications before discharge. Loopback's algorithms considered over one thousand variables and looked at a wide variety of data sources including claim data, EHR data, and pharma point-of-sale data.[250] Using this approach, the University of Tennessee Medical Center ensured the delivery of medications to high-risk patients prior to discharge. This reduced thirty-day readmissions by more than 20 percent as compared to patients with similar risks who did not get their medications delivered.[251]

By focusing on a gap that current readmission risk prediction models did not adequately address, specific to medication adherence, Loopback Analytics was able to align to a real problem with tangible financial implications. In the end, the solution paid for itself, which may be the most important consideration of all.

There is an enormous amount of interest in consumer health applications today; most will try and fail because digital health firms often make the mistake of thinking they have great technology and a very competent workflow. They find out that the sales cycle can come to an abrupt stop for a variety of reasons. One example of a mistake that digital health companies make is to develop a solution that requires people to change how they work. Clinicians on the verge of burnout do not have an additional ten minutes to learn a new system or complete an additional task. For example, asking a nurse to spend ten more minutes doing something to enable deployment of a new solution ignores that nurses are already overstretched and understaffed. So the chances that a solution will get implemented are greatly diminished because the intended target user will not use it. The path of least resistance is, therefore, to integrate seamlessly into the workflow. Big technology firms spend a lot of time and money through focus groups and design-thinking workshops to get this right, and even they often fail.

An often-overlooked aspect of solution development is compliance. Healthcare is a heavily regulated industry, and Silicon Valley engineers and technologists often do not understand that they are obligated to ensure compliance. For many startups, this is partly due to the pressure to grow, especially when there is VC money sitting on them. These companies tend to focus first on staying in business and worry about compliance later. It is often too late. Smiley stresses that "healthcare regulations are incredibly complicated, and unless you are a real student of that and you keep up with it, how they may vary by state and so forth, it is easy to get tripped up."[252] Just ask Zenefits and Theranos, the two healthcare unicorns that were badly damaged due to regulatory compliance issues.

Universal theme #3: Find a champion (or champions).

A truism in healthcare is that everyone wants to work with somebody who has already done it zillion times before. This is a risk-averse community and for good reasons.

Few digital health companies get to see the market for their offerings take off without some failure and experimentation. The one thing in common among those that do succeed is that they had an anchor client who became an unpaid evangelist for the solution. However, sitting behind the journey from pilot phase implementation and enterprise-wide roll-out is a hard ROI consideration at every stage that ensures that the healthcare enterprise is capturing incremental benefits in terms of increased revenues, reduces costs, or improved quality of care.

How do you find a champion? Let us take a step back and understand the seismic shift that has happened in the past few years in the structure of the healthcare industry. Between 2010 and 2016, the general trend towards consolidation among hospitals and physician groups continued, with a 29 percent increase in market concentration (a measure of the extent of consolidation) for primary care physicians.[253] Consequently, technology budgets are getting consolidated among fewer buyers who are looking to use their increased buying power to negotiate better terms with the technology provider community. Simultaneously, as the market shifts away from FFS towards VBC and PHM, we see the emergence of new titles such as CDO, CPHO, and Chief Patient Experience Officer, many of whom have become important stakeholders in technology buying decisions, traditionally the province of a CIO. The emergence of new technology buying centers in large enterprises aligns with what Gartner refers to as "bi-modal" IT when describing the reality of many technology environments today. In bi-modal IT, there is a traditional mode that encompasses legacy technology environments that need renovation and maintenance, often referred to as systems of record, which are traditionally within the purview of the CIO's responsibilities. New and innovative solutions represent the other mode that are mostly stand-alone cloud-based platforms, such as digital health and analytics solutions, often referred to as systems of engagement. Emerging platforms in the systems of engagement are increasingly funded, deployed, and controlled by non-IT executives with CIOs playing supporting roles. The shift in ownership for technology platforms, especially for digital health solutions, is a growing trend, and because many of the non-IT roles and titles with technology budgets did not exist a few years ago, they imply the emergence of new champions for solution providers. The absence of prior relationships with technology vendors among this new community of stakeholders could potentially level the playing field for new entrants against the big incumbent technology firms.

For most technology solution providers, the natural tendency is to assume that the CIO of a healthcare enterprise is the champion for the solution. Emerging non-IT roles with budget and decision authority mean a broader set of stakeholders to cover and a potentially larger group of potential champions who can be at any level in the organization and not just senior executives. In fact, there are often multiple champions for a company or product within an enterprise. It all depends on how an organization is structured. The typical first points of contact for technology firms today have expanded beyond the CIO to include CMIO, CTO, and CPHO. With innovation high on the agenda of most CEOs, the chief innovation officer has become another port of call for technology sales executives. However, chief innovation officers may not have ongoing responsibilities for ensuring the continued success of the platform or solution, and early-stage companies could get stuck in the pilot phases of innovation and fail to graduate to enterprise-wide adoption at scale to solve bigger problems. Technology solution providers who make an entry through the innovation office have to quickly identify and build relationships with economic buyers and other stakeholder groups that have long-term ownership for a particular solution area such as PHM or digital patient engagement.

In the current context, digital health firms should not focus on trying to find the one executive with enterprise-wide authority and control over how to unlock insights from the data. Instead, the approach that is likely to succeed is one where a solution finds a champion within the client organization who is also an individual with enterprise-wide influence, will evangelize the solution provider and the solution, and stay around long enough to experience the benefits of the efforts.

General Principles

The pendulum continues to swing between centralization and decentralization in healthcare enterprises. Some large enterprises have appointed data czars and chief architects to collect data from all parts of the enterprise, ingest it into data lakes (a term that refers to storage repositories for large amounts of structured and unstructured data in native formats such as databases, text, and images), and unlock new insights. Only the largest entities attempt this top-down approach, spending millions of dollars on infrastructure, data collection, and data preparation before they figure out what to do with it. These entities typically work with large global technology firms who have the experience and expertise to mitigate the risks of large-scale projects.

Healthcare enterprises that take a more incremental approach to big data analytics and digital transformation programs work better for smaller technology firms for whom a gradual approach that focuses on a series of smaller, iterative wins is less risky. In many healthcare enterprises, budgets for initial projects for new solution areas such as advanced analytics and digital health typically can be in the hundreds or even tens of thousands of dollars. Most healthcare enterprises can easily fund them from their innovation or R&D budgets. Innovation funds that are discretionary budgets with easier approval processes allow a new solution provider to demonstrate value in a few months and gain the confidence of stakeholders regarding the solution's benefits. Solution providers often have to first make the sale at a departmental level before aiming for an across-the-board, long-term commitment within the larger enterprise. The downside to this approach is that without a champion with enterprise-level influence and authority, many solutions get stuck at a departmental level for an extended period, sometimes years, in what is often referred as "pilot purgatory".

Despite the emerging opportunities for digital health and analytics solutions, the solution provider landscape can appear to be crowded, and healthcare providers may find it overwhelming to decide on whom to place their bets. Consider diabetes, one of the major chronic conditions that impact healthcare costs in the United States. The Centers for Disease Control estimated that in 2015, an estimated 30.3 million individuals representing 9.3 percent of the US population had diabetes;[254] the American Diabetic Association estimated the annual cost of diabetes at $245 billion in 2012.[255] It fair to assume that the healthcare sector is looking for solutions to this problem; the startup ecosystem seems to be eager to oblige. AngelList, a site that publishes job openings in startups, lists 189 diabetes startups as of September 2017 that are focused on helping solve this problem; the challenge is that health systems are not looking to try out every new diabetes solution that comes their way.

A major conundrum for digital health and analytics companies trying to secure their first project is the need for evidence. Health systems look for an evidence base when adopting a new solution in a clinical setting, partly out of consideration for patient safety. This conundrum presents a chicken-and-egg problem for digital health companies. An evidence base is needed to increase adoption. However, increased adoption leads to an evidence base. In its classic form, the evidence-based approach involves a research study that results in a published paper that can lead to broad adoption. Some studies go on to build seminal influence in a particular area. An example of this is the Coleman Care Transitions Model that came out of a project funded by the California Healthcare Foundation in 2007. Developed under a team led by Dr. Eric Coleman, the care transitions model focuses on managing patients during the first few weeks after discharge from an acute care setting; the model eventually led to best practices for readmissions reductions. The conundrum for digital health companies is that they may have come up with an innovative approach to solving a problem, but they need a healthcare enterprise to deploy and use it, and someone within that enterprise to write up an academic paper based on the deployment. If the deployment is a success, it typically results in a research paper that is accepted as evidence within the clinical community for wider adoption.

The evidence-based approach to gaining credibility and acceptance for a solution is a common path for many new healthcare solutions. However, many solutions that gain clinical acceptance and produce a research paper may not see a clear pathway to revenues, especially if the initial clinical sponsor for the project loses interest or is unable to devote time and attention to help the solution gain wider acceptance. To avoid this dilemma, digital health companies must identify a cohort of patients who are likely to benefit from the pilot phase deployment and use the cohort to generate new referrals for the solution, rather than relying on a clinician sponsor to generate new referrals to sustain the solution.

Large and progressive healthcare enterprises, such as AMCs, typically run new projects and evaluate new solutions on an ongoing basis as part of their innovation and R&D programs. Projects funded by innovation programs are opportunities for young companies to gain visibility and earn credibility as healthcare solution providers. However, before starting on a new innovation project, solution providers must have discussions with stakeholders about the next steps and ask questions such as: where is this going to go? It is important to be aware of and possibly even negotiate a series of steps beyond the initial program and identify additional use cases, departments, or functions to try out a new solution. This process could take a long time, sometimes two or three years, given the pace at which most health systems operate.

A related challenge for many digital health companies is that they often have one anchor client. If they are lucky, this may be a client who is a reputed healthcare enterprise and by association provides some credibility to the solution provider. However, these clients can be demanding, and may also pose a significant business and financial business risk to a smaller provider whose future depends almost completely on a single client. Solution providers must quickly move to secure a long-term relationship with their first client and leverage the momentum to enter into similarly transformative relationships with other health systems. The long-term survival of these companies depends on their ability to discover the pathway and accelerate their journey down the path. However, this is easier said than done, and many companies fail to complete the journey.

The only reliable way to address long-term survival risks for a solution provider is to deliver tangible and measurable benefits that are large multiples on the initial investment for clients and to convert the client into vocal champions and evangelists for the solution. Smiley offers some additional advice on this, using a baseball analogy to illustrate the importance of small victories on the path to long-term success. "It is better to go for some singles and doubles to sustain you through the long desert path that I think it takes to contract with large healthcare enterprises. I also believe that it can be a significant risk to a small startup that does not have robust funding, and they can just run out of cash before they get the big, transformative deal done."[256]

8 Growth Strategy Frameworks

Every technology firm has its strategic advantage, which, when positioned with clarity and accuracy, will deliver the kind of traction and growth that they need. Firms rarely know where they fit in the competitive landscape or have a particular interest in how they are positioned in the marketplace. This can be especially true of firms that have developed horizontal offerings that are applicable in multiple use cases or vertical industry segments. In my work with a wide range of technology firms, I see even some of the biggest global technology brands struggle with a strategic positioning message for healthcare markets. At the same time, I see smaller firms that are laser-focused on their target markets and have a clear vision and purpose that come through in their messaging and positioning. (Obviously, several large companies have well-defined positions for their target markets, just as there are niche firms that seem to be unable to express who they are or what they represent.)

The lack of clarity in positioning and messaging arises from a range of reasons: lack of strategic focus on a particular market, lack of rigorous and intentional effort to define and articulate a position in the market, or a deliberate intention to avoid defining their position until the offerings and value proposition are validated by the markets to a certain degree.

It is important for any technology firm to have a framework of reference to map the market landscape and assess its competitive position.

In chapter 5, I outlined the four broad segments in the

technology vendor landscape. To recap, *custodians* are the owners of the data and workflow and include the big EHR vendors such as Epic and Cerner. The *enablers* are big tech firms that have invested in building digital health platforms. These include companies such as Salesforce Health Cloud, GE Health Cloud, and IBM Watson Health. Importantly, this category also includes emerging platforms such as Quest's Quanum and others that are being developed by traditional healthcare providers, often in partnership with a technology firm (such as Inovalon, in the case of Quest Diagnostics). The *arbitrageurs* are global consulting firms that provide technology services. These include Accenture, Deloitte, Cognizant, Infosys, and a slew of smaller and mid-market firms. These firms typically do not develop proprietary platforms and focus instead on providing services for custom development and implementation of third-party platforms. Some of these companies have lately started acquiring IP-led companies. The *innovators* are digital health startups, and they cover a wide range of VC-funded companies, many of which are featured in this book, including Validic, Jvion, and Loopback Analytics.

This segmentation of technology vendors is less about trying to force-fit a company into a category and more about understanding the competitive nature of each category. Technology firms may operate in more than one of these categories. For instance, custodians can also be enablers by building digital experience platforms that sit on the underlying transactional systems. However, it is unlikely that enablers can be custodians as well unless they own a clinical information system such as an EHR platform. Similarly, enablers can be arbitrageurs by offering services to implement, integrate, and maintain the enabling platforms. However, we see fewer instances of arbitrageurs playing the role of enablers, although that is changing due to ongoing M&A and strategic alliances as well as IP development efforts by pure-play services firms.

Regardless of what categories vendors find themselves in, they must develop pertinent go-to-market strategies, customer targeting, and sales approaches. Various buy-side factors come into the equation depending on the type solution a vendor represents. Here are some examples: solution complexity and risk levels drive the number of stakeholders that need to sign off; an economic buyer's budget authority determines how many levels of approvals may be required; enterprises use annual budgeting cycles to decide if a solution purchase will happen in the current fiscal year or not; even with budget approvals, whether the purchase will be accounted for as a capital or operating expense can seal the fate of a sale. Buyers also compartmentalize their vendors and tailor their approaches accordingly when making purchase decisions. For example, a CIO who is tasked with outsourcing IT operations for cost reduction will consider a certain type of vendor and follow a more formal procurement process (often through a request for proposal), involving multiple stakeholder groups and multiple rounds of down-selection and site visits that take place over several months. A senior executive who has an immediate need to drive business performance metrics may sign off very quickly on an innovative new technology solution that can accelerate growth. The emerging class of digital health solutions, especially enabling platforms that are intended for enterprise-wide adoption to roll out multiple solutions, typically need both business stakeholders and the IT function to sign off. These are often non-trivial purchase decisions due to either the strategic nature of the platform purchase or the size and scale of the technology vendor, which expects to build an enterprise-wide long-term relationship regardless of the entry-level transaction. Irrespective of the nature of the offering, it is increasingly common to have business stakeholders and the IT function involved in the purchase of a digital health solution.

The big challenge for technology firms (besides constantly developing a pipeline of qualified opportunities) is accelerating the movement of an opportunity through a pipeline.

Figure 2: Technology solutions growth model: based on Ansoff Matrix

One of my preferred management models to help develop growth strategy is the Ansoff Matrix, developed by mathematician Igor Ansoff in the '50s.[257] I have presented a slightly modified version of the model here that is pertinent to the technology industry, specifically healthcare IT.

The Ansoff Matrix is a framework for a product market strategy to help determine where a product or offering fits in a firm's market. Markets and products are classified as new or existing. The chances of success for an offering will depend on which market segment it is targeting. From the matrix in figure 1, it is easy to see that the fastest path to near-term growth is to sell more of an offering to an existing set of customers in a target market. The same offerings can be positioned successfully in new markets, as can new offerings to existing customers by cross-selling and up-selling. Global technology firms derive most of their annual revenues from their existing footprint of clients through a tried-and-tested process of account penetration, and cross-selling and up-selling products and services. Damo Consulting's research indicates that, in some large technology firms, 95 percent or more of annual revenue is attributed to a set of active accounts at the beginning of the year.

Much of the focus of this book is on the remaining 5 percent, the big winners of tomorrow and the net new logos of today. The costs of acquiring a new logo are very high in a market seemingly saturated with technology products and solutions. Established firms looking to sell new offerings are best served by taking these offerings to existing clients, and, in many cases, the solutions are co-developed with a willing and strategic customer. It is for this reason that many of the executives I interviewed in this book indicated that their default mode for buying a new technology solution is to go to their existing EHR vendors. However, success by default is far from assured, especially when the vendor and its solution are not seen as a logical match for a perceived need. The same executives who default to EHR vendors also point out that EHR vendors are behind the innovation curve, compared to other technology firms and startups. Global IT services companies, perceived as low-cost extensions of the IT resource pool, face a similar struggle to be considered for innovation programs involving cutting-edge digital health platform solutions.

By definition, digital health startups have a limited footprint in the market, and their growth is dependent on gaining that single anchor client, penetrating that account, and then expanding quickly to others. Unlike large tech firms that have ample free cash flow to support new market development, digital health startups have a relatively short window to acquire clients and demonstrate and build a sustainable revenue model. In the Ansoff Matrix, they are mostly operating in the top right quadrant, where acquisition costs are high, and sales cycles can last a year or more. I have discussed several tactical solutions to this conundrum, including partnering with large consulting firms and identifying champions who can provide the much-needed referrals to accelerate the client acquisition process. Since startups typically have just one main offering or solution, their opportunities to expand within their existing accounts with new offerings are limited, and their best bet, therefore, is to replicate their initial success quickly with similar clients in adjacent markets. Either way, their single biggest priority is to escape from the high mortality of the top right quadrant.

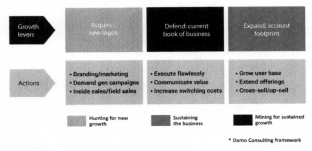

Growth levers	Acquire: new logos	Defend: current book of business	Expand: account footprint
Actions	• Branding/marketing • Demand gen campaigns • Inside sales/field sales	• Execute flawlessly • Communicate value • Increase switching costs	• Grow user base • Extend offerings • Cross-sell/up-sell
	Hunting for new growth	Sustaining the business	Mining for sustained growth

* Damo Consulting framework

Figure 3: The ADE™ framework

The ADE™ framework, a companion to the Ansoff Matrix developed by my firm Damo Consulting, provides a high-level prescription for the growth challenges of technology firms of all sizes and stages of maturity. The framework identifies three levers: *acquire*, *defend*, and *expand* (A, D, and E) and a set of indicative tactical actions to effectively manage the levers. The differences in firms' size and stage of maturity relate to the degree of emphasis on specific aspects of the framework.

Startups, as well as companies with new digital health solutions, are mostly in the *acquire* phase, given the early stage of market maturity for these solutions. The emphasis is therefore on aggressive branding, marketing, and demand generation through a combination of personal referrals, event promotions, content marketing, marketing automation, inbound/outbound campaigns, and inside sales operations. Many companies in this stage also invest heavily in the field sales staff. However, investing in a large field sales organization can be risky for smaller and underfunded firms with weak or emerging pipelines and long sales cycles. In extreme cases, hiring too many field sales staff too early sets up companies for an accelerated cash burn rate, leading to financial trouble if deals do not close in time. The resulting churn in sales staff can jeopardize active deals in the pipeline and cause disruption and loss of momentum in the market. Large tech firms typically overcome this by giving existing sales staff sales quotas for new solutions. However, the flip side is that sales staff are trained to pursue any deal that has a chance of an early close, and they often neglect newer offerings that require more effort and take longer to close.

Technology firms that have managed to acquire an initial set of anchor clients have to pay a great deal of attention to defending these accounts, not necessarily from competition, but from attrition. Early wins for new solutions can have high mortality rates unless they are properly fed and cared for, and most vendors pull out all the stops to ensure flawless execution that exceeds the client's needs. Executing well on ongoing engagements does two things for the solution provider: It blocks the door to new entrants by raising the bar on performance, and it increases switching costs by getting clients used to the new solution, which then is progressively integrated into enterprise systems. The incumbency factor is often the strongest protection against competition from other technology firms, and it takes a bold CIO with a tolerance for cost and risk to switch solutions, especially when the original solution implementation involved capital expenditure that may not have been fully amortized. The upsides for technology firms from investing heavily in existing accounts also include deep relationship-building opportunities that may yield future champions for new solutions, a ready and willing partner to try product enhancements, and a reference base of satisfied clients ready to accept and try new products.

The successful companies in the era of the Big Unlock are the ones that are sitting comfortably in all three stages of the ADE™ framework. These are companies that have found a market segment and a loyal client base that accepts their solutions, reciprocates by investing in the partnership, and willingly tries out new offerings. Such companies can be found among large global tech firms as well as innovative new VC-funded startups. The fastest-growing firms are the ones that are allocating capital to all three stages of the ADE™ framework with free cash flow generated from their client engagements. At the same time, some firms have free cash flow but are not well-positioned to take their share and more of the emerging digital health opportunities. The global IT services companies based in India are an example. Many of these companies have announced large share buybacks in 2017, an indicator possibly of their inability to deploy free cash flow rapidly enough for accelerated growth or an aversion to the risks involved in pursuing inorganic growth too aggressively. At least one of these firms, Cognizant Technology Solutions, has been the target of activist investors looking for large cash reserves to be deployed to spur growth or to be returned to shareholders.[258] Weakening growth for global IT services firms is further exacerbated by technology changes (notably the shift towards cloud computing and the growing trend towards automation in all aspects of business operations) that threaten the IT service provider firms' outdated business models based on labor arbitrage. At the other end of the spectrum are the truly innovative digital health startups that are in a race against time to establish themselves before they run out of cash (and their VCs run out of patience). A lucky few among these have found homes in M&A transactions with larger VC-funded companies or big technology firms with cash flow, including the India-based multinationals.

There is no single prescription for all firms within a market or even within a market segment that can guarantee growth and long-term viability. The Ansoff Matrix and the ADE™ framework serve as foundational tools to do a rigorous assessment of the competitive position of these companies and develop capital allocation and execution strategies that serve them best.

9 Concluding Thoughts: Working in Healthcare B2B Technology

Working in the healthcare sector requires a tremendous amount of patience and a willingness to stay invested. The truth of the matter is that health systems are slow at bringing in innovation, partly due to patient safety concerns but also due to the time and effort involved in gaining the support of a wide range of stakeholders for a new approach. Onboarding new solutions, designing patient experiences, training staff, integrating with other systems, and a whole host of other issues contribute to long adoption cycles.

Hospitals need immediate returns and cannot afford to invest in technology that does not pay back in the short term. For many health systems, the pathway is to identify promising new solutions and technologies through an innovation office and run a pilot. A small number of these pilots then make the transition to enterprise adoption. This process can take a long time due to the conservative and risk-averse nature of health systems. Additional challenges such interoperability issues with EHR systems can further delay enterprise-wide adoption. Either way, the huge chasm between a pilot project and an enterprise platform is a big hurdle that innovative new startups need to cross. They have to negotiate a pathway upfront for enterprise adoption and understand the milestones involved in the process. Along the way, many solutions pivot from the original product strategy to align with a health system's needs to help achieve goals for both parties.

The good news is there is a growing acknowledgment that data is a corporate asset to be unlocked to create value. For innovative solutions that capture new data sources or find creative ways to combine existing data sources to develop new and more efficient ways to improve financial and operational outcomes, finding budgets for pilots is relatively easy. While going beyond the pilot to large-scale implementation is a challenge, having an anchor client can ease the process of gaining broader acceptance in the market. In many cases, healthcare enterprises take on financial risk by making equity investments in promising startups through an investment fund. Having a prominent client as a shareholder also mitigates risks and uncertainties for startups. Many health systems such as UPMC and Kaiser Ventures provide this kind of funding and often become the first anchor client as well.

The pathway for digital health solution providers in the payer market looks a little bit different than the pathway for providers. The payer market is more consolidated as an industry, compared to providers. Payers also tend to build custom technology solutions in-house or with preferred technology services partners. The bigger health insurers use global consulting firms, who in turn sometimes bring in innovative startups as part of a solution framework. Large healthcare enterprises often see smaller solution providers and startups as risky bets and hesitate to contract directly with such firms; the alternative for digital health startups looking to break in is to align with a big global consulting firm that implicitly underwrites the technology and financial risks for payers from the involvement of smaller companies and startups in solution development.

Despite the various options available to digital health startups, many firms fail to transition from initial successes into viable and profitable businesses for the long-term. The Kaufmann Foundation, which tracks entrepreneurial activity in the United States, states that new ventures are more likely to fail than succeed;[259] there has been a widely held belief for some time that nine out of ten Silicon Valley startups fail.[260] In the interviews I conducted with VCs as part of the research for this book, I learned that there is a high mortality rate for technology startups in early stages of a client relationship and the reasons are many: the quality of the product, its usability in a given context, and buy-in from ground-level users of the product in an enterprise, to name a few. A common pitfall startups face is when the person signing the check, typically a C-level executive, buys into the promise of the solution but fails to involve other stakeholders at operational levels early on in the process. Operational stakeholders are individuals who can potentially become champions for the new solution; conversely, they may also become opponents of the solution, often because they were not involved at the start of the solution evaluation process. Most solution providers are trying to accelerate sales cycles, and to them it feels counterintuitive to try to slow down the process in order to secure buy-in from a large group of stakeholders. There are no easy answers to the question of how to find the balance between trying to speed up sales cycles and obtaining the endorsement of a large group of influencers to ensure long-term commitment to the success of the solution. However, having a strong alignment with a compelling market need at an enterprise that feels an urgency to act is probably the best place to be for a digital health company. As healthcare moves progressively toward VBC, advanced analytics and digital health solutions will find more and more traction as stakeholders are compelled to act. Indeed, many solution providers note that the acceleration of solution adoption tends to be in line with the pace of the shift toward VBC and APMs. This cuts across all types of entities, regardless of their size and structure.

Perhaps the best situation for digital health and advanced analytics providers is to have plenty of opportunities to fail early. These failures help solution providers learn to develop effective blocking and tackling techniques in building consensus among stakeholders, build knowledge and learning from customer feedback, and identify the many externalities—such as macro-level policy changes that impact buying decisions—that are out of control. The learnings from failed campaigns, if they come early enough, help firms evolve and survive without running out of resources as they build their own unique roadmap for success.

A question that might cross the minds of technology firms is: why waste time trying to battle the challenges in a slow-moving, conservative sector such as healthcare when there may be better opportunities elsewhere? The answer comes from Neil Smiley. "In my consulting career, I probably worked across ten different industries, and there are not any that are as messed up as healthcare, nor is there another one I would rather be working with."[261]

Acknowledgments

In doing my research for the book, I was very pleasantly surprised that nearly everyone I reached out to for help readily offered their time and insights. Although the names are too many to list here, I do owe special thanks to the following individuals from the healthcare community: Ed Marx of Cleveland Clinic, Lidia Fonseca of Quest Diagnostics, Suresh Krishnan of Amita Health, and Neil Gomes of Jefferson Health. From the technology community, I would like to express my gratitude to Neal Singh of Caradigm, Drew Schiller of Validic, Shantanu Nigam of Jvion, Anand Shroff of Health Fidelity, Neil Smiley of Loopback Analytics, Sid Chatterjee of Persistent Systems, and Guy Mansueto and Dr. Anil Jain of IBM Watson Health. I was fortunate to get the venture capital community's perspective from Sam Brasch of Kaiser Ventures and Jim Pavlik of Baird Capital. Barbra Sheridan McGann of HfS Research provided me with a ton of material along with her insights, which have found their way into the book.

My team at Damo Consulting put in many hours to transcribe the many interviews, edit (and greatly improve) my manuscript, and design the images. Thank you, Arpita, Suni, and Sanjith.

Thanks also to my publishers: Ed Murray at CIO magazine and Heather Perry at Archway.

Last but not least, thank you, dear reader, for picking up this book.

References

Chapter 1

1   Meeker, Mary. "Internet Trends 2017 – Code Conference." KPCB.com. Last modified May 31, 2017. http://www.kpcb.com/internet-trends.

2   International Data Corporation. "Worldwide Semiannual Big Data and Analytics Spending Guide." IDC.com. Accessed 2017. http://www.idc.com/getdoc.jsp?containerId=IDC_P33195.

3   Pennic, Jasmine. "Report: Healthcare Analytics Market Expected to Reach \$43B by 2024." HIT Consultant. Last modified July 13, 2016. http://hitconsultant.net/2016/07/13/report-healthcare-analytics-market/.

4   Meeker, Mary. "Internet Trends 2017 – Code Conference." KPCB.com. Last modified May 31, 2017. http://www.kpcb.com/internet-trends.

5   U.S. Centers for Medicare & Medicaid Services. "National Health Expenditures 2015 Highlights." CMS.gov. Last modified 2015. https://www.cms.gov/Research-Statistics-Data-and-Systems/Statistics-Trends-and-Reports/NationalHealthExpendData/downloads/highlights.pdf.

6   Institute for Healthcare Improvement. "IHI Triple Aim Initiative: Better Care for Individuals, Better Health for Populations, and Lower Per Capita Costs." IHI.org. Accessed 2017. http://www.ihi.org/Engage/Initiatives/TripleAim/Pages/default.aspx.

7   Thune, Sen. John, Sen. Lamar Alexander, Sen. Pat Roberts, Sen. Richard Burr, and Sen. Mike Enzi. "Where Is HITECH's \$35 Billion Dollar Investment Going?" Health Affairs Blog. Last modified March 4, 2015. http://healthaffairs.org/blog/2015/03/04/where-is-hitechs-35-billion-dollar-investment-going/.

8   Quest Diagnostics. Progress on the path to value-based care. Accessed 2017. http://ddx.questdiagnostics.com/2017study.

9   Singh, Neal (CEO of Caradigm) in discussion with the author, May 23, 2017.

10 NEJM Catalyst. Disconnects in Transforming Health Care Delivery: How Excutives, Clinical Leaders, and Clinicians Must Bridge Their Divide and Move Forward Together. NEJM Catalyst, 2017. PDF e-book.

11 Hamblen, Matt. "CEOs rate productivity 'very low' from emerging tech." Computerworld. Last modified April 24, 2017. http://www.computerworld.com/article/3192085/internet-of-things/ceos-rate-productivity-very-low-from-emerging-tech.html.

12 Intel. "50 Years of Moore's Law." Intel.com. Accessed 2017. https://www.intel.com/content/www/us/en/silicon-innovations/moores-law-technology.html.

13 Padmanabhan, Paddy. The Democratization of Analytics: Are we all turning into Data Scientists? Damo Consulting, June 2015. http://www.damoconsulting.net/wp-content/uploads/2016/01/Democratization-of-Analytics-by-Damo-Consulting-June-20151-1.pdf.

14 U.S. Centers for Medicare & Medicaid Services. "MACRA: Delivery System Reform, Medicare Payment Reform." CMS.gov. Last modified September 8, 2017. https://www.cms.gov/Medicare/Quality-Initiatives-Patient-Assessment-Instruments/Value-Based-Programs/MACRA-MIPS-and-APMs/MACRA-MIPS-and-APMs.html.

15 Marx, Ed (CIO of Cleveland Clinic) in discussion with the author, May 4, 2017.

16 Medicare Access and CHIP Reauthorization Act of 2015, Pub. L. No. 114-10, 129 Stat. 87 (2015).

17 Belliveau, Jacqueline. "25% of Healthcare Payments Tied to Alternative Payment Models." RevCycle Intelligence. Last modified October 26, 2016. https://revcycleintelligence.com/news/25-of-healthcare-payments-tied-to-alternative-payment-models.

18 Caradigm. "Bundled Payments for Care Improvement (BPCI) Survey: What do Providers think about BPCI and how far along are they?" Caradigm White Papers, 2017. https://www.caradigm.com/media/1559/caradigm_bpci_survey.pdf.

19 Kliff, Sarah. "How much does hip surgery cost? Somewhere between $10,000 and $125,000." The Washington Post. Last modified

February 12, 2013. https://www.washingtonpost.com/news/wonk/wp/2013/02/12/how-much-does-hip-surgery-cost-somewhere-between-10000-and-125000/?utm_term=.48ab9095cebc.

20 American College of Physicians. "Patient-Centered Medical Home." ACPOnline.org. Accessed 2017. https://www.acponline.org/practice-resources/business-resources/payment/models/pcmh.

21 Pennic, Jasmine. "Chilmark Report: 2017 State of the ACO Value-Based Model & Its Market Evolution." HIT Consultant. Last modified March 6, 2017. http://hitconsultant.net/2017/03/06/chilmark-aco-value-based-model-report/.

22 Muhlestein, David and Mark McClellan. "Accountable Care Organizations In 2016: Private And Public-Sector Growth And Dispersion." Health Affairs Blog. Last modified April 21, 2016. http://healthaffairs.org/blog/2016/04/21/accountable-care-organizations-in-2016-private-and-public-sector-growth-and-dispersion/.

23 Singh, Neal (CEO of Caradigm) in discussion with the author, May 23, 2017.

24 Fonseca, Lidia (CIO of Quest Diagnostics) in discussion with the author, May 31, 2017.

25 Quest Diagnostics. Progress on the path to value-based care. Accessed 2017. http://ddx.questdiagnostics.com/2017study.

26 Padmanabhan, Paddy. "What Quest Diagnostics' new study tells us about healthcare IT and value-based care." CIO. Last modified June 5, 2015. https://www.cio.com/article/3199670/healthcare/what-quest-diagnostics-new-study-tells-us-about-healthcare-it-and-value-based-care.html.

27 Frost & Sullivan. "Healthcare Data Analytics Moves beyond Siloed Business Intelligence to Coordinated Population Health Management and Precision Care." Frost & Sullivan press release, May 11, 2017. https://ww2.frost.com/news/press-releases/healthcare-data-analytics-moves-beyond-siloed-business-intelligence-coordinated-population-health-management-and-precision-care/.

28 Sawyer, Bradley and Nolan Sroczynski. "How do health expenditures vary across the population?" Peterson-Kaiser Health System Tracker. Last modified January 31, 2017. http://www.healthsystemtracker.org/chart-collection/health-expenditures-vary-across-population/.

29   Colby, Sandra L. and Jennifer M. Ortman. The Baby Boom Cohort in the United States: 2012 to 2060. (United States Census Bureau, Report no. P25-1141, May 2014).

30   Nicks, Denver. "Customer Satisfaction With Health Insurance Hits 10-Year Low." Money. Last modified November 17, 2015. http://time.com/money/4116325/health.

31   Hidalgo, Jason. "Here's how millennials could change health care." USA Today. Last modified February 7, 2016. http://www.usatoday.com/story/news/politics/elections/2016/02/07/heres-how-millennials-could-change-health-care/79818756/.

32   Tecco, Halle and Megan Zweig. "Digital Health Funding 2017 Midyear Review: A record breaking first half." Rock Health. Accessed 2017. https://rockhealth.com/reports/2017-midyear-funding-review-a-record-breaking-first-half/.

33   Padmanabhan, Paddy. "How technology and data shape digital marketing in healthcare in an on-demand era." CIO. Last modified November 7, 2016. http://www.cio.com/article/3137460/healthcare/how-technology-and-data-shape-digital-marketing-in-healthcare-in-an-on-dem.

34   Tecco, Halle. "2016 Year End Funding Report: A reality check for digital health." Rock Health. Accessed January 2017. https://rockhealth.com/reports/2016-year-end-funding-report-a-reality-check-for-digital-health/.

35   Gandhi, Malay and Teresa Wang. "Digital Health Consumer Adoption: 2015." Rock Health. Accessed 2015. https://rockhealth.com/reports/digital-health-consumer-adoption-2015/.

36   Gartner. "Gartner Says 6.4 Billion Connected 'Things' Will Be in Use in 2016, Up 30 Percent From 2015." Gartner press release, November 10, 2015. http://www.gartner.com/newsroom/id/3165317.

37   Pratt, Mary K. "Wearables in the enterprise? Yes, really!" CIO. Last modified February 24, 2016. http://www.cio.com/article/3037352/wearable-technology/wearables-in-the-enterprise-yes-really.html.

38   Accenture. "Internet of Health Things Survey." 2017. https://www.accenture.com/t20170215T191150__w__/us-en/_acnmedia/PDF-42/Accenture-Health-2017-Internet-of-Health-Things-Survey.pdf.

39   Hidalgo, Jason. "Here's how millennials could change health care." USA Today. Last modified February 7, 2016. http://www.usatoday.com/story/

news/politics/elections/2016/02/07/heres-how-millennials-could-change-health-care/79818756/.

40 Brüls, Annette. "First Live Experience of Sugar.IQ with Watson for People with Diabetes." Medtronic. Last modified September 26, 2016. https://www.medtronicdiabetes.com/blog/first-live-experience-of-sugar-iq-with-watson-for-people-with-diabetes/.

41 Miller, John. "Big Pharma's bet on Big Data creates opportunities and risks." Reuters. Last modified January 26, 2016. http://www.reuters.com/article/us-pharmaceuticals-data-idUSKCN0V41LY.

42 Metz, Rachel. "The Struggle for Accurate Measurements on Your Wrist." MIT Technology Review. Last modified June 22, 2015. http://www.technologyreview.com/review/538416/the-struggle-for-accurate-measurements-on-your-wrist.

43 Lee, Stephanie M. "Why Wearables Are Silicon Valley's Next Patent Fight." *BuzzFeed News*. Last modified June 17, 2015. https://www.buzzfeed.com/stephaniemlee/why-wearables-are-silicon-valleys-next-patent-fight?utm_term=.og7V55qmW#.hx9Y77Xm9.

44 IMS Institute for Healthcare Informatics. "Patient Adoption of mHealth: Use, Evidence and Remaining Barriers to Mainstream Acceptance." IMSHealth.com. Last modified September 2015. http://www.imshealth.com/files/web/IMSH%20Institute/Reports/Patient%20Adoption%20of%20mHealth/IIHI_Patient_Adoption_of_mHealth.pdf.

45 Corbin, Kenneth. "How CIOs Can Prepare for Healthcare 'Data Tsunami'." CIO. Last modified December 16, 2014. http://www.cio.com/article/2860072/healthcare/how-cios-can-prepare-for-healthcare-data-tsunami.html.

46 Meeker, Mary. "Internet Trends 2017 – Code Conference." KPCB.com. Last modified May 31, 2017. http://www.kpcb.com/internet-trends.

47 Markets and Markets. "Healthcare Analytics Market worth 24.55 Billion USD by 2021." Markets and Markets press release, November 3, 2016. http://www.marketsandmarkets.com/PressReleases/healthcare-data-analytics.asp.

48 Fonseca, Lidia (CIO of Quest Diagnostics) in discussion with the author, May 31, 2017.

49 Schiller, Drew (cofounder and CEO of Validic) in discussion with the author, May 5, 2017.

50   Food and Drug Administration. "FDA allows marketing of first direct-to-consumer tests that provide genetic risk information for certain conditions." FDA press release, April 6, 2017. https://www.fda.gov/newsevents/newsroom/pressannouncements/ucm551185.htm.

51   National Human Genome Research Institute. "The Cost of Sequencing a Human Genome." Genome.gov. Last modified July 6, 2016. https://www.genome.gov/27565109/the-cost-of-sequencing-a-human-genome/.

52   Meeker, Mary. "Internet Trends 2017 – Code Conference." KPCB.com. Last modified May 31, 2017. http://www.kpcb.com/internet-trends.

53   Brogan, Jacob "Who Owns Your Genetic Data After a Home DNA Test?" Slate. Last modified May 23, 2017. http://www.slate.com/blogs/future_tense/2017/05/23/ancestrydna_s_terms_and_conditions_sparked_a_debate_about_ownership_of_genetic.html.

54   U.S. National Library of Medicine. "What is informed consent?" Genetics Home Reference. Last modified September 19, 2017. https://ghr.nlm.nih.gov/primer/testing/informedconsent.

55   Hawaii Medical Service Association. "Risk Adjustment, Quality Measures, and Care of Older Adults." HMSA.com. Last modified July 26, 2017. https://hmsa.com/portal/provider/Risk_Adjustment_Quality_Measures_Care_of_Older_Adults_Webinar_072617_SLIDES.pdf.

56   Padmanabhan, Paddy. "Big data analytics and NLP: How health plans can make more money -- and keep it." *CIO*. Last modified August 26, 2016. https://www.cio.com/article/3112869/analytics/big-data-analytics-and-nlp-how-health-plans-can-make-more-money-and-keep-it.html.

57   Padmanabhan, Paddy. "Big data analytics and NLP: How health plans can make more money -- and keep it." *CIO*. Last modified August 26, 2016. https://www.cio.com/article/3112869/analytics/big-data-analytics-and-nlp-how-health-plans-can-make-more-money-and-keep-it.html.

58   Padmanabhan, Paddy. "A $280 billion healthcare problem ripe for technology innovation and predictive analytics." CIO. Last modified September 27, 2016. https://www.cio.com/article/3124425/healthcare/a-280-billion-healthcare-problem-ripe-for-technology-innovation-and-predictive-analytics.html.

59   Carter, Kara, Razili Lewis, and Tim Ward. "Improving healthcare for people with special or supportive-care needs." McKinsey&Company. Last modified September 2016. http://www.mckinsey.com/industries/

healthcare-systems-and-services/our-insights/improving-healthcare-for-people-with-special-or-supportive-care-needs?cid=other-eml-alt-mip-mck-oth-1609.

60   Office of the Press Secretary. "FACT SHEET: Launching the Data-Driven Justice Initiative: Disrupting the Cycle of Incarceration." The White House, June 30, 2016. https://www.whitehouse.gov/the-press-office/2016/06/30/fact-sheet-launching-data-driven-justice-initiative-disrupting-cycle.

61   U.S. National Archives and Records Administration. Code of Federal Regulations. Title 42. Confidentiality of Substance Use Disorder Patient Records. 2017.

62   Gebremedhin, Dan and Matthew Schuster. "Overview: Health tech startups innovating the behavioral health space." MobiHealthNews. Last modified August 29, 2016. http://www.mobihealthnews.com/content/overview-health-tech-startups-innovating-behavioral-health-space.

63   Monegain, Bernie. "HHS aims to grow behavioral health workforce with $44.5 million investment." Healthcare IT News. Last modified September 23, 2016. http://www.healthcareitnews.com/news/hhs-aims-grow-behavioral-health-workforce-445-million-investment.

64   Padmanabhan, Paddy. "A $280 billion healthcare problem ripe for technology innovation and predictive analytics." CIO. Last modified September 27, 2016. https://www.cio.com/article/3124425/healthcare/a-280-billion-healthcare-problem-ripe-for-technology-innovation-and-predictive-analytics.html.

65   Padmanabhan, Paddy. "How Quest and Inovalon have unlocked value in healthcare analytics." CIO. Last modified March 16, 2016. https://www.cio.com/article/3045227/analytics/how-quest-and-inovalon-have-unlocked-value-in-healthcare-analytics.html.

66   Fonseca, Lidia (CIO of Quest Diagnostics) in discussion with the author, May 31, 2017.

67   Padmanabhan, Paddy. "How unlikely collaborations are changing the future of healthcare." CIO. Last modified March 10, 2017. https://www.cio.com/article/3179467/healthcare/how-unlikely-collaborations-are-changing-the-future-of-healthcare.html.

68   Schiller, Drew (cofounder and CEO of Validic) in discussion with the author, May 5, 2017.

69 U.S. Centers for Medicare & Medicaid Services. "HCAHPS: Patients' Perspectives of Care Survey." CMS.gov. Last modified September 25, 2014. https://www.cms.gov/Medicare/Quality-Initiatives-Patient-Assessment-Instruments/HospitalQualityInits/HospitalHCAHPS.html.

70 Padmanabhan, Paddy. "Healthcare's new challenge: online reputation management." CIO. Last modified February 10, 2017. https://www.cio.com/article/3168340/healthcare/healthcares-new-challenge-online-reputation-management.html.

71 Padmanabhan, Paddy. "Healthcare's new challenge: online reputation management." CIO. Last modified February 10, 2017. https://www.cio.com/article/3168340/healthcare/healthcares-new-challenge-online-reputation-management.html.

72 Padmanabhan, Paddy. "How technology and data shape digital marketing in healthcare in an on-demand era." CIO. Last modified November 7, 2016. http://www.cio.com/article/3137460/healthcare/how-technology-and-data-shape-digital-marketing-in-healthcare-in-an-on-dem.

73 Padmanabhan, Paddy. "How technology and data shape digital marketing in healthcare in an on-demand era." CIO. Last modified November 7, 2016. http://www.cio.com/article/3137460/healthcare/how-technology-and-data-shape-digital-marketing-in-healthcare-in-an-on-dem.

74 Heiman, Harry J. and Samantha Artiga. "Beyond Health Care: The Role of Social Determinants in Promoting Health and Health Equity." The Henry J. Kaiser Family Foundation. Last modified November 4, 2015. http://kff.org/disparities-policy/issue-brief/beyond-health-care-the-role-of-social-determinants-in-promoting-health-and-health-equity/.

75 Central New York Care Collaborative. "Central New York Care Collaborative Announces Partnership with IBM Watson Health on Regional Population Health Management System." CNY Care Collaborative. Accessed 2017. https://cnycares.org/news/ibm-watson-health-regional-phm/.

76 New York State Department of Health. "Delivery System Reform Incentive Payment (DSRIP) Program." Health.NY.gov. Last modified

August 2017. https://www.health.ny.gov/health_care/medicaid/redesign/dsrip/.

77   Padmanabhan, Paddy. "Social determinants: powering the next big leap for healthcare analytics." CIO. Last March 23, 2017. https://www.cio.com/article/3183578/healthcare/social-determinants-powering-the-next-big-leap-for-healthcare-analytics.html.

78   Nag, Sid. "Forecast Analysis: Public Cloud Services, Worldwide, 1Q16 Update." Gartner. Last modified May 2, 2016. https://www.gartner.com/doc/3303417/forecast-analysis-public-cloud-services.

79   U.S. Department of Health & Human Services. "Guidance on HIPAA & Cloud Computing." HHS.gov. Last modified June 16, 2017. https://www.hhs.gov/hipaa/for-professionals/special-topics/cloud-computing/index.html.

80   Padmanabhan, Paddy. "Healthcare data breaches: It's no longer about healthcare or medical data." CIO. Last modified August 16, 2016. http://www.cio.com/article/3107927/healthcare/healthcare-data-breaches-its-no-longer-about-healthcare-or-medical-data.html.

81   Myers, Andrew. "Stanford's John McCarthy, seminal figure of artificial intelligence, dies at 84." Stanford News. Last modified October 25, 2011. http://news.stanford.edu/news/2011/october/john-mccarthy-obit-102511.html.

82   Clark, Liat. "Google's Artificial Brain Learns to Find Cat Videos." Wired. Last modified June 26, 2012. https://www.wired.com/2012/06/google-x-neural-network/.

83   International Data Corporation. "Worldwide Cognitive Systems and Artificial Intelligence Revenues Forecast to Surge Past $47 Billion in 2020, According to New IDC Spending Guide." IDC press release, October 26, 2016. http://www.idc.com/getdoc.jsp?containerId=prUS41878616.

84   Mukherjee, Sy. "You Can Now Download an Artificial Intelligence Doctor." Fortune. Last modified January 10, 2017. http://fortune.com/2017/01/10/healthtap-dr-ai-launch/.

85   Gartner. "Hype Cycle Research Methodology." Gartner. Accessed 2017. http://www.gartner.com/technology/research/methodologies/hype-cycle.jsp

86 Accenture. "Artificial Intelligence: Healthcare's New Nervous System." 2017. https://www.accenture.com/us-en/insight-artificial-intelligence-healthcare.

87 Dall, Tim, Ritashee Chakrabarti, Will Iacobucci, Alpana Hansari, and Terry West. The Complexities of Physician Supply and Demand 2017 Update: Projections from 2015 to 2030. (IHS Markit, Washington, DC, February 28, 2017).

88 Jain, Anil (Chief Innovation Officer of IBM Watson Health) in discussion with the author, June 8, 2017.

89 Wikipedia. s.v. "Algorithm." Accessed 2017. https://en.wikipedia.org/wiki/Algorithm.

90 Wikipedia. s.v. "Learning" Accessed 2017. https://en.wikipedia.org/wiki/Learning.

91 McGann, Barbra (Chief Research Officer of HfS Research) in discussion with the author, May 10, 2017.

92 McGann, B. (2017, May 10). An Interview with Barbra McGann, Chief Research Officer at HfS Research. (P. Padmanabhan, Interviewer)

93 Hamblen, Matt. "CEOs rate productivity 'very low' from emerging tech." Computerworld. Last modified April 24, 2017. http://www.computerworld.com/article/3192085/internet-of-things/ceos-rate-productivity-very-low-from-emerging-tech.html.

94 Monegain, Bernie. "Healthcare top target for cyberattacks in 2017, Experian predicts." Healthcare IT News. Last modified December 1, 2016. http://www.healthcareitnews.com/news/healthcare-top-target-cyberattacks-2017-experian-predicts.

95 IBM Institute for Business Value. Healthcare rallies for blockchains: Keeping patients at the center. IBM, 2016. https://www-01.ibm.com/common/ssi/cgi-bin/ssialias?htmlfid=GBE03790USEN&.

96 Mearian, Lucas. "IBM Watson, FDA to explore blockchain for secure patient data exchange." CIO. Last modified January 12, 2017. http://www.cio.com.au/article/612599/ibm-watson-fda-explore-blockchain-secure-patient-data-exchange/.

97 American Hospital Association. "Fast Facts on US Hospitals." AHA.org. Last modified January 2017. http://www.aha.org/research/rc/stat-studies/fast-facts.shtml.

98 Marx, Ed (CIO of Cleveland Clinic) in discussion with the author, May 4, 2017.

99 Noseworthy, John, James Madara, Delos Cosgrove, Mitchell Edgeworth, Ed Ellison, Sarah Krevans, Paul Rothman, Kevin Sowers, Steven Strongwater, David Torchiana, and Dean Harrison, "Physician Burnout Is A Public Health Crisis: A Message To Our Fellow Health Care CEOs." Health Affairs Blog. Last modified March 28, 2017. http://healthaffairs.org/blog/2017/03/28/physician-burnout-is-a-public-health-crisis-a-message-to-our-fellow-health-care-ceos/.

100 Wachter, Bob. "How Technology Led a Hospital to Give a Patient 38 Times His Dosage." Wired. Last modified March 30, 2015. https://www.wired.com/2015/03/how-technology-led-a-hospital-to-give-a-patient-38-times-his-dosage/.

101 van Biesen, Tim, Josh Weisbrod, Michael Brookshire, Julie Coffman, and Andy Pasternak. "Front Line of Healthcare Report 2017: Why involving doctors can help improve US healthcare." Bain & Company. Last modified May 11, 2017. http://www.bain.com/publications/articles/front-line-of-healthcare-report-2017.aspx.

102 NEJM Catalyst. Disconnects in Transforming Health Care Delivery: How Excutives, Clinical Leaders, and Clinicians Must Bridge Their Divide and Move Forward Together. NEJM Catalyst, 2017. PDF e-book.

103 Krishnan, Suresh (Chief Technology Officer of Amita Health) in discussion with the author, May 11, 2017.

104 Marx, Ed (CIO of Cleveland Clinic) in discussion with the author, May 4, 2017.

105 Gomes, Neil (CDO of Jefferson Health) in discussion with the author, May 12, 2017.

106 Gomes, Neil (CDO of Jefferson Health) in discussion with the author, May 12, 2017.

107 Gomes, Neil (CDO of Jefferson Health) in discussion with the author, May 12, 2017.

108 Chandler, Adam. "How Ransomware Became a Billion-Dollar Nightmare for Businesses." The Atlantic. Last modified September 3, 2016. https://www.theatlantic.com/business/archive/2016/09/ransomware-us/498602/.

109 Cuthbertson, Anthony. "Ransomeware Attacks Rise 250 percent in 2017, Hitting U.S. Hardest." Newsweek. Last modified May 23, 2017. http://www.newsweek.com/ransomware-attacks-rise-250-2017-us-wannacry-614034.

110 Nerney, Chris. "Hacking attacks against providers soared in 2016." Healthcare IT News. Last modified April 20, 2017. http://www. hiewatch.com/news/hacking-attacks-against-providers-soared-2016.

111 Experian® Data Breach Resolution. "Fourth Annual 2017 Data Breach Industry Forecast." Experian. Accessed 2017. http://www.experian. com/assets/data-breach/white-papers/2017-experian-data-breach-industry-forecast.pdf.

112 Shahani, Aarti. "Premera Blue Cross Cyberattack Exposed Millions Of Customer Records." NPR.org. Last modified March 18, 2015.

113 Padmanabhan, Paddy. "IoT and healthcare IT security: from firefighting to building code upgrades." CIO. Last modified October 26, 2016. http://www.cio.com/article/3134546/security/iot-and-healthcare-it-security-from-firefighting-to-building-code-upgrades.html.

114 Kan, Michael. "An IoT botnet is partly behind Friday's massive DDOS attack." PCWorld. Last modified October 21, 2016. http://www.pcworld. com/article/3134056/hacking/an-iot-botnet-is-partly-behind-fridays-massive-ddos-attack.html.

115 Padmanabhan, Paddy. "The NHS ransomware event and security challenges for the U.S healthcare system." CIO. Last modified May 15, 2017. https://www.cio.com/article/3196706/cyber-attacks-espionage/the-nhs-ransomware-event-and-security-challenges-for-the-u-s-healthcare-system.html.

116 Padmanabhan, Paddy. "Connected Health and IoT in healthcare delivery: Are we ready?" CIO. Last modified February 29, 2016. http://www. cio.com/article/3039261/healthcare/connected-health-and-iot-in-healthcare-delivery-are-we-ready.html.

117 Padmanabhan, Paddy. "3 best practices in healthcare IT security: How Group Health Cooperative does it." CIO. Last modified January 27, 2016. http://www.cio.com/article/3026464/security/3-best-practices-in-healthcare-it-security-how-group-health-cooperative-does-it.html.

118 Padmanabhan, Paddy. "3 best practices in healthcare IT security: How Group Health Cooperative does it." CIO. Last modified January 27, 2016. http://www.cio.com/article/3026464/security/3-best-practices-in-healthcare-it-security-how-group-health-cooperative-does-it.html.

119 Padmanabhan, Paddy. Healthcare data breaches: It's no longer about healthcare or medical data. Last modified August 16, 2016. http://www.

cio.com/article/3107927/healthcare/healthcare-data-breaches-its-no-longer-about-healthcare-or-medical-data.html.

120 Miliard, Mike. "Bon Secours says data breach affects 655,000 patients." Healthcare IT News. Last modified August 15, 2016. http://www.healthcareitnews.com/news/bon-secours-says-data-breach-affects-655000-patients.

121 Castellucci, Maria. "Nearly 90% of healthcare lawyers say industry is at greater risk of data breaches than others." Modern Healthcare. Last modified October 14, 2016. http://www.modernhealthcare.com/article/20161014/NEWS/161019954.

122 Constantin, Lucian. "Advocacy group calls on healthcare industry to adopt medical device security principles." CIO. Last modified January 19, 2016. http://www.cio.com/article/3024382/security/advocacy-group-calls-on-healthcare-industry-to-adopt-medical-device-security-principles.html.

123 Padmanabhan, Paddy. "A major medical device maker's unique approach to data security." CIO. Last modified June 20, 2017. https://www.cio.com/article/3202264/healthcare/a-major-medical-device-makers-unique-approach-to-data-security.html.

124 Food and Drug Administration. Postmarket Management of Cybersecurity in Medical Devices: Guidance for Industry and Food and Drug Administration Staff. (December 28, 2016). https://www.fda.gov/downloads/MedicalDevices/DeviceRegulationandGuidance/GuidanceDocuments/UCM482022.pdf.

125 Food and Drug Administration. Postmarket Management of Cybersecurity in Medical Devices: Guidance for Industry and Food and Drug Administration Staff. (December 28, 2016). https://www.fda.gov/downloads/MedicalDevices/DeviceRegulationandGuidance/GuidanceDocuments/UCM482022.pdf.

126 Food and Drug Administration. Postmarket Management of Cybersecurity in Medical Devices: Guidance for Industry and Food and Drug Administration Staff. (December 28, 2016). https://www.fda.gov/downloads/MedicalDevices/DeviceRegulationandGuidance/GuidanceDocuments/UCM482022.pdf.

127 Singh, Neal (CEO of Caradigm) in discussion with the author, May 23, 2017.

128 U.S. Department of Health & Human Services. "Covered Entities and Business Associates." HHS.gov. Last modified June 16, 2017. http://www.hhs.gov/hipaa/for-professionals/covered-entities/.

129 Snell, Elizabeth. "2016 Healthcare Data Breaches Largely From Employee Error." Health IT Security. Last modified January 20, 2017. https://healthitsecurity.com/news/2016-healthcare-data-breaches-largely-from-employee-error.

130 Weldon, David. "5 things that top CSO candidates need on a resume." CIO. Last modified January 20, 2016. http://www.cio.com/article/3024521/careers-staffing/5-things-that-top-cso-candidates-need-on-a-resume.html.

131 Padmanabhan, Paddy. "3 factors that will impact the growth of IoT in healthcare." CIO. Last modified January 14, 2016. http://www.cio.com/article/3022679/internet-of-things/3-factors-that-will-impact-the-growth-of-iot-in-healthcare.html.

132 Constantin, Lucian. "Advocacy group calls on healthcare industry to adopt medical device security principles." CIO. Last modified January 19, 2016. http://www.cio.com/article/3024382/security/advocacy-group-calls-on-healthcare-industry-to-adopt-medical-device-security-principles.html.

133 Mom, Mitchell and Ashlee Adams. "Digital Health Funding 2016 Midyear Review." Rock Health. Last modified July 13, 2016. https://rockhealth.com/reports/digital-health-funding-2016-midyear-review/.

134 Accenture. "Internet of Health Things Survey." 2017. https://www.accenture.com/t20170215T191150__w__/us-en/_acnmedia/PDF-42/Accenture-Health-2017-Internet-of-Health-Things-Survey.pdf.

135 Pedersen, Craig A., Philip J. Schneider, and Douglas J. Scheckelhoff. "ASHP national survey of pharmacy practice in hospital settings: Prescribing and transcribing—2016." American Journal of Health-System Pharmacy 74, no. 17 (September 1, 2017). doi: 10.2146/ajhp170228.

136 Washington, Vindell, Karen DeSalvo, Farzad Mostashari, and David Blumenthal. "The HITECH Era and the Path Forward." The New England Journal of Medicine 377 (September 7, 2017): 904–6. doi:10.1056/NEJMp1703370.

137 Excerpts from the American Recovery and Reinvestment Act of 2009 (ARRA). HealthIT.gov. Accessed 2017. https://www.healthit.gov/sites/default/files/hitech_act_excerpt_from_arra_with_index.pdf.

138 Conn, Joseph. "Federal health IT payments top $28 billion after December surge." Modern Healthcare. Last modified February 13, 2015. http://www.modernhealthcare.com/article/20150213/NEWS/302139932/federal-health-it-payments-top-28-billion-after-december-surge.

139 Gandhi, Malay and Teresa Wang. "Digital Health Consumer Adoption: 2015." Rock Health. Accessed 2015. https://rockhealth.com/reports/digital-health-consumer-adoption-2015/.

140 HL7 International. "FHIR Overview." HL7.org. Last modified April 19, 2017. https://www.hl7.org/fhir/overview.html.

141 Washington, Vindell, Karen DeSalvo, Farzad Mostashari, and David Blumenthal. "The HITECH Era and the Path Forward." The New England Journal of Medicine 377 (September 7, 2017): 904–6. doi:10.1056/NEJMp1703370.

142 Marx, Ed (CIO of Cleveland Clinic) in discussion with the author, May 4, 2017.

143 Boulton, Clint. "Google's Apigee buy validates API economy." CIO. Last modified September 8, 2016. http://www.cio.com/article/3118346/application-development/google-s-apigee-buy-validates-api-economy.html.

144 Padmanabhan, Paddy. Why healthcare needs to care about Google's acquisition of Apigee. CIO. Last modified September 15, 2016. https://www.cio.com/article/3120434/healthcare/why-healthcare-needs-to-care-about-googles-acquisition-of-apigee.html.

145 Yamnitsky, Michael. "The API Management Solutions Market Will Quadruple By 2020 As Business Goes Digital." Forrester. Last modified June 7, 2015. http://blogs.forrester.com/michael_yamnitsky/15-06-07-the_api_management_solutions_market_will_quadruple_by_2020_as_business_goes_digital.

146 Greene, Diane. "Google to acquire Apigee." Google Cloud Platform Blog. Last modified September 8, 2016. https://cloudplatform.googleblog.com/2016/09/Google-to-acquire-apigee.html.

147 Institute for Healthcare Improvement. "IHI Triple Aim Initiative: Better Care for Individuals, Better Health for Populations, and Lower

Per Capita Costs." IHI.org. Accessed 2017. http://www.ihi.org/Engage/
Initiatives/TripleAim/Pages/default.aspx.

148 HL7 International. "FHIR Overview." *HL7.org*. Last modified April 19, 2017. https://www.hl7.org/fhir/overview.html.

149 HL7. Comparison - FHIR v3.0.1. Retrieved from HL7: https://www.hl7.org/fhir/comparison.html

150 U.S. Department of Health & Human Services. "Health Information Privacy." HHS.gov. Accessed 2017. http://www.hhs.gov/hipaa/.

151 Padmanabhan, Paddy. "Healthcare analytics, big data oil and the multilane expressway." CIO. Last modified July 19, 2016. http://www.cio.com/article/3097267/analytics/healthcare-analytics-big-data-oil-and-the-multilane-expressway.html.

152 Schiller, Drew (cofounder and CEO of Validic) in discussion with the author, May 5, 2017.

153 Gomes, Neil (CDO of Jefferson Health) in discussion with the author, May 12, 2017.

154 Padmanabhan, Paddy. "Invisible analytics and the last mile in healthcare." CIO. Last modified April 13, 2016. https://www.cio.com/article/3055576/analytics/invisible-analytics-and-the-last-mile-in-healthcare.html.

155 Conn, Joseph. "EHR vendors fall short on usability testing." Modern Healthcare. Last modified September 9, 2015. http://www.modernhealthcare.com/article/20150909/NEWS/150909913.

156 Gomes, Neil (CDO of Jefferson Health) in discussion with the author, May 12, 2017.

157 Davenport, Thomas H. and D.J. Patil. "Data Scientist: The Sexiest Job of the 21st Century." Harvard Business Review, October 2012.

158 Davis, Paul M. "McKinsey Report Highlights the Impending Data Scientist Shortage." Pivotal. Last modified July 23, 2013. http://blog.pivotal.io/data-science-pivotal/news-2/mckinsey-report-highlights-the-impending-data-scientist-shortage.

159 Burtch, Linda. "Data scientists: salary survey shows pay, demand continue to rise." Analytics. Accessed 2017. http://analytics-magazine.us2.list-manage1.com/track/click?u=2f228f4c6b94e453302788f09&id=f1e4ef9465&e=f721062dd7

160 Burning Glass Technologies. "The Quant Crunch: How the Demand for Data Science Skills is Disrupting the Job Market." IBM.com,

2017. http://www-01.ibm.com/common/ssi/cgi-bin/ssialias?htmlfid=
IML14576USEN&.

161 Wikipedia. s.v. "Regression toward the mean." Accessed 2017. http://
en.wikipedia.org/wiki/Regression_toward_the_mean.

162 Wang, Hao, Richard D. Robinson, Carlos Johnson, Nestor R. Zenarosa,
Rani D. Jayswal, Joshua Keithley, and Kathleen A. Delaney. "Using
the LACE index to predict hospital readmissions in congestive heart
failure patients." BMC Cardiovascular Disorders 14, no. 97 (August
7, 2014). doi: 10.1186/1471-2261-14-97.

163 Boston University School of Medicine. "Project RED (Re-Engineered
Discharge)." Boston University School of Medicine. Last modified
2014. http://www.bu.edu/fammed/projectred/.

164 Padmanabhan, Paddy. "Premera data breach: 3 things healthcare
enterprises could do." CIO. Last modified March 20, 2015. http://www.
cio.com/article/2899664/data-breach/premera-data-breach-3-things-
healthcare-enterprises-could-do.html?nsdr=true.

165 Padmanabhan, Paddy. "Healthcare analytics: Early days for many,
significant progress for some." CIO. Last modified November 30, 2015.
https://www.cio.com/article/3008628/analytics/healthcare-analytics-
early-days-for-many-significant-progress-for-some.html.

166 Brasch, Sam (partner, Kaiser Ventures) in discussion with the author,
June 2, 2017.

167 Nash, Kim S. "Allergan Acquisitions Jump-Start IT Efficiency." The
Wall Street Journal. Last modified April 22, 2016. http://blogs.wsj.com/
cio/2016/04/22/acquisitions-let-allergan-jump-start-it-efficiency/.

168 IBM. "IBM Closes Deal to Acquire Merge Healthcare." IBM press
release, October 13, 2015. https://www-03.ibm.com/press/us/en/
pressrelease/47839.wss.

169 IBM. "IBM Acquires Explorys to Accelerate Cognitive Insights for
Health and Wellness." IBM press release, April 13, 2015. https://www-
03.ibm.com/press/us/en/pressrelease/46585.wss.

170 IBM. "IBM to Acquire Phytel to Help Healthcare Providers Deliver
Higher Value Care." IBM press release, April 13, 2015. https://www-03.
ibm.com/press/us/en/pressrelease/46584.wss.

171 IBM. "IBM Watson Health Closes Acquisition of Truven Health
Analytics." IBM press release, April 8, 2016. https://www-03.ibm.com/
press/us/en/pressrelease/49474.wss.

172 Capgemini. "Capgemini Completes the Acquisition of US-based IGATE Corporation." Capgemini press release, July 1, 2015. https://investors.capgemini.com/capgemini-completes-the-acquisition-of-us-based-igate-corporation.

173 Xerox. "Xerox Completes Sale of its Information Technology Outsourcing Business to Atos." Xerox press release, June 30, 2015. https://www.news.xerox.com/news/Xerox-completes-sale-of-its-ITO-business-to-Atos.

174 Roumeliotis, Greg. "Japan's NTT Data agrees to buy Dell's IT services unit for $3 billion." Reuters. Last modified March 28, 2016. http://www.reuters.com/article/us-dellitservices-m-a-nttdatacorp-idUSKCN0WU03Q.

175 HP. "HP to Acquire EDS for $13.9 Billion." HP press release, May 13, 2008. http://www8.hp.com/us/en/hp-news/press-release.html?id=169924#.V0ZoWBVcSko.

176 Clark, Don and Tess Stynes. "HP Enterprise to Spin Off, Merge Services Business." The Wall Street Journal. Last modified May 24, 2016. http://www.wsj.com/articles/hp-enterprise-to-spin-off-merge-services-business-1464121433?tesla=y.

177 Quest Diagnostics. "Fact Sheet." Quest Diagnostics.com. Accessed September 15, 2017. http://newsroom.questdiagnostics.com/index.php?s=30664.

178 Padmanabhan, Paddy. "How unlikely collaborations are changing the future of healthcare." CIO. Last modified March 10, 2017. https://www.cio.com/article/3179467/healthcare/how-unlikely-collaborations-are-changing-the-future-of-healthcare.html.

179 Padmanabhan, Paddy. "IBM's insatiable appetite for healthcare data." CIO. Last modified August 13, 2015. http://www.cio.com/article/2970229/big-data/ibm-s-insatiable-appetite-for-healthcare-data.html.

180 Padmanabhan, Paddy. "A $280 billion healthcare problem ripe for technology innovation and predictive analytics." CIO. Last modified September 27, 2016. https://www.cio.com/article/3124425/healthcare/a-280-billion-healthcare-problem-ripe-for-technology-innovation-and-predictive-analytics.html.

181 Padmanabhan, Paddy. "It's a B2B world for digital health startups: Here's how it works." CIO. Last modified September 6, 2017. https://

www.cio.com/article/3222846/it-industry/its-a-b2b-world-for-digital-health-startups-heres-how-it-works.html.

182 NEJM Catalyst. Disconnects in Transforming Health Care Delivery: How Excutives, Clinical Leaders, and Clinicians Must Bridge Their Divide and Move Forward Together. NEJM Catalyst, 2017. PDF e-book.

183 Small, Carla E., Matthew Murphy, Kevin Churchwell, and John Brownstein. "How a Startup Accelerator at Boston Children's Hospital Helps Launch Companies." Harvard Business Review. Last modified June 5, 2017. https://hbr.org/2017/06/how-a-startup-accelerator-at-boston-childrens-hospital-helps-doctors-launch-companies.

184 Studer Group. *Physician Burnout: Diagnosing, Preventing and Treating Physician Burnout*. Accessed 2017. https://www.studergroup.com/industry-impact/physician-burnout.

185 KPMG International. "Beyond Implementation: Optimizing EHRs to realize results." *KPMG.com. Accessed 2017.* http://www.kpmg-institutes.com/content/dam/kpmg/healthcarelifesciencesinstitute/pdf/2017/beyond-implementation-optimizing-ehrs-to-realize-results.pdf.

186 Landi, Heather. "Survey: Only 31 Percent of Healthcare Providers Use EHR Analytics Capabilities." Healthcare Informatics. Last modified May 4, 2017. https://www.healthcare-informatics.com/news-item/analytics/survey-only-31-percent-healthcare-providers-use-ehr-analytics-capabilities.

187 Singh, Neal (CEO of Caradigm) in discussion with the author, May 23, 2017.

188 Brasch, Sam (partner, Kaiser Ventures) in discussion with the author, June 2, 2017.

189 Padmanabhan, Paddy. "Salesforce dreams of a world beyond Patient Records with Health Cloud." CIO. Last modified September 14, 2015. https://www.cio.com/article/2983269/healthcare/salesforce-dreams-of-a-world-beyond-patient-records-with-health-cloud.html.

190 Apple. "Apple Advances Health Apps with CareKit." Apple press release, March 21, 2016. http://www.apple.com/pr/library/2016/03/21Apple-Advances-Health-Apps-with-CareKit.html.

191 Singh, Neal (CEO of Caradigm) in discussion with the author, May 23, 2017.

192 HP. "HP to Acquire EDS for $13.9 Billion." HP press release, May 13, 2008. http://www8.hp.com/us/en/hp-news/press-release.html?id=169924#.V0ZoWBVcSko.

193 Das, Arpita Bose, Natteri, Bharath, and Gopalakrishnan, Meera. "Healthcare IT Services: Q1 2017 Update." Damo Consulting. Last modified 2017. https://www.damoconsulting.net/downloads/healthcare-services-q1-2017-update/.

194 Cognizant. "Cognizant to Acquire TriZetto, Creating a Fully-Integrated Healthcare Technology and Operations Leader." Cognizant press release, September 15, 2014. http://investors.cognizant.com/2014-09-15-Cognizant-to-Acquire-TriZetto-Creating-a-Fully-Integrated-Healthcare-Technology-and-Operations-Leader.

195 Wipro. "Wipro to Acquire HealthPlan Services, a Leading Technology and Business Process as a Service Provider in the US Health Insurance Market." Wipro press release, February 11, 2016. http://www.wipro.com/newsroom/press-releases/Wipro-to-acquire-healthplan-services-a-leading-technology-and-business-process-as-a-service-provider-in-the-us-health-insurance-market/.

196 Knowledge@Wharton. "Has the 'Dream Run' for Indian IT Ended?" Knowledge@Wharton. Last modified April 14, 2017. http://knowledge.wharton.upenn.edu/article/dream-run-indian-ended/.

197 Damo Consulting. "Healthcare IT services market: the outlook for 2017." Damo Consulting. Last modified 2017. http://www.damoconsulting.net/downloads/healthcare-services-market-outlook-2017/.

198 American Medical Association. "AMA CEO Outlines Digital Challenges, Opportunities Facing Medicine." American Medical Association press release, June 11, 2016. https://www.ama-assn.org/ama-ceo-outlines-digital-challenges-opportunities-facing-medicine.

199 IMS Institute for Healthcare Informatics. "Patient Adoption of mHealth: Use, Evidence and Remaining Barriers to Mainstream Acceptance." IMSHealth.com. Last modified September 2015. http://www.imshealth.com/files/web/IMSH%20Institute/Reports/Patient%20Adoption%20of%20mHealth/IIHI_Patient_Adoption_of_mHealth.pdf.

200 American Medical Association. "Digital Health Study: Physicians' motivations and requirements for adopting digital clinical tools." American Medical Association. Last modified 2016. https://www.

ama-assn.org/sites/default/files/media-browser/specialty%20group/
washington/ama-digital-health-report923.pdf.

201 Morris, Mitchell, Ken Abrams, Natasha Elsner, and Wendy Gerhardt. "Practicing value-based care: What do doctors need?" Deloitte University Press. Last modified October 20, 2016. https://dupress. deloitte.com/dup-us-en/industry/health-care/physician-survey-value-based-care-models.html.

202 HL7 International. "FHIR Overview." HL7.org. Last modified April 19, 2017. https://www.hl7.org/fhir/overview.html.

203 Mangan, Dan. "Health Plans Pay Patients to Get Cheaper Care." NBCNews.com. Last modified March 28, 2016. http://www.nbcnews.com/business/consumer/health-plans-pay-patients-get-cheaper-care-n546831.

204 Shroff, Anand (CTO and cofounder of Health Fidelity) in discussion with the author, January 2017.

205 Padmanabhan, Paddy. "Healthcare consumerism is here – or is it really?" CIO. Last modified November 6, 2015. http://www.cio.com/article/3002110/healthcare/healthcare-consumerism-is-here-or-is-it-really.html.

206 Padmanabhan, Paddy. How technology-enabled partnerships empower consumers battling healthcare costs. Last accessed April 01, 2016. https://www.cio.com/article/3050740/consumer-electronics/how-technology-enabled-partnerships-empower-consumers-battling-healthcare-costs.html.

207 U.S. Department of the Treasury. "Health Savings Accounts (HSAs)." Treasury.gov. Last modified December 1, 2015. https://www.treasury.gov/resource-center/faqs/Taxes/Pages/Health-Savings-Accounts.aspx.

208 U.S. Department of the Treasury. "Treasury Modifies 'Use-or-Lose' for Health Flexible Spending Arrangements." U.S. Department of the Treasury press release, October 31, 2013. https://www.treasury.gov/press-center/press-releases/Documents/103113FSA Fact Sheet.pdf.

209 Edwards, Haley Sweetland. "How You Could Get Hit With a Surprise Medical Bill." Time. Last modified March 7, 2016. http://time.com/4246845/health-care-insurance-suprise-medical-bill/?xid=bbm.

210 Gittlen, Sandra. "Survey Snapshot: Genomic Data Is Far from Clinical Use." NEJM Catalyst. Last modified March 23, 2017. http://catalyst.nejm.org/survey-snapshot-genomic-data-clinical-use/.

211 Marx, Ed (CIO of Cleveland Clinic) in discussion with the author, May 4, 2017.

212 Brasch, Sam (partner, Kaiser Ventures) in discussion with the author, June 2, 2017.

213 Evans, Bill and Sue Shiao. "Streamlining Enterprise Sales in Digital Health." Rock Health. Accessed 2017. https://rockhealth.com/reports/streamlining-enterprise-sales-in-digital-health/.

214 U.S. Department of Health & Human Services. "HITECH Act Enforcement Interim Final Rule." HHS.gov. Last modified June 16, 2017. https://www.hhs.gov/hipaa/for-professionals/special-topics/HITECH-act-enforcement-interim-final-rule/.

215 Murillo, Angelica and Halle Tecco. "Q1 2017: Business as usual for digital health." Rock Health. Accessed 2017. https://rockhealth.com/reports/q1-2017-business-as-usual-for-digital-health/.

216 U.S. Centers for Medicare & Medicaid Services. "Hospital Readmissions Reduction Program." Medicare.gov. Accessed May 2017. https://www.medicare.gov/hospitalcompare/readmission-reduction-program.html.

217 Nigam, Shantanu (CEO of Jvion) in discussion with the author, May 8, 2017.

218 American Hospital Association. "Fast Facts on US Hospitals." AHA.org. Last modified January 2017. http://www.aha.org/research/rc/stat-studies/fast-facts.shtml.

219 American Hospital Association. "Underpayment by Medicare and Medicaid Fact Sheet." AHA.org. Last modified December 2016. http://www.aha.org/content/16/medicaremedicaidunderpmt.pdf.

220 U.S. Centers for Medicare & Medicaid Services. "NHE Fact Sheet." CMS.gov. Last modified June 14, 2017. https://www.cms.gov/research-statistics-data-and-systems/statistics-trends-and-reports/nationalhealthexpenddata/nhe-fact-sheet.html.

221 Johnson, Carolyn Y. "Why America's health-care spending is projected to soar over the next decade." The Washington Post. Last modified February 15, 2017. https://www.washingtonpost.com/news/wonk/wp/2017/02/15/u-s-health-care-spending-projected-to-soar-to-5-5-trillion-by-2025/?utm_term=.1be120dd3c68.

222 U.S. Centers for Medicare & Medicaid Services. "NHE Fact Sheet." CMS.gov. Last modified June 14, 2017. https://www.cms.gov/

research-statistics-data-and-systems/statistics-trends-and-reports/ nationalhealthexpenddata/nhe-fact-sheet.html.

223 Murillo, Angelica and Halle Tecco. "Q1 2017: Business as usual for digital health." Rock Health. Accessed 2017. https://rockhealth.com/ reports/q1-2017-business-as-usual-for-digital-health/.

224 Marx, Ed (CIO of Cleveland Clinic) in discussion with the author, May 4, 2017.

225 Schiller, Drew (cofounder and CEO of Validic) in discussion with the author, May 5, 2017.

226 Gomes, Neil (CDO of Jefferson Health) in discussion with the author, May 12, 2017.

227 HIMSS North America. "2017 HIMSS Leadership and Workforce Survey." HIMSS.org. Accessed 2017. http://www.himss.org/sites/ himssorg/files/FileDownloads/2017%20LEADERSHIP%20and%20 WORKFORCE%20SURVEY_Summary_Findings_Final.pdf.

228 Gittlen, Sandra. "Survey Snapshot: Genomic Data Is Far from Clinical Use." NEJM Catalyst. Last modified March 23, 2017. http://catalyst. nejm.org/survey-snapshot-genomic-data-clinical-use/.

229 Fonseca, Lidia (CIO of Quest Diagnostics) in discussion with the author, May 31, 2017.

230 DamoDigital. "Thought leadership: winning the battle for attention in B2B technology marketing." Damo Consulting. Last modified June 2017. https://www.damoconsulting.net/downloads/thought- leadership-winning-battle-attention-b2b-technology-marketing/.

231 Content Marketing Institute. B2B Content Marketing: 2017 Benchmarks, Budgets, and Trends—North America. Accessed 2017. http://contentmarketinginstitute.com/wp-content/uploads/2016/09/ 2017_B2B_Research_FINAL.pdf.

232 DamoDigital. "2017 Content Marketing Survey Report for Healthcare B2B Marketers." Damo Consulting. Last modified March 2017. https:// www.damoconsulting.net/downloads/2017+Content+Marketing+ Survey+Report+for+Healthcare+B2B+Marketers.

233 Mack, Heather. "Mercom: healthcare IT funding reached $5B in 2016." MobiHealthNews. Last modified January 16, 2017. http://www.mobihealthnews.com/content/mercom-healthcare- it-funding-reached-5b-2016.

234 Pavlik, Jim (partner at Baird Capital) in discussion with the author, June 1, 2017.

235 Tecco, Halle. "2016 Year End Funding Report: A reality check for digital health." Rock Health. Accessed January 2017. https://rockhealth.com/reports/2016-year-end-funding-report-a-reality-check-for-digital-health/.

236 Murillo, Angelica and Halle Tecco. "Q1 2017: Business as usual for digital health." Rock Health. Accessed 2017. https://rockhealth.com/reports/q1-2017-business-as-usual-for-digital-health/.

237 Venrock. (2017). 2017 Healthcare Prognosis. Retrieved from Venrock: http://hcprognosis.venrock.com/

238 Adams, Ashlee, Mark Shankar, and Halle Tecco. "50 things we now know about digital health consumers." Rock Health. Accessed 2016. https://rockhealth.com/reports/digital-health-consumer-adoption-2016/.

239 Brasch, Sam (partner, Kaiser Ventures) in discussion with the author, June 2, 2017.

240 Healthcare Growth Partners. "Health IT & Health Information Services: HIT Market Review." HGP.com. Last modified January 2017. http://www.hgp.com/assets/pdf/hitis-market-review-2017-01.pdf.

241 Schiller, Drew (cofounder and CEO of Validic) in discussion with the author, May 5, 2017.

242 Pavlik, Jim (partner at Baird Capital) in discussion with the author, June 1, 2017.

243 Smiley, Neil (CEO of Loopback Analytics) in discussion with the author, April 27, 2017.

244 Schiller, Drew (cofounder and CEO of Validic) in discussion with the author, May 5, 2017.

245 Schiller, D. (2017, May 05). Interview with Drew Schiller, Co-founder & CEO of Validic. (P. Padmanabhan, Interviewer)

246 Nigam, Shantanu (CEO of Jvion) in discussion with the author, May 8, 2017.

247 Gomes, Neil (CDO of Jefferson Health) in discussion with the author, May 12, 2017.

248 Gomes, Neil (CDO of Jefferson Health) in discussion with the author, May 12, 2017.

249 Schiller, Drew (cofounder and CEO of Validic) in discussion with the author, May 5, 2017.

250 Smiley, Neil (CEO of Loopback Analytics) in discussion with the author, April 27, 2017.

251 Mason, Kimberly (University of Tennessee Medical Center at Knoxville, TN) in discussion with the author, February 14, 2017.

252 Smiley, Neil (CEO of Loopback Analytics) in discussion with the author, April 27, 2017.

253 Weil, A.R. "Market Concentration." Health Affairs 36, no. 9 (September 2017): 1527. doi:10.1377/hlthaff.2017.1012.

254 Centers for Disease Control and Prevention. National Diabetes Statistics Report, 2017. (Atlanta, GA, 2017).

255 American Diabetes Association. "Economic Costs of Diabetes in the U.S. in 2012." Diabetes Care 36, no. 4 (2013): 1033–46. doi:10.2337/dc12-2625.

256 Smiley, Neil (CEO of Loopback Analytics) in discussion with the author, April 27, 2017.

257 Wikipedia. s.v. "Ansoff Matrix." Accessed 2017. https://en.wikipedia.org/wiki/Ansoff_Matrix.

258 Hufford, Austen and David Benoit. "Activist Elliott Management Calls for Change at Cognizant." The Wall Street Journal. Last modified November 28, 2016. https://www.wsj.com/articles/activist-elliott-management-calls-for-change-at-cognizant-1480343701.

259 Ewing Marion Kauffman Foundation. "Startup Survival, Failure and Growth." Kauffman.org. Accessed September 2017. http://www.kauffman.org/key-issues/startup-survival-failure-growth.

260 Griffith, Erin. "Why startups fail, according to their founders." Fortune. Last modified September 25, 2014. http://fortune.com/2014/09/25/why-startups-fail-according-to-their-founders/.

261 Smiley, Neil (CEO of Loopback Analytics) in discussion with the author, April 27, 2017.

Index

B

Bain 81, 170, 211
Baird Capital 167, 172, 199, 224
Banner Health 91
Barbra McGann 73, 210
Beckman Coulter 92
Behavioral Health 44–45, 121
Big Data ix, 1–3, 8–10, 21, 31, 37,
    41–43, 47, 60–61, 66, 78,
    101, 108, 112, 138, 140–141,
    144, 152, 167–168, 182, 201,
    205–206, 216
Big Unlock xi, xiv, 1, 4, 16, 21,
    59, 62, 65, 74, 86, 105, 126,
    173, 193
Binary Fountain 52
Blockchain 59, 74–75, 77–78
Blood pressure monitors 38
Blue Cross 86, 150, 170, 212
Bon Secours Health System 91
Boston Children's Hospital
    122, 219
Boston University Medical
    Center 114
Brad Rutter 65
Bundled payments 12, 14, 151,
    158, 202
Business associate agreements
    (BAA) 63–64, 95–97, 153
Business Intelligence (BI) 21, 107,
    115, 203

C

Caradigm 3, 12, 16, 94–95, 129,
    199, 202–203, 213, 219
CareKit 128, 219

Care management 2, 12, 20–21,
    23, 50, 56–57, 82, 110, 134,
    143, 151
CareQuality 54, 101
Castlight 26, 138, 171
Centers for Medicare and
    Medicaid Services (CMS) 3,
    12, 16, 19, 28, 41–43, 51, 53,
    145, 201–202, 208, 222
Central New York Care
    Collaborative 55–56, 208
Chief Digital Officer (CDO)
    8–9, 23, 84, 180, 211, 216,
    223–224
Chief Executive Officer (CEO) 3,
    5, 16, 38, 44, 46, 50, 68, 74,
    88–89, 104, 139, 145, 150,
    156, 173, 181, 202–203, 205,
    207, 210–211, 213, 216, 219–
    220, 222–225
Chief Information Officer (CIO)
    xi, xiii, 6, 9, 11, 17, 23, 36, 46,
    54, 67, 86, 89–90, 96, 124,
    128, 133, 158, 180–181, 189,
    193, 199, 202–219, 221–223
Chief Medical Information Officer
    (CMIO) 36, 181
Chief Population Health Officer
    (CPHO) 9, 23, 38, 55,
    180–181
Children's Health Insurance
    Program (CHIP) 3, 149, 202
Chris Grant 90–91, 96, 212
Cigna 27, 56, 138, 150
Cleveland Clinic x, xi, 11, 80, 84,
    101, 119, 130, 141, 148, 151,

Made in the USA
Middletown, DE
10 May 2018